FORT COLLINS AT 150

A Sesquicentennial History

By Wayne C. Sundberg

A publication of Visit Fort Collins in cooperation with
the Fort Collins Area Chamber of Commerce
and the City of Fort Collins

With All Best Wishes,
Wayne C. Sundberg

HPNbooks
A division of Lammert Incorporated
San Antonio, Texas

First Edition

Copyright © 2014 HPNbooks

ISBN: 978-1-939300-74-4

Library of Congress Card Catalog Number: 2014955842

Fort Collins at 150—A Sesquicentennial History

author:	Wayne C. Sundberg
contributing writer for sharing the heritage:	Joe Goodpasture

HPNbooks

president:	Ron Lammert
project manager:	Bart Barica
administration:	Donna M. Mata, Melissa G. Quinn
book sales:	Dee Steidle
production:	Colin Hart, Evelyn Hart, Glenda Tarazon Krouse, Christopher Mitchell, Tony Quinn

CONTENTS

ACKNOWLEDGMENTS

Over forty years of research and writing has gone into this publication celebrating Fort Collins 150th birthday. I fell in love with Fort Collins forty-eight years ago, after moving here. I began teaching at Lincoln Junior High in late August, 1966. One of my first assignments was to teach a course on Colorado history. Out of this I created an interest in Fort Collins history and developed an elective course covering our city's past, which I taught to both seventh graders and to students at CSU until I retired in 1993. I continue to be involved in many aspects of local history, doing walking tours, making presentations, and writing articles and books. I greatly appreciate this fantastic opportunity Ron Lammert of HPNbooks has given me with the writing of this Sesquicentennial history of Fort Collins, and to the unbelievable number of local businesses and organizations who have signed on to have their business profiles in the book.

The book's sponsor, the Fort Collins Convention & Visitors Bureau/Visit Fort Collins, has been of tremendous support and encouragement, over the past twelve months. The help from the bureau's staff has been invaluable.

A number of sources were used for the book, including my own extensive, and very disorganized, archive! Material from two late local historians, who were also long-time friends of mine, provided me with a wealth of information—David Watrous did extensive newspaper research which he printed in notebooks, and Arlene Ahlbrandt researched, collected, and wrote on a wide ranging variety of area history topics. I found many interesting tidbits of history in their materials which were used in the book. The late Evadine Swanson's book, *Fort Collins Yesterdays*, was useful as a fact checking source. The extensive postcard collection of my late friend and neighbor, Jane Bass, provided me with several Fort Collins images that have not before been published. My friend and fellow author, Malcolm "Mac" McNeill, provided valuable advice along the way as well as sharing some of his photos.

One should not neglect to mention the 1911 monumental publication of early newspaperman, Ansel Watrous, *The History of Larimer County, Colorado*. It is the starting place for much of the research on this area, as are the online digital copies of many of the city's early newspapers, and the microfilm and files at the Fort Collins Museum of Discovery's local history archive. Lesley Drayton and Jayne Hansen, of the archive, were always there to help and to provide the digital images that I needed.

I wish to thank City Manager Darin Atteberry and Mayor Karen Weitkunat for their wonderful letters of support, as well as the letters from the Chamber's David May and Doug Ernest on behalf of the Poudre Landmarks Foundation.

The most valuable support and help for this project came from my wife, Joan Day. She painstakingly read and edited my manuscript chapters—sometimes twice, as the copy evolved—and made critical comments that helped to greatly improve the text. I drew extensively from her family collection—Great Uncle Myron Akin's diaries, several Akin family photographs, and stories from the late "Cousin" Wayne Akin, who lived to the age of 102! Joan encouraged, prodded, and suggested many great changes that helped me to finish this project—finally!! This is definitely "Our Book!"

—Wayne C. Sundberg

Note: Photographs without a credit line are from the author's private collection.

OVERVIEW

FORT COLLINS: THE SETTING

Fortunate Fort Collins! Tree City USA! Lilac City! One of the top ten cities for retirees!! Bike Fort Collins! Gateway to the Poudre Canyon! All of these descriptors have been applied to Fort Collins at one time or another. The city sits in an ideal location, making it attractive to visitors and residents alike. Geographically it is on the western edge of the Great Plains, at the base of the foothills of the Rocky Mountains. Thirty miles to the north, forming part of the Colorado-Wyoming border is the Cheyenne Ridge, described in James Michener's epic novel, *Centennial*, as the "Gangplank." The ridge and foothills place Fort Collins in a semi-protected basin, where many storms are diverted away from the city.

The Cache la Poudre River emerges from its beautiful canyon ten miles from downtown Fort Collins, flowing along the north side of "Old Town" before turning southeast, where thirty miles lower down, it joins the South Platte River just east of Greeley. The Poudre provides water for a myriad of irrigation canals and reservoirs surrounding the city and giving rise to a thriving agricultural area—both presently and historically. The Poudre also provides many recreational opportunities. People use the river and canyon year-round, with use peaking in the summer. Many campgrounds dot the river bank in the Poudre Canyon. During the peak run-off of the late spring and summer, rafters and kayakers dominate many stretches of the river, as do both fly and bait fishermen (and fisherwomen). Hiking trails, of varying degrees of difficulty and length, wander up the sides of the canyon. And the canyon has been a favorite motor route since the early days of auto transportation, due to its geologic diversity and natural beauty. Completion of an unpaved highway through the canyon in the 1920s made the whole area accessible to people. Today, the all-weather highway, Colorado 14, makes the canyon very compatible to recreationalists and travelers year-round. Skiers headed for Steamboat Springs or cross country skiers wanting to travel the trails near Cameron Pass find the well-maintained road to be an excellent travel route.

Forming the border between Colorado and Wyoming, north of Fort Collins, is the Cheyenne Ridge (James Michener's "Gangplank").

Above: Emerging from the mouth of the Poudre Canyon ten mile northwest of downtown Fort Collins is the beautiful Cache la Poudre River winding through Pleasant Valley.

Below: One of the area's historic irrigation canals, part of the lifeblood of Northern Colorado's agriculture.

Bordering Fort Collins on the west are ridges of foothills. Between the first two ridges is the beautiful Horsetooth Reservoir, covering part of Pleasant Valley. The namesake geologic formation, Horsetooth Rock, dominates the second ridge, and led to a fable attributed to the early Native Americans—"The Legend of Horsetooth." According to the story, as written by Hugo Evon Frey many years ago, the valley the Native Americans called the "Valley of Contentment," was filled with abundant game—bison, deer, and pronghorn. They couldn't enter the valley to hunt because it was guarded by a fearsome giant who would slay any who tried to hunt there. At night, while the giant slept,

a large nighthawk flew above and screeched a warning any time someone tried to enter the valley. But let Frey's own words tell the tale:

But it became known that this giant, in his sleep, exposed his great heart at certain times of the full moon.... The Indians called on their great most powerful chief to lead them against the giant. When Chief Maunumoku learned of the moonlight vigil of the nighthawk, he determined to lure the bird away with the aid of a large white rabbit. He stealthily approached the sleeping giant. He could see the great breast, heaving in stertorous breathing, and he saw the titanic heart outlined against the sky.

Maunumoku grasped a glittering tomahawk out of the skies, brilliantly studded with stars, and with a mighty stroke, he cleft the giant's heart. Blood spurted as though from a volcanic crater out of the gaping wound as the giant struggled to rise. The giant's roar made the earth tremble, as Maunumoku struck again, once on the right and once on the left, leaving huge ugly wounds. The gushing blood filled the valleys, reddening the cliffs, and the stricken giant soon lay still and quiet. The great body and heart turned to granite, and this is the mountain now known as HORSETOOTH.

It is always nice to know the true story of our geologic past, and to learn why the sandstone rocks are red!

Above: Horsetooth Reservoir with its namesake mountain, Horsetooth Rock, or the giant's stone heart is looming over the west side!

PHOTOGRAPH COURTESY OF RYAN BURKE, PHOTOGRAPHER FOR THE FORT COLLINS CONVENTION AND VISITORS BUREAU/VISIT FORT COLLINS.

Left: Horsetooth Rock.

CHAPTER 1

THE CACHE LA POUDRE RIVER ALWAYS ATTRACTED PEOPLE

Archeological excavations at the
Lindenmeier site in the 1930s.

The human history of the Cache la Poudre River goes back at least 12,000 years when Folsom People used the area as a seasonal hunting ground. Evidence of their occupation and use was found at the Lindenmeier site, north of Fort Collins, on the city's Soapstone Natural Area. The location is considered to be a World Heritage archaeological site. Smithsonian digs during the 1930s uncovered tools, weapons, and animal bones, but no human remains. Other native tribes inhabited the area over the ensuing millennia following herds of game animals, prior to the seasonal occupations of modern tribes—Arapaho, Cheyenne, and Utes.

In the early 1800s, trappers, traders, and explorers traversed the area. The name, Cache la Poudre, comes from one of those early groups, with members of French ancestry, who hid some gun powder near the banks of a yet unnamed stream. There are a myriad of tales as to the source of the name. One of the simplest tells of a group of French-Canadian trappers along the river. When they were attacked by Native Americans, the leader yelled to the others, in French, "Cache la poudre," (hide the powder!), thus creating the river's name! Or is it the popular legend about trappers or traders from either the Hudson Bay Company or the American Fur Company whose wagon train was stopped by an enormous snow storm in November, 1836, forcing them to lighten their load? According to the story, they dug a large pit and hid (cached) some of their supplies including 100 kegs of gun powder (la poudre). This is a nice tale but it begs the question, how did General Dodge know to note in his journal, "…passed the mouth of the Cache la Poudre", a year-and-a-half earlier, in July 1835? The river had no known name when Major Long passed its mouth in the summer of 1820, so sometime in those fifteen years between 1820 and 1835, the river acquired its name. It possibly received its name in the winter of 1824-1825 when traders with the Rocky Mountain Fur Company, led by William Ashley, made some temporary "caches" near the river while trading with local Native Americans for furs. As it stands today, the source of the name and when it was given to the river is lost in the mists of time.

The Poudre is one of three major streams feeding the South Platte River in Northern Colorado, the other two being Big Thompson and St. Vrain. The main stem of the river, starting at Poudre Lake on the Continental Divide in Rocky Mountain National Park flows north, then east down to its confluence with the South Platte, a

distance of 126 miles. Its main tributaries are the North Fork, the Big South, and the Little South, with lesser feeder streams like Box Elder, Fossil Creek, Joe Wright Creek, The Elkhorn, and Spring Creek. The river carries two national designations. Since the river has no impoundments, seventy-six miles of the upper Poudre was designated as Colorado's only "Wild and Scenic River" in 1986. Because of its importance in both irrigation and in the development of Western water law, ten years later, the lower forty-four miles was selected as the "Cache la Poudre River National Heritage Area," the first such designation west of the Mississippi River. In addition, the river through the canyon carries the state designation, "Cache la Poudre-North Park Scenic & Historic Byway," as one of twenty-five state byways.

Above: Caching (hiding) la Poudre (powder) along the river.

Bottom, left: The lower forty-four miles of the Cache la Poudre River is a national heritage corridor.

Pleasant Valley near Bellvue, site of the first settlement, Colona.

Since the days of migrating Native America groups, the river has been part of many trails. People noted the ambiance of the Poudre in letters, diaries and in published journals. One of the earliest was written by later settler, Antoine Janis. He wrote:

> On the first of June, 1844, I stuck my stake on a claim in the valley, intending the location selected for my home should the country ever be settled. At that time the streams were all very high and the valley black with buffalo. …I thought the Poudre valley was the loveliest spot on earth, and think so yet.

Horace Greeley, publisher of the *New York Tribune*, visited the Colorado gold mining camps in 1859 and passed through Larimer County in June of that year. He encountered a bridgeless Cache la Poudre at flood stage, describing it as, "…by far the most formidable stream between the South Platte and the Laramie." He witnessed the difficult fording of the Poudre by three heavily loaded wagons pulled by oxen. John Provost's ferry had been swept downstream two nights before. The Greeley party decided to overnight on the south bank until the next day. He writes of their adventurous crossing in his book, *Overland Journey to California in 1859*:

> So the Frenchman (his guide) on his strong horse took one of our lead mules by the halter and the Indian took the other and we went in, barely escaping an upset from going down the steep bank, obliquely, and thus throwing one side of our wagon much above the other, but we righted in a moment and went through, the water being at least three feet deep for about one hundred yards, the bottom broken by boulders, and the current very swift.

Greeley continued his journey after safely crossing the Poudre, and wrote a little more of his impressions of the river and its valley:

Cache la Poudre has quite a fair belt of cottonwood, thenceforth there is scarcely a cord of wood to a township for the next fifty or sixty miles…. The high prairie on either side is thinly, poorly grassed, being of moderate fertility at best, often full of pebbles of the average size of a goose egg, and apparently doomed to sterility by drouth. …It will in time be subjected to systematic irrigation….

Descriptions are varied according to whether the visit was made in a "wet year" or a "dry one." J. R. Todd, in 1907, related a

story, printed in Ansel Watrous' monumental *History of Larimer County, Colorado, 1911*, of his experience passing through the area in 1852:

The waters of the river were as clear as crystal all the way down to its confluence with the Platte. Its banks were fringed with timber not as large as now, consisting of cottonwood, box elder, and some willow. The waters were full of trout of the speckled or mountain variety. The undulating bluffs sloped gently to the valley which was carpeted with luxuriant grasses. It was June, the mildest and most beautiful part of the summer in the western country, when the days were pleasant, the nights cool and mornings crisp and bracing. The sky was scarcely ever obscured by clouds, and its vaulted blue, golden tinted in the morning and evening, was a dream of beauty. Not an ax had marred the symmetry of the groves of trees that lined its banks. Nor a plow, or spade, or hoe had ever broken its virgin soil. Wild flowers of the richest hue beautified the landscape….

Very contrasting descriptions! These vivid descriptions were as different as the groups who passed through, be they small groups, wagon trains, early cattle drives, or stage coach riders. Each saw the countryside through their own eyes, depending on the season of the year, and many left other colorful written narratives.

Above: The Antoine Janis cabin at its original site.

Below: Antoine Janis, one of the founders of Colona and LaPorte.

Right: The Spring Canyon Stage Swing Station building near Spring Canyon Dam.

Below: Overland Trail Ruts from the 1860s—north of Fort Collins.

THE OVERLAND TRAIL

Many people passed through the area over the decades—Native Americans, trappers and traders, part Cherokee miners, and emigrants. The outbreak of the Civil War in 1861 took many of the federal soldiers from the frontier to fight in the East. Northern Plains tribes saw an opportunity to "push the white man from their land." They closed down the main Oregon-California Trail up the North Platte River and part way across the Dakota Territory, which is present-day Wyoming. The route of the Overland Stage Line then followed up the South Platte River to Latham, near the

Top, left: LaPorte Home Station.

Top, right: The Overland Stage Line marker at LaPorte.

Below: Virginia Dale Home Station—now being restored.

confluence of that river with the Cache la Poudre. The stage road followed up the north side of the Poudre to the small town of LaPorte. The stage company established a cut-off route to Denver with a foothills route north. Little "swing stations," where the horse teams were changed, were built every 10 to 12 miles. In this area, they carried names like Sherwood's, Spring Canyon, and Stonewall Stations. Home stations like LaPorte and Virginia Dale were located 25 to 30 miles apart. At these stations, passengers could get meals—some good and some terrible. They could also stay overnight, if they were willing to give up their seat on the stagecoach. Completion of the transcontinental railroad in 1869 ended the need of cross-country stage lines.

By 1860 settlers had established farms and small settlements near the river. Antoine Janis kept his vow to return in 1859 when he, his brother, Nicolas, and several other men founded a town named Colona up the Poudre near Pleasant Valley. One account says there were fifty cabins at the little town. Because there was not a good place to cross the river, the group laid out the LaPorte town sites less than a mile downstream a year later. This community flourished during the 1860s, with stores, homes, several saloons, and a German brewery. When Colorado became a territory in 1861, LaPorte was one of the contenders to be the territorial capital. The next year, with the arrival of the new route of the Overland Stage Line and the building of a home station there, LaPorte became the focal point of Northern Colorado.

Left: Part of the Colona platting document.

Right: Colona town site.

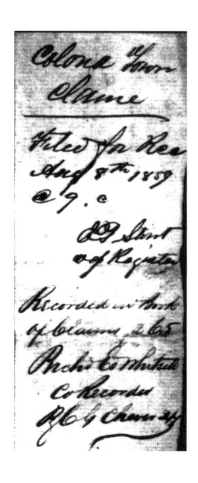

This page: There have been several spring floods along the Poudre River over the past 150 years.

CAMP VS. FORT

Right: Lieutenant Colonel William O. Collins the city's namesake.

Below: Portions of Colonel Collins order establishing the Fort, August 20, 1864.

Opposite, top: Casper Collins drew a plat of the Fort just before it was finished.
COURTESY OF COLORADO STATE UNIVERSITY MORGAN LIBRARY, SPECIAL COLLECTIONS.

Opposite, bottom: Joseph (Joe) Mason, an early settler, who help pick out the site for the Fort in the summer of 1864.
PHOTOGRAPH COURTESY OF THE LOCAL HISTORY ARCHIVE AT THE FORT COLLINS MUSEUM OF DISCOVERY.

A small, temporary military post was built on Janis' land west of LaPorte by troops of the 9th Kansas Volunteer Cavalry in July, 1862. In military parlance a "fort" implies permanence while a "camp" is a temporary post. The Kansas troops named it "Camp Collins" in honor of Lieutenant Colonel William O. Collins of the 11th Ohio Volunteer Cavalry. Collins was the popular regional commander out of Fort Laramie. The mission of the soldiers on the Poudre was to patrol the stage road and protect the settlers. Troops of the 1st Colorado took over the camp in early 1863. They were relieved by Company F, 11th Ohio Volunteer Cavalry in May 1864. Disaster struck these troops in early June. The winter had been very snowy in the mountains and the Poudre was running bank-full when a large thunderstorm occurred up the Poudre Canyon. A large torrent of water burst from the canyon's mouth, flooding the valley. The flood waters swept away Camp Collins, virtually "lock, stock, and barrel!" No troops were lost, but most of their equipment went downstream. When the waters receded, temporary headquarters were set up in LaPorte, and word of the destruction was sent to Fort Laramie.

The oft reported date for the flood, published in early sources, is June 9, 1864. A recently discovered copy of letter by Lieutenant Ewell Drake, the camp's adjutant, dated June 12, puts the date of the flood that latter night:

I drop you a line under very unfavorable circumstances—I arrived here last Thursday—found the river unusually high—the Captain [Evans] all O.K.—Last night he went down to Big Thompson seventeen miles distant to attend a dance—at one o'clock last night the Cache la Poudre let forth its torrents submerging our whole camp—for a time every thing looked serious—but our troops got out of their cabins without any serious inconvenience at LaPorte, one mile below us a child was drowned.

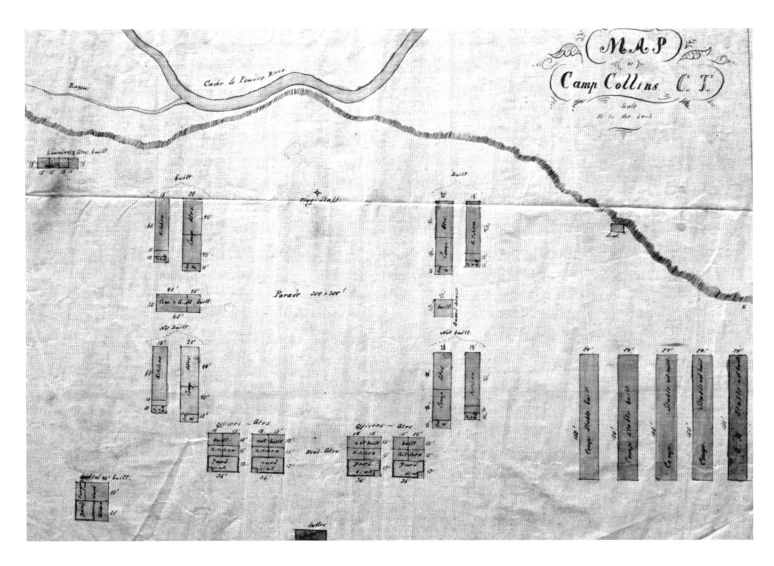

Captain Evans was stranded on the south side of the river, which Drake described as being, "...more than two miles wide." It would take Evans a couple of days to get back across the river to join his command.

Once he had accessed the damage to Camp Collins, Captain William H. Evans, the camp's commander, sent Lieutenant James Hanna and a small party down the river to find a new location. They met early settler, Joseph Mason, who pointed out a site a mile down from his farm on the south side of the river, where the ground was above the river, with a large area to the south that was unclaimed with no squatters on it. Captain Evans sent a report up to Fort Laramie, 154 miles away, about the possible new spot, four miles downriver from LaPorte. On August 8, Colonel Collins and a detachment began a six-day ride south to his troops at the flood site at LaPorte.

THE BIRTH OF A SESQUICENTENNIAL

Shortly after his arrival, Colonel Collins rode down the Poudre to look over the proposed site. Finding it to his liking, he sketched a rough layout for the new post. On August 20, 1864, a date since celebrated as the birth date of Fort Collins, he wrote Special Order #1 where he verbally described his vision for what he called, "...a permanent post on the Cache la Poudre River...." He included the structures he wanted built. He also proposed an approximately four mile square military reservation, which when surveyed included over 6,000 acres south of the fort buildings. Collins left and the 11th Ohio began building the new fort. He came back in late September and made some adjustments to his original plan, with Special Order #8, dated October 1. He must have brought his son, Caspar, with him

(Copy)

Executive Mansion
November 14. 1864.
Let the tract of land
within described be set
apart as a Military res-
ervation, pursuant to the
recommendation of the
acting Secretary of the
Interior.
A. Lincoln

Above: President Lincoln's November 1864 order setting aside the land for the Fort Collins Military Reservation.

Below: Fort sketch with select buildings.

because Caspar created a hand-drawn plat on linen, showing most buildings as completed, but a few "not built." Those were never constructed. In late October, the core fort was finished. Stores and supplies were moved from LaPorte and the soldiers moved in. The post "Order Book" has an entry headed "Camp Collins, C. T." (Colorado Territory) for October 21. Two days later, the heading read "Fort Collins, C. T." so the final moving day must have been the October 22. One hundred and fifty years later, in 2014, Fort Collins celebrates its "sesquicentennial.

In the style of most western military posts built where large trees were scarce, the post did not have a log stockade. Most of the buildings were small structures built with logs hauled from the foothills. West of town, one of the canyons filled in with today's Horsetooth Reservoir and a dam, has the name Soldier Canyon. This canyon would have given the soldiers excellent access to the foothill trees used as building logs. Other buildings were constructed of soft cement called grout, hence the later name of the two-story cement Sutler's Store, "Old Grout." Log warehouses were located on the west side and stables to the east—downwind!

As the Civil War drew to its bloody conclusion, different units were sent to the western frontier. Over the next two years units of the 5th and 6th United States Volunteers, the 21st New York Cavalry, the 1st and 7th Michigan Cavalries, and the 13th Missouri Veterans Volunteer Cavalry inhabited the fort for short periods of time. The demise of the small, "permanent" fort began in the fall of 1866 when General William T. Sherman ordered the fort be closed and the stores, and even some of the building logs, transported to another post. After some protests by local citizens, the final closure came in March 1867. All that remained was Auntie Stone's cabin, the Sutler's Store, and a couple of other buildings, which were soon occupied by settlers. The tangible fort was gone, but the Fort Collins Military Reservation land remained on the government rolls for another five years before Washington could figure out how to open it for homesteading. The records of its existence had been lost in the various files of the Civil War forts.

Left: Fort headquarters.

Center: Troop barrack.

Bottom: Left to right, Sutler's Store, officers quarters and headquarters.

PHOTOGRAPHS ON THIS PAGE ARE FROM THE
REMINGTON COLLECTION, LOCAL HISTORY ARCHIVE,
FORT COLLINS MUSEUM OF DISCOVERY.

THE FLEDGLING TOWN

Above: This log cabin, built for Lewis and "Auntie" Elizabeth Stone on the Fort land, was the first private residence in town.
PHOTOGRAPH COURTESY OF THE LOCAL HISTORY ARCHIVE AT THE FORT COLLINS MUSEUM OF DISCOVERY.

Right: Elizabeth Hickok Robbins "Auntie" Stone, sometimes referred to as "the Founding Mother of Fort Collins."

Elizabeth Hickok Robbins Stone and her husband, Lewis, an older couple in their sixties, had been invited to come to the new fort in early October 1864 by Dr. Timothy Smith, the post surgeon. An order, in the post "Order Book" dated October 8 stated: "Leave is hereby given to Mr. Lewis Stone to build and keep a mess house at this post...." The mess house would be the Stone's private home and would be used to "board" (feed) the officers, who were given money to buy their own food. Mrs. Stone was by all accounts an excellent cook, and very popular with the lonely soldiers, who are said to have nicknamed her "Auntie," a title that stuck for the rest of her long life. Sixty-five year old Auntie was widowed a second time when Lewis died in January 1866. That spring, she invited her widowed, thirty-six year old niece, Elizabeth Keays, and her ten year old son, Wilbur, to come from Illinois, and live with her. They made the journey with Henry Clay Peterson, who had gone back to Ohio, to get his brother and sister-in-law, Fountain and Carrie Peterson.

Mrs. Keays kept a diary of the trip describing the hardships of cross-country travel in a wagon. The group left Illinois in April 1866, and arrived at the fort after dark on May 31. She only wrote in her diary for another week, talking about how busy fort life was for her and "Auntie." Part of her entry for June 1 is most intriguing. She writes that the soldiers are, "...beginning Mr. Fount Petersons [sic]

house for Photographing." Her entry on June 6, "Mr. Fount Peterson is under full headway taking Ambrotypes...." There are several fort photographs from that time that must be Peterson's pictures. Her diary ends that day.

The two Elizabeths prepared meals not only for the remaining officers, but for members of the small community as well. One photo, probably taken by Fount Peterson, shows "Dinner at Auntie Stone's Cabin," with aunt and niece in aprons. The scattered settlers created numerous opportunities for social gatherings; having meals, dances, and holiday gatherings, as well as weddings. The widow Mrs. Keays began teaching her son, Wil, and Harry Cooper, in an upstairs room of the Stone cabin, creating the first school in Fort Collins. Others asked if she would also teach their children. Soon her school had outgrown the tiny cabin room, so classes were moved to one of the abandoned fort warehouses. H. C. Peterson and some others organized School District #5, in 1866, for Fort Collins. Mrs. Keays resigned in December, and on the thirtieth of that month married Harris Stratton at his home in the former fort's headquarters building. Judge Jesse Sherwood performed what would be the first wedding in Fort Collins.

The abandonment of the military post led to a small influx of new settlers since the land was technically still a military reservation. The future of the town was in limbo. Few new buildings were built between 1866 and 1872. There were enough people to carry a vote in 1868, moving the county seat of Larimer County from LaPorte to Fort Collins. The upstairs of the former Sutler's Store, Old Grout, became the county courthouse. The mercantile space downstairs housed the post office. Various fraternal and religious groups met in the upstairs room. This building was truly Fort Collins first "community center." Mrs. Stone's cabin became a hotel, as she took in visitors who got off the Overland Stage at Mason's Store, Old Grout, half a block away.

On December 4, 1871, Harris Stratton, serving as a correspondent for the *Rocky Mountain News*, wrote a long descriptive article about the town as the citizens were waiting

for the federal government to make a decision on the status of the military reservation land:

> They have made quite an improvement at this place within the past six months. A schoolhouse has been erected that is a credit to the people. ...Dr. McClanahan has completed and now occupies a convenient dwelling here. Jone[s] & son of Greeley have opened a branch store here and are making a good beginning. The old firm of Stover and Matthews [sic] are driving at their goods business and have prospered so well that they have opened a branch house in Laporte. Whedbee and McClanahan have a snug little drug store and do a good business, as they well deserve. Harry Conley has completed his hotel and now has the best public house in this part of the country. The flouring mill here has recently changed hands and will be run by a man who has experience in the Rough and Ready Mill at Littleton.

The small public school built that same year a few blocks east "Old Grout" along the "Denver Road" (present-day Riverside), began accepting students. Judge Howes led the effort to raise $1,100 for the construction and furnishing of the school. The District #5 board hired Alice Watrous as the building's first teacher for first grade through eighth grade for the fall term, 1871.

Auntie Stone's niece, Elizabeth Keays, married Harris Stratton in December of 1866 in what is said to be the first wedding in Fort Collins.

Above: This sketch of the Fort done years later shows the stage road to the Spring Canyon station; part of which is today's Canyon Avenue.

PHOTOGRAPH COURTESY OF JANE BASS POSTCARD COLLECTION.

Below: The former Fort Sutler's Store, called "Old Grout," was the town's first store and post office.

PHOTOGRAPH COURTESY OF THE LOCAL HISTORY ARCHIVE AT THE FORT COLLINS MUSEUM OF DISCOVERY.

FORT COLLINS BECOMES AN OFFICIAL TOWN

The federal government finally released the Military Reservation land in the spring of 1872. The Larimer County Land Improvement Company, sometimes called the "Agricultural Colony," was organized and began taking up claims on that land. They solicited members and in November 1872, the group hired twenty-three year old, Franklin C. Avery, to plat a small area around the former fort. Avery had come west with the Union Colonists in 1870, and had helped plat their town, Greeley. At that town site he used east-west street names like Oak, Mulberry, Olive, etc. He named the north-south streets for the colony's founders. Greeley later changed from those names to numbered streets and avenues. His "Old Town" Fort Collins plat was a rectangle, oriented with streets running parallel to the river and the cross streets going from northeast to southwest, the same way the fort had been laid out.

In January 1873 the town company had acquired more land and had more members. They again employed Avery to create a larger town. Since he was a trained surveyor, he must have been thrilled to plat the town using baselines and meridians, i.e. east-west and north-south survey lines. He named the main north-south streets for the town founders— Cowan, Stover, Whedbee, Peterson, Mathews, Remington, Mason, Meldrum, the Sherwood brothers, and Whitcomb. Avery even put in a connecting walkway, Trimble Court, to connect "Old Town" with "New Town," the area west of College and south of Mountain. The main street he labeled College, acknowledging the fact that the Agricultural College of Colorado had been designated for the site in 1870, after some of the early residents donated land to the Colorado Territory for the college. One diagonal street is readily apparent on the town plat—Canyon Avenue. It was the former route for the mail coaches between the Spring Canyon swing station and the fort. In naming the east-west streets,

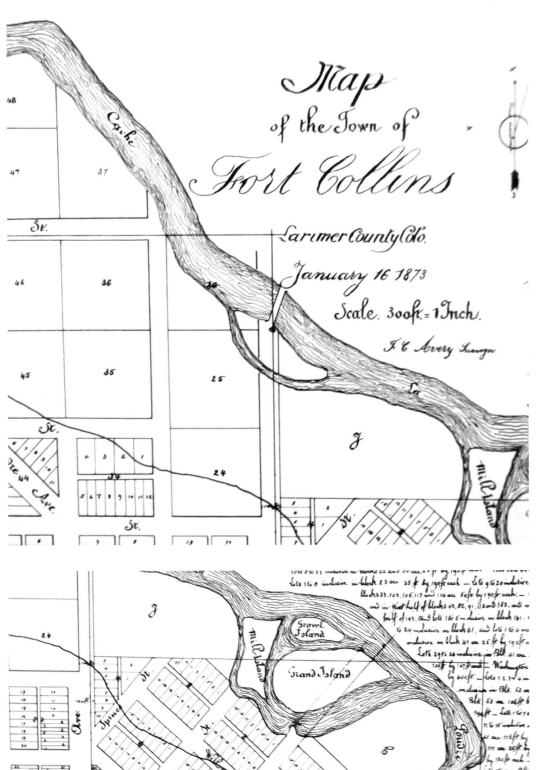

Map
of the Town of
Fort Collins
Larimer County Colo.
January 16 1873
Scale. 300ft. = 1 Inch.
F. C. Avery Surveyor

Left: Part of Franklin Avery's 1873 plat of the town of Fort Collins.

Below: Most of the north-south streets were named for town founders—William C. Stover, Henry Clay Peterson, and several others.

he again used the same idea he had used in Greeley, naming those streets for eastern trees and bushes—Olive, Cherry, Oak, Mulberry, Magnolia, and so on. The exceptions were Mountain and LaPorte Avenues. Avery laid out numbered blocks with numbered lots on each block. Most of the lots were long and narrow, especially in the residential areas, but the streets were very wide. One theory is that he was a good planner and made them wide enough that a fully loaded freight wagon could turn around in the street without having to back-up!

The commissioners also appointed a town "board of trustees," the first city council for Fort Collins. This board consisted of some of the town's founding fathers and street namesakes: Benjamin T. Whedbee, G. G. Blake, Henry Clay Peterson, William C. Stover, and W. S. Vescelius. Whedbee was elected chair this board, making him the "de facto" first mayor.

Top: William C. Stover.

Right: Benjamin T. Whedbee was the president of first town board of trustees making him the first "mayor" of Fort Collins.

Below: Henry Clay Peterson.

On February 3, 1873, the Larimer County Commissioners met and responded to a citizen petition:

> A petition was presented to the Board by the tax payers of Fort Collins praying for the incorporation of said town, and the commissioners being satisfied that two-thirds of the tax payers in said limits had subscribed said petition do therefore order that the said town be incorporated under the name Fort Collins....

This is the birth announcement of the City of Fort Collins; hence 2013 was the 140th birthday of the city.

This issue became a moot point, as several saloons and a pool hall were built in the business district. Those early trustees soon had to deal with the question of licensing saloons. This would be a hot political issue for the next two decades, as "wets" and "drys" vied for control over this aspect of life in the new town.

Left: Jay H. Boughton.

Below: Jay H. Boughton and his brother, Clark, built the first commercial building on College Avenue shortly after the town was platted.

The trustees tackled a couple of pressing issues for the newborn town: Building a bridge across the Poudre River at the north end of College Avenue and getting the new town organized.

Now that the town was platted and incorporated, the Larimer County Land Improvement Company could begin selling lots, and promoting the town. Different kinds of lots were for sale as stocks in the new town, for $50 for a regular residential lot, $150 for a residential lot plus a lot outside the platted town site, and $250 for a residential and a business lot. A lottery drawing was held to see who got the prime pieces of real estate. Jay H. Boughton and his brother, Clark, acquired a lot in the 100 block of North College Avenue, and immediately put men to work to build a small false-front, wooden structure. This would become the first business building erected on College Avenue. The town company was also clear on another issue, in the promotional flyer called Circular No. 1:

What we do not want is [sic] whiskey saloons or gambling halls. There is not a place in the county where liquor is legally or publically sold as a beverage, neither do we intend that there shall if we can help it.

LARIMER COUNTY EXPRESS.

VOL. I.   FORT COLLINS, COLORADO, SATURDAY, APRIL 26, 1873.   NO. 1.

"BOOMING"
THE NEW TOWN

Above: Fort Collins first newspaper,
The Larimer County Express.
PHOTOGRAPH COURTESY OF THE LOCAL HISTORY
ARCHIVE AT THE FORT COLLINS MUSEUM OF DISCOVERY.

Right: J. S. McClelland.

By April 26, 1873, the fledgling town saw its first newspaper in print, the *Larimer County Express*. The publisher was Joseph S. McClelland, a Civil War veteran who came to Colorado in 1872, working on a Denver newspaper for a few months. In early 1873, he moved his family to Fort Collins to establish the *Express*. The four page paper contained quite a bit of advertising, with ads for local businesses as well as businesses in Greeley and Denver. There were "wire stories" taken from the telegraph lines, as well as gossipy bits about the townspeople and their businesses. Newspapers at this time were meant to be published for mail subscribers, and therefore ran booster articles promoting the area. One such story, copied from the Boulder "News," was titled the "Mines of The Cache-A-La-Poudre," "An Interesting Country." It described the foothills and mountains west of Fort Collins, telling of small mineral strikes in those areas. Another piece, "Answers To Questions—Addressed to the Officers of the Fort Collins Agricultural Colony, concerning Fort Collins, Colorado and the Country generally." It addressed such questions as: "How are your winters?" "Are there any government lands to be taken near Fort Collins?" "Is there danger from Indians?" Each had answers, but no indication who wrote the questions. The second page of the paper had a descriptive story about "The New Agricultural Hotel," being built at the southeast corner of Mountain and Mason,

by Alonzo Scranton. It was "a few doors west of the *Express* office" with two stories with fifty feet fronting on Mountain Avenue and seventy feet on Mason Street and containing "upwards of forty capacious [sic] rooms." It was a much needed addition to the new town.

Since Fort Collins was established as an agricultural colony, there were stories about that topic. One article told of "Bachelder's 'Vermont' Sheep Rancho", which W. N. Bachelder had established near the mouth of Spring Canyon in 1871. He bred and raised Merino sheep, which he had brought in from the East, and in turn sold part of his stock to other farmers. There were two other stories about

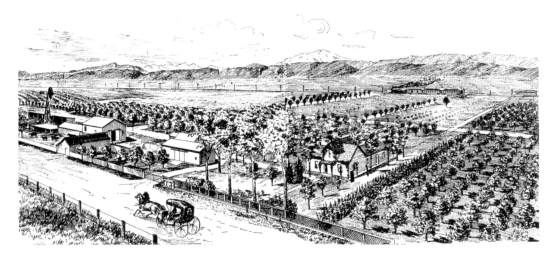

the founding of the "Larimer County Stock Growers" organization and the "Fort Collins Farmers' Club." Another article complimented C. (Charles) Boettcher for building the first hardware store in town (in the 200 block of Jefferson Street).

A little "teaser" sentence told of a big event for the new town. "All the bodies in the old cemetery have been exhumed and removed to the new cemetery ground and reinterred." The city fathers did not want a cemetery in the middle of the downtown; the fort burial ground was located where the Oak Street Plaza is now. The new cemetery, located off the southeast corner of Laurel and Stover Streets, would take the name "Mountain Home."

Not everyone saw the tiny town as something to brag about. Isabella Bird, a refined English woman who traveled all over the world, came through Fort Collins in the fall of 1873. She wrote a series of letters to her sister back in England, describing the places she visited. They were later published in a book, *A Lady's Life in the Rocky Mountains*. Her description of this new settlement was less than flattering. After a six-and-a-half hour ride from Greeley in an open wagon under the hot sun, she arrived in Fort Collins. She wrote, the town "consists a few frame houses put down recently on the bare and burning plain." The dwelling in which she stayed was "freer from bugs than the one in Greeley, but full of flies. The lower floor of this inn swarms with locusts in addition to thousands of black flies. The latter cover the ground and rise buzzing from it as you walk." Her vivid description continued, "These new settlements are altogether revolting, entirely utilitarian, given to talk of dollars as well as the making of them, with coarse speech, coarse food, coarse everything, nothing wherewith to satisfy the higher cravings if they exist, nothing on which the eye can rest with pleasure."

Top: J. S. McClelland, the Express *founder, had a large orchard south of Fort Collins.*

Above: The raising of sheep for wool and the feeding of lambs for meat were important agricultural endeavors for many years.
PHOTOGRAPH COURTESY OF JANE BASS POSTCARD COLLECTION.

from the mountains in full view of the everlasting snow range, and with a boundless view of the plains to the east as far as vision can reach…. The location of the agricultural college of Colorado, at this place secures its literary advantages, and in the enterprise of its people it is behind none. It has two newspapers, a flouring mill, churches, schools, stores and shops, and room for many more, which will be in high demand. At present the town has no railroad connections, but two roads are projected, one to connect with the U. P. R. R. from Julesburgh [sic] via Greeley with Laramie City by way of the Cache a la Poudre valley…. The town and county has no debt and taxation is light.

Boughton sold the *Standard* a few months later as his health deteriorated. He died in October 1874 at the age of twenty-three. Few of the "pioneers" were old men or women when they came to the area, as we are led to believe by the photos we see of them, usually taken years later.

The town he had helped establish was struggling for its survival. The population had gone from about 600 souls in 1873 to around 400 in 1874, a loss of one-third of its citizens!

Top: This view shows Jefferson Street, looking east, in 1878.

Above: The rail line through the middle of Fort Collins, along Mason Street, literally saved the town in 1877.
PHOTOGRAPH COURTESY OF JANE BASS POSTCARD COLLECTION.

Below: Mountain Home Cemetery was the first city-owned cemetery.
PHOTOGRAPH COURTESY OF THE LOCAL HISTORY ARCHIVE AT THE FORT COLLINS MUSEUM OF DISCOVERY.

By the second year of the town's existence, a second newspaper appeared on the scene, the *Fort Collins Standard*. Clark Boughton, the editor and founder, came to the Colorado Territory with his brother, the town attorney Jay H. Boughton, in 1872, to try to find a cure for his lung ailments. He became involved in town affairs and was elected county superintendent of schools. The *Standard* also was a newspaper, publishing "booster" editorials promoting the Fort Collins area:

Fort Collins, the county seat of Larimer County, is situated on the south bank of the Cache a la Poudre River, on the broad beautiful table of bench land four miles out

A RAILROAD HELPS SAVE THE TOWN

Bird's narrative had hinted at one problem facing the new town—locust. During the first three years of the community's life, it almost died. The years 1873 thru 1876 saw hordes of locust descending on the area. They devoured virtually every living plant, destroying the hard work of the farmers. This, coupled with the first banker leaving town with all the money under his sway, made the town's future look bleak. In 1877 there were much fewer locusts and an offer from W. A. H. Loveland to build his Colorado Central Railroad through town on its way to connect with the mainline of the Union Pacific in Cheyenne. This gave town folks renewed hope. The city's board of trustees granted the Colorado Central a right-of-way down the middle of Mason Street "forever!" That railroad literally saved the town from extinction.

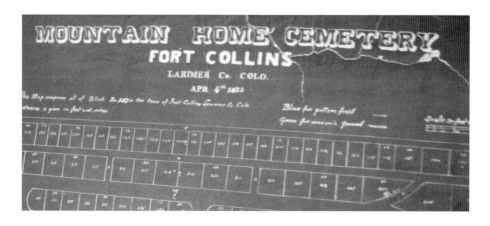

CHAPTER 2

TOWN GROWTH TRULY BEGINS

As the 1870s came to a close, Fort Collins had become a nice little Western community of mostly wooden structures that was transitioning to one with more buildings made of brick and stone. "Auntie" Elizabeth Stone and Henry C. Peterson had gone into business together, for a second time, and built a brick yard on the eastside of town just above the river. This provided locally kilned bricks for these buildings. The first brick home was built in 1871 for Peterson near the Peterson and Stone Mill at Willow and Lincoln Streets. William C. Stover built the first brick commercial building on the corner of Linden and Jefferson Streets in 1874. This two-story structure housed his mercantile enterprise. In 1879, Franklin Avery completed the main part of his home at the northeast corner of Mountain and Meldrum, built of red sandstone from the new stone quarries west of town. He moved in with his new bride, Sara Edson Avery. Family members occupied the home until the mid-twentieth century.

Fort Collins first "grist" mill,
built by Elizabeth "Auntie" Stone and
Henry C. Peterson in 1869.
PHOTOGRAPH COURTESY OF THE LOCAL HISTORY
ARCHIVE AT THE FORT COLLINS MUSEUM OF DISCOVERY.

*Above: Fort Collins first brick house built
for Henry C. Peterson near the mill,
which was torn down in 1911.*

*Right: William C. Stover had the first brick
store in Fort Collins built in 1874.*

The year before, 1878, the population had increased enough that the small school on Riverside Avenue was overcrowded. The male electors of District #5 voted by a majority of 31 to 14 to fund a school bond sale for $7,500 for a substantial new building. The brick, granite, and sandstone Remington Street School opened its doors to students for the fall term 1879. That same year the new "Main" building opened its doors on the campus of the "Agricultural College of Colorado" on the south edge of town. Classes at the "Aggies" school could now begin.

As the town entered the decade of the eighteen-eighties, a period of unprecedented growth, many of the blocks and lots within Mr. Avery's 1873 plat began to be filled with homes and businesses. So many beautiful homes and decorative business blocks were built that local historian Richard Baker labeled it "The Elegant Eighties," in a series of articles he wrote for the weekly newspaper, the *Triangle Review*. It was a perfect characterization of that era.

Some earlier wooden structures were replaced for various reasons. One powerful reason was fire, the scourge of many early towns. Jacob Welch's two-story wood frame dry goods store was totally destroyed by fire during the night of February 3, 1880, with loss of two of his employees' lives.

Above: The original part of Franklin C. Avery's sandstone home as it appeared shortly after it was built in 1879.

Left: The town's first substantial brick and stone school—the Remington Street School.

Below: An early view of the first building on the campus of the Agricultural College of Colorado, later nicknamed "Old Main."

Right: The Opera House under
construction, 1881.

Below: The Opera House, which is said to
have brought culture and refinement of the
early town.

The two lived in rooms on the upper floor. Tillie Irving, the firm's bookkeeper, and A. F. Hopkins, one of the store's salespeople, were burned to death before they could escape. Citizens demanded better fire protection so on May 21, 1881, a "Hook and Ladder Company" was organized, and a fine brick structure to house the fire department and city hall was completed on Walnut Street in July 1882. Many fires plagued the city over the next few years, so the "fire laddies" would get immeasurable practical experience. In fact there were so many fires that Ansel Watrous printed a speculation in his Fort Collins *Courier* that men from the railroads and other manual jobs might be setting the fires. Saloons, at this time, offered free drinks to those who helped fight fires and Watrous insisted that this practice must cease!

New brick and stone structures were being built in all parts of the town. The Tedmon House, a three-story brick hotel, was constructed across the street west of William Stover's store in 1880. The most

"elegant" new building of the beginning of this decade was the Opera House Block on the west side of the 100 block of North College. Several business people and lot holders went into the enterprise together— F. C. Avery, J. H. Boughton, P. S. Balcom, L. W. Welch, M. F. Thomas, and Dr. C. P. Miller. Their three-story building, fronting 200 feet on College Avenue, would contain business storefronts on the ground floor, offices and apartments on the second and third floors, and a spacious opera house performance hall occupying the north half of the building. Welch's new dry goods store would occupy the corner of the building at College and Mountain, the next space was for the Windsor Hotel with Avery's Larimer County Bank in the next section of the building. After only seven years on College Avenue, Judge Boughton's wood-framed law office had to be moved around the corner on to Mountain Avenue, so that construction could begin in March. The spacious building was completed a year later. The Fort Collins *Courier* on

Early photograph of the "fire laddies" and
their hose cart.

March 3, 1881, ran a long article on the structure titled, "A Monument to Enterprise: The Fort Collins Opera House—The Largest and Best Building in Colorado Outside of Denver." The paper was enthralled with the one-thousand seat performance hall, "...a hall in which first class concerts and dramatic entertainments can be given, with all the essentials for the most complete presentations of drama and opera, this hall is unequaled by any in the state." Over the years, a couple of operettas were performed in the hall but never a full-blown opera.

The completion of the Opera House block created a new dilemma for the small town: What would happen if one of their three-story buildings caught fire? Throwing buckets of water up three-stories was not very effective. The issue of a city water system had been voted on previously, but nothing had been done to start building a water system.

The impetus for a water system came in the form of a destructive fire on September 14, 1882. The nearly completed two-story, brick Keystone Block at the corner of Linden and Jefferson, belonging to Frank Stover, caught fire causing the adjoining building owned by T. H. Robertson and W. S. Haynes to also catch fire. The "Hook and Ladder" boys responded along with several citizens. The bucket brigade and a small pump proved ineffective, and the two buildings were a total loss. Following the fire, the Fort Collins *Courier* printed a descriptive story about the big fire: "Lines of buckets were formed from every available source of water supply and a steady stream of water was soon poured on the roof (pumped from a cistern in the basement of an adjoining building).... It soon became evident, however, that the Keystone Block could not be saved...." Several fire fighters suffered injuries from falling or thrown buckets.

Five days later, a vote of 273 for and 182 against approved an $85,000 expenditure for a municipal water system.

The building of the water works took only a matter of months. A contract was signed with Russell & Alexander, contractors from Colorado Springs, in early November 1882. Work began near the corner of present-day Overland Trail and Bingham Hill Road on constructing the pump house; digging the supply ditch to carry water from the Cache la Poudre River to the water works; installation of the below ground turbine water wheels and other machinery; digging a reservoir behind the pump house; and laying several miles of wrought iron pipe into town. Work proceeded through the winter of 1882-1883. Finally, on May 31, the *Daily Express* could report "Testing the Water Works." Hoses were attached to two newly installed fire hydrants and two streams of water were sprayed ninety feet into the air. Two more successful tests were conducted on June 4,

showing that the town was now ready to fight fires in any building. This meant, to the delight of the citizens, they could now have water piped into their homes for various domestic uses.

Additional "elegant" homes and business blocks came to occupy many of the lots in this flourishing town which created the lovely historic character the town continues to enjoy today. The population increased nearly fifty percent during the decade—from 1,356 in 1880 to 2,011 in 1890. Since town growth had tended to move southeast, residences began to surround the city's cemetery, "Mountain Home" at Laurel and Stover Streets. A large acreage part of the former McAdams farm, over a mile west of town at the far end of Mountain Avenue, was purchased by the city for a new cemetery site in 1887. Bodies were exhumed at Mountain Home and reburied at the new "Grand View" cemetery. The Mountain Home site was then vacated for residential development.

Frank P. Stover, long-known as the "City Druggist," standing in the doorway of his drug store when it was in the Tedmon House at Linden and Jefferson Streets.

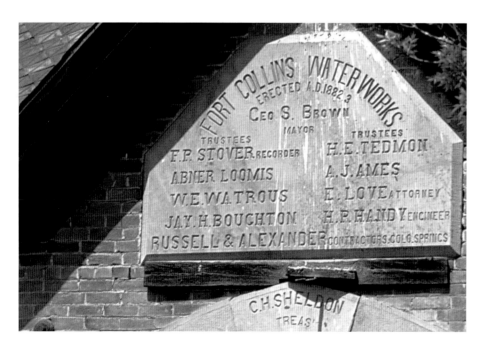

A modern water system, an electric light company in 1887, and the first telephone in 1886 showed that Fort Collins was transitioning from a frontier town to a modern city. The town's growth meant that more public school classrooms were needed. Ground was broken for another brick and stone school, named Franklin, in 1886. The school and Larimer County's new courthouse, across the street from one another at Mountain and Howes Streets, both opened the following year. The Franklin School became the home of the town's first high school curriculum in 1889. Prior to that, students who wanted education beyond the kindergarten through eighth grade public school program had to attend a prep school at the "Aggies" college.

As the new courthouse was nearly finished, it became the site of frontier justice—the city's first and only lynching. James Howe, a day laborer and a member of the city's hose cart team, came home drunk to the duplex in the 300 block of Walnut that he shared with his wife, Eva. There had been earlier reports of spousal abuse by James, and Eva was packed and ready to take their young daughter, Gertrude, back to Ontario to live with her parents. James became enraged, pulled out his pocket knife, and began stabbing her. She struggled free and made it to the fence out front. Passersby heard her scream, "murder," before she collapsed and died. The town marshal was notified and came to arrest James Howe, who had passed out on the bed. That night, according to the local papers, the lights in that part of town were "mysteriously extinguished and a masked band of vigilantes broke into the jail. They took James to the nearly completed courthouse, had a quick trial by the law of "Judge Lynch" and hanged James from some of the construction scaffolding. This was Fort Collins first and only lynching. It also led the outraged citizens to create a battered women's protective group.

The next ten years proved to be challenging. While Colorado had a booming economy fuelled by the silver mining in the mountains, the demonetization of silver in 1893 and the "Panic of 1893" caused national business downturn, which was minimized in Colorado by new gold discoveries in the Cripple Creek mining district. While agriculture had come out of the 1880s in a somewhat weakened state, the sheep feeding industry was just beginning to emerge by 1890. Fort Collins continued to grow though the nineties with the notable additions of Franklin Avery's red sandstone and brick flatiron business block at the corners of College, Mountain and Linden Streets, Judge Jay H. Boughton's spacious three-story wood framed house built at 113 North

Sherwood, and Montezuma Fuller's lovely brick home at 226 West Magnolia Street. Fuller, the town's first important architect, designed and built many homes, business buildings, schools, and churches during this decade and on into the next century. The city's railroad link, the Colorado and Southern, completed is lovely new passenger depot in the 100 block of West LaPorte Avenue in May 1899.

Above: Franklin School, home of the first high school program in 1889.

Below: The Larimer County Courthouse built on "Courthouse Square" in 1887.

The contentious municipal election of April 7, 1896, brought the anti-saloon element into power. Led by Mayor Fredrick Baker, one of their first acts of the new city trustees was to pass an ordinance prohibiting open saloons and the sale of intoxicating liquors of all kinds within the town's boundaries. This "dry" ordinance would stay in effect for the next seventy-three years and color the character of the city in many ways.

Mayor Baker also took on the role of futurist in a column, "Fort Collins 100 Years Hence," published in the Weekly *Courier*, January 2, 1896.

A man is entirely safe in predicting how Fort Collins will look 100 years hence, because he will not be here to corrected, no matter how far he is 'off.' If I should wake up 100 years from now I would expect to find Fort Collins with a population of 100,000 people, nine-tenths of whom would be engaged in the manufacture of batteries, [push] buttons, wire, and wheels. All houses…to have them cooled in summer and heated in winter by electricity. …Women would have pockets in their clothing. I would expect to see men and women dressed very much alike and they would all be so busy that there would be no time for social meetings or neighborly visits. Stores and other places of business would be open all night and all cooking would be done by electricity.

If you wished to communicate with a person in New York or California you would sit at your table or desk and simply touch a button and your communication would be produced in writing to whomever you had called with the button. [The Internet?!] …I would expect to find horses selling for $1,000 and farmer doing all their work by means of batteries, buttons, and wires.

The 1895 home of Judge Jay H. Boughton and his family in the 100 block of North Sherwood Street.

His musings were quite prophetic! Mayor Baker could not resist adding a last comment of a political nature, "And no man or woman would be allowed to vote unless they understood electrical engineering."

In a related political vein, there was a statewide movement in the early 1890s to give women the right to vote in state elections. When the ballot issue came to a vote in the November election of 1893, Larimer County voters—all male—had voted in favor of the issue—1.138 for and 555 against. Colorado became the first state where the male voters granted this right to women. In the election of 1894, "Auntie" Elizabeth Stone, a few weeks before her ninety-third birthday, was taken to the polls in a "wheeled chair" to cast her very first vote after living the entire nineteenth century without that right. In the city election in April 1895, Alice Edwards was elected as an alderman to the city council. For some reason her term only lasted eight months. She resigned in mid-November. A year later, Grace Espy Patton ran for state superintendent of public instruction and won. It would not be until the Nineteenth Amendment became the law of the land in 1921 that women received the right to vote for, and to serve in national offices.

The dawn of the twentieth century brought renewed prosperity to the town, along with a radical change in architectural design. No more Victorian style designs. It was the new, modern twentieth century and buildings must reflect this new attitude of modernity. New structures became less decorative with a more utilitarian design.

THE DAWNING OF THE NEW "MODERN" TWENTIETH CENTURY

The dawn of the new century brought with it an agricultural "boom." The introduction of the sugar beet seeds to Northern Colorado by Charles Boettcher, who had brought seeds back with him from Germany, created a new industry. The cultivation of massive irrigated, and very labor intensive, fields of sugar beets led to the building of a series of sugar beet processing plants in Northeastern Colorado. A group of local business people created the Fort Collins Sugar Manufacturing Company and raised money to build a sugar factory north of the downtown. The plant, capable of producing 1,200 tons of sugar per season, went into operation in January 1904. Buckingham Place, a residential area, was developed the year before for German workers (from Russia) who were being brought in from the Dakotas and Nebraska, where they had

Above: The turn of the twentieth century brought a radical change from the decorative Victorian architectural style to a very plain style for the new century.
PHOTOGRAPH COURTESY OF JANE BASS POSTCARD COLLECTION.

Below: A very elderly Elizabeth "Auntie" Stone from an 1894 newspaper.

Above: The Fort Collins Sugar Factory
provided an economic boom for farmers
and many others in Fort Collins.

PHOTOGRAPH COURTESY OF THE LOCAL HISTORY
ARCHIVE AT THE FORT COLLINS MUSEUM OF DISCOVERY.

Right: Fort Collins' sugar
manufacturing factory.

immigrated to in the late nineteenth century. Thirteen small "beet worker shacks" were built there to house these new workers and their families. The Great Western Sugar Company purchased the controlling interest in the plant during the summer of 1904 after its first successful sugar manufacturing "campaign."

Above: The German-Russian beet field workers were provided with "beet worker shacks."

Left: Beet worker shacks, c. 1910.

Above: Thousands of lambs were fed and fattened in the area, each year, in the early 1900s.

PHOTOGRAPH COURTESY OF JANE BASS POSTCARD COLLECTION.

Right: Lamb feeding, c. 1910.

The lamb feeding industry greatly expanded during this time. The large, leafy sugar beet tops were very good feed for livestock and the beet pulp left over after the sugar beets were processed was recycled back to the farmers as additional livestock feed. By the latter part of this decade, 300,000 to 500,000 fattened lambs were being shipped out of the Fort Collins area, mostly to Eastern markets. Fort Collins

branded itself the "Lamb Feeding Capital of the World," and introduced "Lamb Days" in September 1909. Over 20,000 people attended this free lamb feed. This festival only lasted three years. By 1911 the demand for lamb as a food source had declined enough that much smaller numbers of lambs were purchased for local feeding. Despite this downturn, agriculture grew as fast as the city's economy.

Above and bottom, left: Smoke fills the air from the barbecue pits on "Lamb Day," September 29, 1909.

Below: "Lamb Day" flyer in 1909.

A high school building was built at 417 South Meldrum in 1903, the same year a Carnegie Library building was constructed at 200 Mathews. A year later the incorporation of the Poudre Valley Gas Company brought manufactured gas into homes for heating and cooking. The 1882-1883 Water Works proved inadequate so a new filter plant was constructed just above the confluence of the main stem of the Cache la Poudre River with its north fork in 1903-1904. The ornate Victorian Commercial Hotel at the corner of Walnut and College was purchased by a group of city business people in 1904. They changed the façade to the new relatively plain twentieth century style and added an ornate stained glass dome to the dining room, changing the name to "The Northern." By 1905, the population of Fort Collins had doubled. Building was booming.

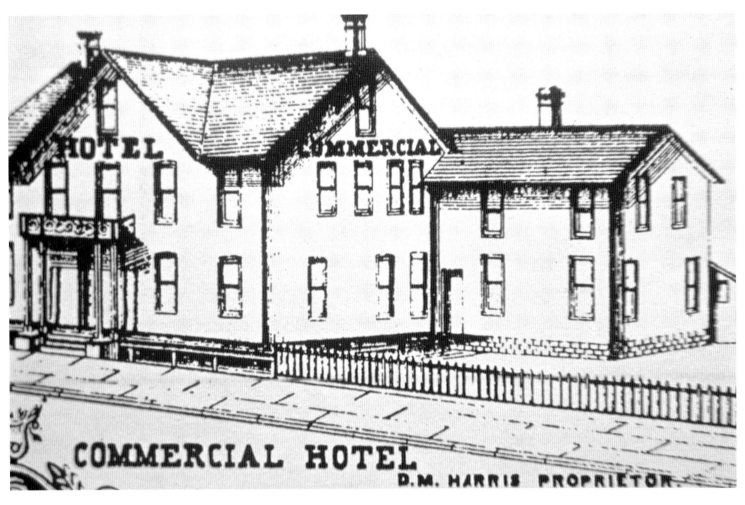

COMMERCIAL HOTEL
D.M. HARRIS PROPRIETOR

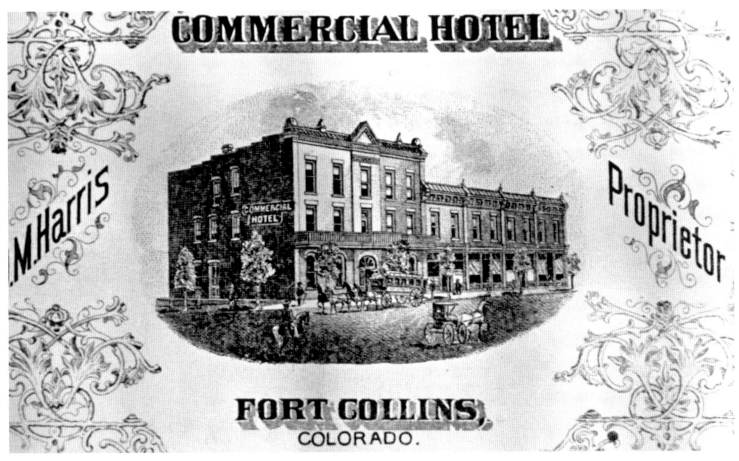

COMMERCIAL HOTEL

D.M.Harris

Proprietor

FORT COLLINS,
COLORADO.

*Above: The Cherry Street home where
actress Hattie McDaniel's family lived in the
early 1900s, when she attended
Franklin School.*

*Right: Town growth meant more students
so a separate high school was built in the
400 block of South Meldrum Street in 1903.*

The *Weekly Courier* for January 4, 1905, headlined, "New Homes for New People" with a subheading "Three Hundred New Buildings Erected in Fort Collins in 1904—Twenty-Eight Others Improved." The story went on to list each one with a brief description. One of those "new" homes, at 317 Cheery Street, was occupied by a family whose daughter would become famous thirty-five years later. Henry McDaniel had moved his family from Denver, seeking better job opportunities in Fort Collins. His daughter, Hattie, attended Franklin School. Within a couple of years, the family moved back to Denver. Hattie later became a band singer and then a bit player in Hollywood movies. Her role as "Mammy" in the 1939 film classic, *Gone with the Wind* won her an Academy Award, making her the first Black person to win an "Oscar." At the time that the McDaniel's family lived here, there was only one other Black family living in Fort Collins. Charles "Charlie" Clay, a former slave in Missouri, had come west during the Civil War, first to Fort Laramie, then to LaPorte. He worked as a cook and a barber at various stage stations over the years, finally landing a job at the Blake House, a Jefferson Street hotel in 1874. His wife, Annie, and their six children were familiar faces over those early days. In his later years, Charlie became the city "scavenger" or trash collector and was very well-respected around town. He died August 31, 1910, and his age was thought to be somewhere close to 100 years old.

The second half of this "boom" decade brought still more change. In 1906 the city granted a franchise to the Denver & Interurban Railway to lay out a streetcar system for the expanding city. Construction began in the summer of 1907 and the first big Woeber Electric streetcars began running on December 30 of that year. The Fort Collins newspapers had a good time with the new streetcars, publishing several little stories about happenings connected with this new institution. One told of a rancher, Clint Farrar, from up by Livermore, who said he was crowded on the street by the big Woeber streetcars. He said if they did not learn to

share the road, he was going to buy a gun and "shoot the derned thing."

The Fort Collins *Weekly Courier* reported on January 8, 1908:

> A man unfamiliar with street car etiquette last night poked his elbow through a window in one of the motor cars, smashing the glass into bits. He was occupying one of the end seats and carelessly swung his strong right arm through the double strength glass. It will cost the company $2. The superintendent announced that this is strictly against the rules. It is also forbidden to shoot out the lights.

Actress Hattie McDaniel with her fellow students. Hattie is in the center, top row, c. 1903.

Right: Fort Collins schools, c. 1910.

Below: Architect Montezuma Fuller in his office in the Avery Block. Featured in the photograph to the right are three of his designs—Laurel Avenue School (bottom, left), LaPorte Street School (top, right), and the original Fort Collins High School (center).

Opposite, top: Looking west across Sheldon Lake at the Prospect Park racetrack.
PHOTOGRAPH COURTESY OF THE LOCAL HISTORY ARCHIVE AT THE FORT COLLINS MUSEUM OF DISCOVERY.

Opposite, bottom: An early trotting horse race at Prospect Park.

West Mt. Ave. Looking East, Ft. Collins, Colo.

The Denver and Interurban Railway operated these large Woeber streetcars in Fort Collins from late 1907 until 1918.
PHOTOGRAPH COURTESY OF JANE BASS POSTCARD COLLECTION.

The *Courier* a week later, January 15:

A passenger on the Mountain Avenue line who got off on the wrong side of the car last night while the car was in motion, was struck by one of the iron trolley poles and knocked down. He was not injured, but the accident indicated that the next man might not be so fortunate; hence the company today inaugurated a new rule. Henceforth passengers will not be permitted to get on or off the car except on the side away from the poles.

And one last account, from the Fort Collins *Express*, July 22, 1908:

Juanita Pherrgo, age 11, 642 S. Howes, thrown off the street car at Laurel & College and knocked unconscious. Man got up...she followed him to the back platform, man got off—the car sped to cross the intersection. The girl had arms full of packages and fell off the car as it sped up. She was unconscious all afternoon.

Other than these and other minor incidents, the street cars ran smoothly and became quite popular for social events and church group's outings to the new park at Lindenmeier Lake.

The Gentleman's Riding and Driving Club laid out a half mile trotting track with grandstands and stables west of Sheldon Lake and ran its first races in early October 1907.

Cowboy Tournaments and Race Meets were also held at this race site named "Prospect Park." Other milestones were when the Y.M.C.A. built its new home at the corner of East Oak and Remington Streets in 1907-1908. Two substantial red brick elementary schools, designed by Montezuma Fuller, were built: Laurel Street School in 1906 on the eastside of town and LaPorte Avenue School in 1907 on the west side.

The January 15, 1908, *Weekly Courier* ran a very descriptive article on the city, stating that it had:

Three parks; Two hospitals; Two cigar factories; Bonded indebtedness of $355,000; Court house valued at $60,000; Five hotels and five restaurants; A $16,000 National Guard Armory; City revenues, estimated at $80,000; Three foundry and machine shops; Home of the state agricultural college; One public library with 5,000 volumes; Three daily and four weekly newspapers; Telephone exchange with 1,500 subscribers; Forty-two school rooms, employing 53 teachers; An opera house, Orpheum and two electric theaters; A $60,000 Y.M.C.A. building nearly completed; Eleven church organizations and ten church edifices; Four passenger trains each way daily between Fort Collins and Denver; Has three National banks and one state bank, with deposits aggregating $2,500,000; Will manufacture 50,000,000 pounds of granulated sugar during the season of 1907-08.

The Union Pacific Railroad began laying tracks parallel to Jefferson/Riverside Streets in 1909, completely changing the appearance of the north side of Jefferson Street. An auction was held for the home and business buildings along that part of the street from Lincoln to College in January, 1910. The purchasers could either tear the structures down for building material or move them to another location. The first Union Pacific train arrived in Fort Collins on July 15, 1911. The end of the first decade of the twentieth century revealed that the town's population had gone from 3,153 in 1900 to 8,210 by 1910, an unprecedented growth! The next three decades would be less spectacular.

Left: Downtown Fort Collins in the early 1900s.
PHOTOGRAPH COURTESY OF JANE BASS POSTCARD COLLECTION.

Below: The Union Pacific Railroad auction of structures on Jefferson Street just west of Lincoln Avenue in 1910.
PHOTOGRAPH COURTESY OF THE LOCAL HISTORY ARCHIVE AT THE FORT COLLINS MUSEUM OF DISCOVERY.

Above: The Armory in the 1960s.

Right: The Fort Collins Armory (top, right) from a 1907 "Sunlight Views" booklet featuring buildings under construction and completed.

BUILDINGS UNDER CONSTRUCTION SUMMER OF 1907

$60,000 Y. M. C. A. BUILDING   ARMORY FOR COMPANY F., C. N. G.

FIRST NATIONAL BANK   FORT COLLINS ORPHEUM THEATER CO.

CHAPTER 3

THE NINETEEN TEENS THRU THE WAR YEARS— CHALLENGES AND SUCCESSES

The years between 1910 and 1920 saw a radical slowdown in population growth, and in the local economy, with a late surge during World War One. The sugar industry and lamb feeding, with their related agricultural endeavors, continued as economic mainstays. Fort Collins was rapidly transitioning from its "horse & buggy" days to a mechanized city. A few smaller industries were begun at this time.

The Agricultural College saw the construction of two new and very substantial buildings in 1910—Guggenheim Hall and the Civil and Irrigation Engineering Building. Guggenheim was built to house the growing home economics department and used construction funds from one of the "Copper Kings," Senator Simon Guggenheim. Inga M. K. Allison, professor of home economics, was named acting head of the department. The "Aggies" college's population had grown from ten students in 1879 to 530 in 1913. Charles A. Lory had taken the reins of the "Aggies" in 1909 and was instrumental in promoting many changes at the college. He would serve as the school's innovative and inspiring leader for thirty-one years. The students built Colorado Field in 1912, the first sodded athletic field in Colorado, and they also created the whitewashed rock "A" on one of the foothills west of town in 1923. The "Aggies" football team, under Coach Harry Hughes, used the field to bring its first conference championship home in November 1915, after they defeated Colorado College.

Top: Fort Collins Post Office under
construction in 1911.

Above: The Fort Collins Post Office
after completion.

drought years at the beginning of the decade, grasshoppers were again a problem for farmers. The college's agricultural departments helped with methods for fighting the pests.

With a fairly large population, 1911 saw contracts being signed to construct the new federal building at the southwest corner of Oak Street and College Avenue. Finished the next year, it would house the U.S. Post Office for most of the twentieth century. Horse importer and business-man, Jesse Harris, took over the mayor's job in 1911. Both he and Akin, a sheep feeder and water developer, were well suited to lead the city with its almost total dependence on agricultural based industries. The former Sheldon sheep ranch land west of town had been purchased by the city in 1907 and, in 1912, the city's parks commission named that tract of land "City Park." The city also purchased the Prospect Park race track land and structures for $10,000 and added it to City Park with the idea that it would serve as a fairground site.

The city entered this decade electrified. Two huge tungsten lamps were hung on both sides of the trolley poles along College Avenue in 1910, but the major downtown side streets continued to have gas street lights. North of the downtown, a private group built a golf course and created the country club that same year. Mayor Myron Akin provided exemplary leadership during his tenure, 1909 to 1911. Partially because of

That same year James Vandewark built his new Riverside Ice and Storage Building in the 200 block of LaPorte Avenue. This new building was needed because the business' former home on Riverside was purchased and demolished by the Union Pacific Railroad. The new structure was unique because of its concrete, steel, and cork construction. Several inside rooms were lined with cork to provide cold storage for fruits, vegetables, eggs, and women's furs! In 1914 the RISCO plant added an ice cream manufacturing component, selling their ice creams under the name Dairy Gold. This era saw train traffic increase through Fort Collins. The Colorado and Southern ran twelve passenger trains and four freight trains through the city each day, linking citizens with cities all over the country including the sheep raising area of the Big Horn Basin in Wyoming. This created a new source for purchasing feed lambs for Eastern markets. Added to this were the trains on the new tracks of the Union Pacific Railroad, crossing the downtowns' north side. Both lines linked the city with the transcontinental rails at Cheyenne.

Denver & Interurban worker clearing snow
from streetcar tracks.

THE BIG BLIZZARD
OF 1913

The year, 1913, ended with a "white bang!" Early on December 1, it began snowing. Newspaper headlines that month told the stories vividly:

SNOWFALL HEAVIEST IN 15 YEARS
Depth is almost record for month of December
Fort Collins Weekly Courier, 12/5/1913.

HEAVY STOCK LOSS
IN THE MOUNTAINS
One man saves only small part of 200 head
Weekly Courier, 12/12/1913

STREET CAR COMPANY
TRIES TO CLEAR TRACKS
Weekly Courier, 12/12/1913

PLOWING SNOW OFF THE ROADS
County having hard time opening highways
Weekly Courier, 12/19/1913

Reports from outlying areas, like Livermore and Rustic in the Poudre Canyon, told of three to six feet of snow. Horse teams pulling plows were unable to make any progress because the snow just compacted in front of the plows. By the end of that first week, thirty-one inches of snow had fallen. Schools were closed and no milk or mail was getting through. Estes Park was cut off from the rest of the Front Range. As soon as roads and railroad tracks were cleared, the strong winds blew the snow right back to clog them up once more! Power poles that had been just recently put up fell down. Somehow telephone service was maintained, probably due to the crank telephones that generated their own electrical charge and the operators who put through each call personally. The December 5 *Express* reported: "The busiest place in Fort Collins today is the telephone exchange. So strenuous did the work become that two of their number fainted at their desks. There was no relaxation for the others as the calls were unceasing." Citizens wanted to make sure that friends and relatives were doing okay!

Let an observer at the time tell the story. Former mayor, Myron Akin, wrote in his 1913 diary:

Monday December 1, Commenced snowing at 6 A.M. & a fierce blizzard raged all day, 12 inches of snow tonight.

Tuesday December 2, Clear and cold about 15 inches of snow. Wayne [his 19 year old son] & I put in the day shoveling snow & hauling alfalfa to the corrals at the B. B. Harris place.

Thursday Terrific blizzard all day—over 31 in of snow on the level tonight. Wayne and I worked with our dairy cows at Harris all day. Uncle Abe tied up at Livermore. All st. car traffic here & at Denver at stand still.

Friday Another day of blizzard 31 in. of snow & more coming. Wayne and I…shoveled snow all day.

Saturday Clear & windy & warm. 40 in of snow in Denver. St. cars & trains blocked in all directions. Never a storm like it in Colorado. 5 ft. of snow in Estes Park. Uncle Abe at Livermore & cannot go up or down from there. Rotary snow plow came from Cheyenne first train in two days. Wayne & I had Fred Fluke, Gordon Stewart & Les Antles helping shoveling snow.

The next weekdays saw them alternating between shoveling snow and hauling hay and straw for their livestock.

Saturday December 13, Street cars running only to sugar factory & to Plum St. ….

Myron also commented on the difficulty of walking, or "wading through the snow," and how good the horse drawn sleighs worked.

Friday December 19, Terrific blizzard all day…. Roads again drifted full of snow.
Sunday Deep snow. Mr. Nightingale lost 69 cattle out of 75 in storm.

Toward the end of December, the newspapers were reporting a frigid "Cold Wave," with temperatures falling below the minus ten degree mark in Fort Collins. The "Big Storm of 1913" just did not want to let loose of the area! An interesting side note, the storm temporarily solved the unemployment situation. The city hired sixty laborers and with ten teams of horses, began clearing the streets. The spring thaw was still a ways off.

Top: View of the "Big Snow" storm of December 1913 into January 1914.

Above: College Avenue after the "Big Snow" "Don't throw that snowball at the camera, kid!"

*Above and below: Views from the 1914
Semi-Centennial Parade at Linden and
Jefferson Streets.*

THE SEMI-CENTENNIAL OF THE BIRTH OF FORT COLLINS, 1914

The newspapers carried several "reminiscent" stories from early settlers, in the mid-nineteen teens, as the fiftieth birthday, or "Semi-Centennial," of the town approached. A large citizen's committee was formed and many activities were planned for July 2, 3, and 4, 1914. A key part of the celebration would be what was called a "Pioneer Reunion." Several Civil War veterans who had been stationed at the Fort Collins military post had returned and settled here after the war. In addition, anyone who had settled here in the 1860s and 1870s was invited to be a part of the reunion. At a "pioneer" banquet, held in a large tent erected at the corner of LaPorte Avenue and Howes Street, many aged pioneers were recognized, and at the "Pioneer Campfire," a prize was given to the "pioneer" who had come to the area the earliest. Unfortunately, the newspapers of that time did not report who took this honor. There was an historic pageant, a parade, and two "Wild West Shows" with rodeos, put on by the Irwin Brothers of Cheyenne Frontier Days fame, at the Prospect Park horse track. There were performances on each of the three days of the "Semi-Centennial."

Above: Victor Akin driving a wagon in the Semi-Centennial Parade promoting local agriculture.

PHOTOGRAPH COURTESY OF JOAN DAY.

Below: Part of Semi-Centennial Parade on College Avenue.

Another highlight of this celebration was the return of "Lamb Day," with a free lamb feed for all who came to Thursday's first day events. The *Morning Express* carried a very "tongue-in-cheek" report about the event in its July 3 edition:

MARY'S LAMB DISAPPEARS, 5,200 HELP HIM VANISH

The hungry crowd was led by Governor E. M. Ammons, to whom the first piece of lamb was offered by a "dainty miss." 'Thank you,' said the governor, passing back the plate and taking the morsel with his fingers. 'I delight in being served by the little ladies.' Now, sometimes things may go wrong between the governor and his people and he may seem to have never a friend in the wide world. But that will be wrong. For that little miss is his friend forever.

The story continued,

The concourse that gathered back of the grandstand at Prospect Park to partake of the lamb feast was the most cosmopolitan that Fort Collins had ever seen...it was frontier and pioneer in every feature. The headdresses of the Indian visitors, the great hats of the cow men, the dainty frocks of school misses, the suits of business men with every variety of masculine gear, from that which belongs behind the counter to that which is in place behind the plow, made it an ensemble worthy of painting.

After "vanquishing" the meal the crowd adjourned to the grandstand for the Wild West Show and Rodeo, with performances by both men and women.

Local celebrity, Frank Miller, performing both shooting and roping tricks while standing on his horse.

PHOTOGRAPH COURTESY OF THE LOCAL HISTORY ARCHIVE AT THE FORT COLLINS MUSEUM OF DISCOVERY.

On Friday, a beef barbeque replaced the lamb feed before the "Wild West Show." The highlight of the show that day was local trick roper and crack shot, Frank C. Miller. The *Express* printed a glowing description of his part of the show in its July 4th edition:

Among the pleasing events that of Frank C. Miller, the Fort Collins expert with the rifle. He astonished those who had seen him before as he has added some numbers to his program that were entirely new. A secret that may be disclosed here is that he is left-handed in handling a rifle though he uses his right hand in preference for all other of his usual performances. Whether it is an acquired habit or whether it came naturally to him from the first he does not remember as he has handled a rifle from his infancy. The elder Miller, his father, was a pioneer of the West, and was proficient with the rifle. Early in the young man's life Miller, Sr., began to drill him in handling weapons and this, aided by his naturally quick eye and accurate hand, has made him one of the most expert riflemen in the West, as well as the best in trick shooting.

He is said to have set up a shooting range in the basement of his father's magnificent 1888 building in Old Town in the early twentieth century. He went on to perform in some big-named rodeos, like Cheyenne Frontier Days and the 101 Ranch Rodeo in Oklahoma. Some accounts say he learned some of his rope tricks from the legendary performer, Will Rogers.

The final day, July 4, had a morning parade, an afternoon rodeo, and evening fireworks at the city playground at LaPorte Avenue and Howes Street. A hot air balloon ascent had to be cancelled because of wind! One highlight of the daily rodeo was the wild mule races, as the *Weekly Courier* indicated the week after the big celebration,

The events at Prospect Park were all entertaining and it is difficult to tell which pleased the crowd most. The wild mule race was certainly one of the leaders and there was plenty of sport watching the stubborn brutes as men tried to haul them on the track with lariats and tried to get them harnessed up and try to make animals go around the track. Most of the animals preferred jumping the fence.

One of the big winners during the celebration was the Denver & Interurban's Fort Collins streetcars. On the last day of the celebration, receipts showed that 15,000 people rode the cars. Post Semi-Centennial estimates put attendance for the three days at over 30,000 happy souls.

MORE AUTOMOBILES
CREATE DEMAND
FOR BETTER
STREETS AND ROADS

As mechanical transportation became more popular and more automobiles showed up on the city streets, the demand for better streets and county roads increased. The road in the Poudre Canyon northwest of Fort Collins was little more than a rocky trail in the early twentieth century and did not go all the way through. People who wanted to access the upper canyon had to make the long journey to Livermore, then west to Log Cabin where the road turned south to Elkhorn, going down

the steep Pingree Hill Road into The Rustic. The Rustic had developed as a health resort in the late 1800s. Hunters and fishermen were frequent visitors to the upper canyon. The Zimmerman family built the magnificent brick Keystone Hotel west of The Rustic. Convict Road gangs were brought in to work on the road to Pingree Park and to improve the dangerous, steep road down Pingree Hill from Elkhorn to The Rustic in the fall of 1911. When these were finished, the convicts were moved to the lower canyon. They finished a road over Water Works Hill in the late winter of 1913. That same year, Fort Collins business interests created the "Poudre Valley Good Roads Association" and began lobbying the State Highway Commission for a road through the canyon. There were two formidable barriers—the Big and Little Narrows—blocking the way. In 1914, along with funds from the Larimer County commissioners, the state appropriated $35,000 to begin constructing a road through the canyon to The Rustic. Thirty-three convicts from the Canon City prison were again brought to the canyon. The first mile of road was built in 26 days at a cost of $730.73. By October, the gravel road was completed to Hewlett Gulch. Local road boosters held a celebration picnic at Farrell Grove complete with fried chicken, salad, biscuits, and other goodies for 600 people, transported in 100 automobiles.

Ten more convicts were added by early 1916, including a doctor from Cripple Creek! Road building had slowed to less than 1,000 feet per month as the canyon walls became steeper and narrowed in closer to the river. The next big challenge was building the

Above and below: Poudre Canyon Road in the early nineteen hundreds.

PHOTOGRAPHS COURTESY OF MALCOLM "MAC" MCNEILL.

Right: Baldwin Tunnel in the Little Narrows of the Poudre Canyon blasted through in 1916.

PHOTOGRAPH COURTESY OF MALCOLM "MAC" MCNEILL.

Below: Fifth and final annual picnic celebration on the nearly completed Poudre Canyon Road, Indian Meadows, October 12, 1920.

PHOTOGRAPH COURTESY OF THE LOCAL HISTORY ARCHIVE AT THE FORT COLLINS MUSEUM OF DISCOVERY.

road through the very constricted part of the canyon known as the Little Narrows. The convict work force, now under the supervision of Captain Charles Baldwin, blasted a tunnel through the granite during June and July 1916. State Senator William Drake drove the first car through the completed tunnel in early July. The tunnel was named the Baldwin Tunnel to differentiate it from "The Tunnel," the Laramie-Poudre irrigation tunnel, which had been put through a few years earlier in the upper canyon. Road construction continued west and the now-annual picnic was held on October 18, 1916, a mile above the Baldwin Tunnel and featured roast corn and fresh, fried Poudre River trout!

The fourth annual picnic was held just below the Big Narrows the following Labor Day, 1917, as the blasting and grading had taken the road two miles into that part of the canyon. By the spring of 1918, the convict camp was moved to the flat a half mile above the Big Narrows. Work now progressed at a faster pace. John McNabb and Norman Fry were contracted to build three bridges in the Indian Meadows area in the fall of 1919, which they finished by early the following March. The big celebration picnic on October 12, 1920, was held in Indian Meadows with 1,200 people in attendance. Speakers featured were Fort Collins Mayor Fred W. Stover, County Commissioner chair, Harris Akin, and Governor Oliver H. Shoup, in addition to several other State and county officials. Festivities included a Wild West show put on by ranchers from Livermore and Log Cabin and feasting on two 450 pound beeves roasted all night long at the site. The hope had been to celebrate completion of the road to The Rustic, but two miles of road were still to be constructed. Some of the celebrants decided to return home by way of the crude, unfinished road through The Rustic. Reported the Fort Collins *Courier* the next day:

> The road was found to be excellent where completed, but as parts of it had not been completed and were a little rough near the upper end, some of the cars forded the Poudre and came back by Pingree hill and the Log Cabin road.

Early the next year when the stretch to The Rustic was finished, the convict camp was moved to Kinikinik to begin rebuilding what was the old Stewart Toll Road. Stewart had built the toll road in the 1880s to provide a route into North Park and to the short-lived mining towns of Lulu City and Teller City. Jackson County workers were improving and widening the road on the west side of Cameron Pass. The roads were finally connected in August of 1926. A big two county celebration was held at the top of Cameron Pass that year on September 6. The opening of the road for the newly emerging auto tourism was a great boon for both counties. Over the years of the twentieth century, the road was improved and sections of paved canyon road were pushed westward. The Poudre, the so-called "Colorado's Trout Route," became very popular with easier automobile travel and several campgrounds were developed along its way, the first of which was to be called Camp Ansel Watrous. The *Courier,* in April 4, 1919, reported "City's First Mountain Park Named After Ansel Watrous." Its location was at one of Watrous' favorite fishing holes in the river. The era of auto tourism had come to Fort Collins and Northern Colorado.

Top: Ansel Watrous Campground signage.
PHOTOGRAPH COURTESY OF THE UNITED STATES FOREST SERVICE.

Above: Early Fort Collins newspaper man and historian, Ansel Watrous, namesake of the campground.
PHOTOGRAPH COURTESY OF THE UNITED STATES FOREST SERVICE.

WAR CLOUDS GATHER OVER THE WORLD, FORT COLLINS PREPARES

By the mid-teens The Great World War had engulfed Europe. America tried to stay out of the conflict while building up its military forces. In early 1916, Battery A was established on the campus of the Colorado Agricultural College. Professor Roy G. Coffin was commissioned as a captain and put in charge of the field artillery company. After Mexican soldiers under Pancho Villa crossed the international border and raided the small town of Columbus, New Mexico, the unit was federalized as a Colorado National Guard unit and ordered to Camp Baldwin in Golden for training before being sent to the southern U.S. border. Other federal troops settled the potential problem with an invasion into Mexico to pursue Villa. Battery A was sent back to Fort Collins. The artillery company continued to train and to recruit more members as the U.S. drew closer to entering the war. In early April 1917, Congress voted to support

Above: George Beach, namesake of the local American Legion Post #4, from the Fort Collins High School Lambkin Yearbook, *1918.*
PHOTOGRAPH COURTESY OF THE LOCAL HISTORY ARCHIVE AT THE FORT COLLINS MUSEUM OF DISCOVERY.

Right: Stuart McKeown, World War I hero, in 1914.
PHOTOGRAPH COURTESY OF THE LOCAL HISTORY ARCHIVE AT THE FORT COLLINS MUSEUM OF DISCOVERY.

President Woodrow Wilson's declaration of war against Germany. By May the company had a strength of 190 enlisted men and 5 officers, when they were ordered to Fort Riley, Kansas, for training. In October, they were made part of the 148th Field Artillery Regiment and sailed for Europe in January 1918.

Many other men from Larimer County were drafted or volunteered for military service and were sent off to various training camps around the country. One soldier who received extra publicity was Lieutenant Stuart McKeown serving in the U.S. Army Air Corps in France. He was shot down in August 1918, crashing his plane into a haystack. He survived with severe burns and other injuries. Taken captive by the Germans, he was subjected to several painful, experimental skin grafts. After being liberated in December, he spent three months in a Paris hospital before being sent home in April 1919 to a hero's welcome. Myron Akin, soon to be McKeown's father-in-law as he was engaged to daughter, Eunice, wrote in his diary on April 4, 1919. "Stuart Rt [sic] from long absence in France—scarred but brave Stuart gave Eunice a diamond." His experiences were later chronicled in the book, *Heaven High, Hell Deep*, written by his friend, Norman Archibald, in 1935. Another was also a pilot, George A. Beach. He trained as a fighter pilot. He was doing additional training in Italy in 1918 when his plane crashed into another plane in a heavy fog and he was killed. He was Fort Collins first war fatality. One of the Fort Collins Legion posts was later named in his honor. Beach's name was printed on a brass plaque mounted shortly after the war on the wall of the high school, at its Meldrum Street location, along with five others of "Our Honored Dead" soldier-graduates killed in the World War: Henry Winter, Charles Conrey, Frank Allen, Harry Gault, and Roscoe Becker.

Plaque from the original high school building, now at Lincoln Middle School, honoring Fort Collins High School graduates killed in World War I.

THE SPANISH INFLUENZA HITS FORT COLLINS

In early October 1918, as Fort Collins was training additional military units at the Aggie's college, the world-wide Spanish Influenza pandemic hit the city and county hard. President Charles Lory ordered the college closed. Newly-built barracks that housed military trainees were converted into hospitals and the trainees were quarantined. Virtually every public gathering was prohibited in the city and schools were closed. Several churches were set up as hospitals, as Red Cross workers and other volunteers tried to provide comfort to critically ill patients. There were several deaths including a very popular assistant botany professor, and also the adjutant to the military department at the college, Lieutenant Harvey E. Vasey who succumbed to the "flu." At one point, there were 185 patients in the college's military barracks alone. As the "flu" threat declined, the college reopened on January 4, 1919, and public gatherings returned to the city.

Former Mayor Akin gave a very personal look at the local epidemic in his 1918 and 1919 diaries. On October 12 he wrote, "All meetings in the city prohibited a/c [account] of Spanish Influenza" On the 19th, "Many sick with Spanish Influenza" The next day, "2nd Sunday of Quarantine vs. Spanish Influenza—No public gathering of any sort allowed." One day later, October 21, "College adjourned for 2 weeks on a/c [sic] Influenza." The two weeks would stretch into January and his daughter, Eunice, who had been instructing at the Agricultural College, came down with the influenza. October 27, "3rd Sunday of quarantine, Eunice still sick with 'Flu,' 5 boys died at the College" November 6, "Eunice sang at 3 funerals today." She was among the fortunate ones who were able to recover quickly. November 17, "No church or SS on a/c of flu quarantine" November 28 (Thanksgiving), "No services or meetings of any kind on a/c of "Flu" quarantine." December 18, "Flu conditions improving." There were no public Christmas gatherings, but some church groups went out caroling. Finally, on December 29, "One church service today 1st since October 6th." The influenza epidemic was slowly losing its grip on the community.

This page: New Birney Safety Cars replaced the big Woeber Streetcars in 1919.

The end of the decade looked promising as Fort Collins was about to enter the twenties. The Denver & Interurban Street Railway, which had operated streetcars in the city since late 1907, had gone into receivership in 1918, so service had been suspended. Fort Collins voters, by a margin of eight times as many votes in favor as those opposed, approved $100,000 to buy the system. The Fort Collins Municipal Railway was created and went into operation in May 1919, with four brand new Birney Safety Streetcars from the American Car Company in St. Louis, Missouri. The cherished streetcar service was restored to Fort Collins. The cost of living was still riding the wartime prosperity. The Hawthorn Garage at College and Olive advertised gas for 24 cents a gallon. On October, 30, 1919, W. C. Johnston's Lincoln Highway Garage, on East Mountain at Remington ran a car ad in the newspaper, "Chevy Touring Car, $875, Roadsters, $855, Sedans, $1,395." In late November, houses were advertised for sale from $600 to $5,000. That fall, apple growers shipped 200 train carloads of the fruit, which required 200 to 300 employees to pick. At the same time, cherry production grossed 2,870,000 pounds at $200 a train carload. The Aggie's college, which had finally reopened in January 1919, with 415 students, saw a fall term enrollment of 743 students, of which 108 were veterans of the World War. "Happy Days" were truly here again!

AND WHAT CAUSED FORT COLLINS TO VIRTUALLY DOZE FOR THE NEXT TWENTY YEARS?

The Happy Days going into the Roaring Twenties did not really create a good time for everyone. The Great World War's "Economic Boom" did not continue. By the 1920s, agriculture in Northern Colorado went into a depression with lower demand and consequently lower farm prices. While Fort Collins' population had only grown by 500 souls during the Teens, the next thirty years showed only static growth averaging less than twenty percent per decade, with the years during the Great Depression of the thirties showing very little change in the population. In May 1920 the McCormick brothers, George and James, publishers of the Fort Collins *Express*, purchased the Fort Collins *Courier*, renaming the new publication, The Fort Collins *Express–Courier*, and promised both a morning and evening edition. The demand for two local newspapers had dropped enough that the community could no longer support two separate publications.

A load of Akin Farm wool in front of the privately owned Poudre Valley Gas Company on Willow Street.
PHOTOGRAPH COURTESY OF JOAN DAY.

The combined paper would continue with the new name until taken over by the *Coloradoan* on April 29, 1945.

The post-war demand for sugar had declined, so the Great Western Sugar Company contracted for 3,000 less acres of sugar beets in 1920. Still, sugar beet growing and the processing of the crop remained one of the mainstay industries in Northern Colorado, as did lamb feeding and the raising of sheep for their wool. In spite of this, some of the local citizens were still doing well since the Larimer County Clerk reported that there were over 500 autos registered in the county as of February 1920.

The Mitchell Well on fire in the summer of 1924.

There was a flurry of activity north of the city in the mid-twenties as many oil and natural gas wells were drilled. Production was promising and by 1928 there were thirty-four producing wells in the Fort Collins and Wellington Fields, but not without

some dangers. On November 11, 1923, the "Discovery Well" near Wellington literally blew its top. It blew a plume of white natural gas into the air with a roar that could be heard in Fort Collins. Charles H. Sherman, field manager for the Union Oil Company, estimated that between 85 and 100 million cubic feet of gas was being lost every day and put the daily loss at $24,000. The blowing well became a local tourist attraction as hundreds journeyed north of the city to see the spectacle up close, but not too close! One Fort Collins entrepreneur set up a small café, the "Inform Bureau Café," near the well, and another started an auto stage line to carry viewers to the oil field. It took oil field workers six weeks to finally cap the well. In another instance, the Mitchell Well, caught fire on July 23, 1924, and burned for a month before being snuffed out by a charge of nitro. It had not been properly capped after it "blew in." The other part of the "Oil and Gas Boom" was the large number of stock speculators who moved to Fort Collins, selling shares in wells—some of which actually existed! Part of this natural gas was piped into Fort Collins by 1925, replacing the Poudre Valley Gas Company's coal gasification plant that had served the city since the late 1800s. Some of the old wells are still operating in the area today as a new era of gas and oil exploration hits the region.

The mid-twenties saw other signs of progress. The newspaper reported on February 28, 1924, that a large force of men was putting in flagstone walks at several intersections where the streets were still unpaved. Despite 1915 and 1921 additions to the 1903 high school building, it had become very overcrowded. Citizens in 1923 voted a $330,000 bond issue for a new high school to be built on the south edge of town on land donated by L. C. Moore. The beautiful colonnaded brick structure was completed in mid-1925 and classes began that fall. That same year a three story brick county hospital was built for $175,000 at the east edge of town on a road called Hospital Lane (present-day Lemay Avenue), on the grounds of the county's "poor farm." Over the years, several additions were built as the Poudre Valley Hospital district was created by voters. Today there are three hospital campuses along with another new name, the University Hospital System, linking

Top: The original Fort Collins High School with its 1915 and 1921 additions.

Center and bottom: The second Fort Collins High School under construction and the finished building.

The ARMSTRONG HOTEL . . . . Fort Collins, Colorado

CENTRALLY LOCATED IN THIS AREA

A CONVENIENT BASE FROM WHICH TO MAKE ONE, AND TWO-DAY MOUNTAIN AND FISHING TRIPS

COFFEE SHOP

CHANDLER W. POST, MGR.
ART QUINLAN   DAVE WARNOCK

DINING ROOM

Above: The Armstrong Hotel was the first local hotel built for the motor tourism trade in 1922.

PHOTOGRAPH COURTESY OF JANE BASS POSTCARD COLLECTION.

Right: Area on the west side of town, west of Overland Trail, owned by the local KKK, city map, March 1929.

PHOTOGRAPH COURTESY OF THE LOCAL HISTORY ARCHIVE AT THE FORT COLLINS MUSEUM OF DISCOVERY.

Below: A fourth floor was added to the Northern Hotel in 1924 and the outside was redecorated in the mid-thirties.

Fort Collins healthcare with the University Hospital in Aurora. In 1922 the first hotel to meet the demands from the motor tourist, The Armstrong Hotel, was built. Two years later, the Northern Hotel added a fourth floor and went through a remodeling to meet this growing tourism industry.

A new social organization emerged in Fort Collins when an advertisement appeared in the *Express-Courier* on August 17, 1924, offering a $10 membership to "100% Americans. A local "klavern" of the Ku Klux Klan was seeking members. Families were encouraged to join, and parades and gatherings were among their activities. The Klan owned a tract of land off the west side of Fort Collins where

some of their gatherings were held. A local grocer, Samuel J. Salyers, campaigned to expose them for what they really stood for—anti-Catholic, anti-Jew, and anti-ethnic groups. The Colorado KKK claimed 30,000 members in 1925, and had actually helped elect a pro-Klan governor, Clarence Morley. By 1926, the Klan power and popularity was on the decline throughout the state, and in Fort Collins it was no longer even a social force.

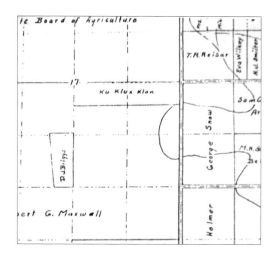

By early 1929 it looked like the economy might be improving. Larimer County ranked third in the state in manufactured products. It claimed a new Ideal Cement Plant, built that same year near LaPorte. There was also a foundry shop, a brick and tile company, canning factories, flour mills, creameries producing butter, cheese, and milk, and the Union Oil Company. The Great Western Sugar Company's factory once again had high sugar and sugar-related products output. In February 1927, the sugar company had platted and registered a community named Alta Vista on land northeast of the factory hoping to encourage their Mexican migrant workers to settle there. The company offered lots, fifty by 85 feet along with straw, dirt, and lime for the building of adobe homes. The lots were free the first year, and then the workers would have to pay $40 per year for the next three years. To serve many of these Spanish-speaking Catholics, Father Joseph Pierre Trudel spearheaded raising money to build Holy Family Church at Whitcomb and Cherry Streets in 1929. As an aside for this apparent "economic boom," the first "talkie"

movie, *The Jazz Singer* starring Al Jolson, appeared on screen at the America Theater in March of that same year.

The economic bubble burst and the whole country plunged into the Great Depression at the end of October 1929. Adding to the gloom of falling farm prices, a five year drought, the so-called "Dust Bowl," set in and hordes of grasshoppers appeared once more after a fifty year hiatus. By September 1934 the Poudre River was at the lowest flow level since the earliest settlement, and the city banned the use of water for lawns and gardens. Many people lost their jobs as businesses closed and unemployment numbers soared. By 1935, thirty-five percent of the residents of Larimer County, about

11,500 people, were receiving federal or county relief assistance. The Civilian Conservation Corps (C.C.C.) had two camps in the area—one at Buckeye and another at Red Feather Lakes, and the W.P.A. (Works Progress Administration) also provided government-supported jobs. One benefit of these programs for Fort Collins was the building of City Park Nine Golf Course in 1938 by the W.P.A. The city took the former fairground/race track site and allegedly added part of Grandview Cemetery for the course. And alcohol, sort of, returned to the city in 1936. Colorado passed a law allowing the sale of 3.2 percent beer in Colorado, and the town's oldest bar opened in 1936— The Town Pump.

Above: City Park Nine golf course ground breaking in 1938.
PHOTOGRAPH COURTESY OF THE LOCAL HISTORY ARCHIVE AT THE FORT COLLINS MUSEUM OF DISCOVERY.

Below: A view of the Buckeye Civilian Conservation Corp camp near Buckeye, north of the city, October 11, 1937.
PHOTOGRAPH COURTESY OF THE LOCAL HISTORY ARCHIVE AT THE FORT COLLINS MUSEUM OF DISCOVERY.

Above: A panel showing the Forney "Farm Welders" products.

Below: Allen "Bert" Christman, Fort Collins aviator killed early in WWII, in his Navy uniform.

Many people found creative ways to survive the economic depression. For example, J. D. Forney, who saw his door-to-door encyclopedia sales drying up, invented an "Instant Heat Soldering Iron" in 1932. It could be operated off a farm tractor or truck battery. He had noticed the need for this type of farm appliance in his sales travels through the rural areas of Colorado, Nebraska, and Kansas. He sold, or more often traded, the soldering iron for various farm products like chickens or vegetables. When the Rural Electrification Administration brought electricity to most rural areas, J. D. invented a transformer to go with the soldering iron. In 1938 he patented the "Forney Farm Welder," which was manufactured in a small plant at the corner of Jefferson and Pine Streets. The manufacturing plant outgrew that location by 1947 and Forney Industries moved to a new plant on LaPorte Avenue.

The "Great Depression" and prolonged drought, along with lobbying by northern Colorado farm groups, pushed the U.S. Congress to authorize a vast water storage and diversion project in August, 1937. Called the "Colorado-Big Thompson Project," it created a system of reservoirs, canals, and the thirteen and a half mile long tunnel, the

Alva B. Adams Tunnel, under the Continental Divide in Rocky Mountain National Park. Construction began in 1938 and would continue for the next twenty years, with World War II slowing construction during the forties. Its purpose was to provide supplemental water to 650,000 acres of land, as well as electricity, in northeastern Colorado. It also created many needed jobs as the project was being built. When the project was completed and its reservoirs were filled by 1957, it proved to be a great boon to agriculture and recreation in northeast Colorado and to the cities in that area.

THE WAR YEARS AND AFTER

As the 1940s rolled in, the European war was spreading as the Nazis took over more countries on that continent. Americans, for the most part, were quite isolationist, but wanted to be prepared if the United States was drawn in to this foreign conflict. Colorado A & M added a pilot training program in June 1940, as part of a national defense plan. By October that year, 3,881 men had registered for the draft in Larimer County. Many local men were already serving in the

various U.S. military services. Allen "Bert" Christman left a successful career with a New York newspaper, having created a popular comic strip, "Scorchy Smith." He enlisted as a pilot in the U.S. Navy Air Service and was commissioned a lieutenant. He transferred to General Claire Chennault's Chinese "Flying Tigers" and was flying "The Hump" in Burma, fighting against the Japanese who had taken over much of China. On January 23, 1942, he was shot down and killed over Rangoon, shortly after the United States was drawn into World War II. He became one of Fort Collins' earliest casualties of that war. The city's first war loss was Ben Schlect, a U.S. Navy radioman, serving on a ship at Pearl Harbor, who was killed during the surprise Japanese attack on that naval base, on December 7, 1941. Another U.S. sailor, Harold D. Webster, of Loveland, died in that same attack.

Just before the country's entry into the war, in what was probably the final local Great Depression W.P.A. project, the sandstone Fort Collins Pioneer Museum was constructed in the 200 block of Peterson Street in Lincoln Park in 1940. The shift to a wartime economy certainly brought the country out of the Depression. Men and women alike signed up to serve in the armed forces. Some young women also moved to the West Coast to work in war manufacturing plants—Fort Collins own versions of "Rosy the Riveter!" By the end of the war, over 4,000 county residents served in the armed forces. Some local businesses were taken over for the war effort. Giddings's Machine Shop at Pine and Willow Streets was leased by the Northern Colorado Manufacturing Company and converted into a plant to produce large valves for U.S. Navy ships and submarines.

The old Pioneer Museum in the 200 block of Peterson was built in 1940 and razed in the late 1970s.

shortage of farm labor. Many of the German and Italian POWs housed in these camps were "loaned out" as farm workers. Since northern Colorado had a fairly large German-Russian population, German POWs could easily communicate in German with many of the farmers. The location of one of these internment camps is marked by two stone entrance columns, with some interpretive signs, just off US Highway 34 south of Windsor.

Numerous scrap metal and paper collection drives were held by various local groups, as well as war bond drives and blood donation efforts. Newspapers during the war years were filled with news of how the various battles were going, as well as news on local military personnel. There were reports of local soldiers, sailors, and airmen who were wounded or killed in action or who were captured and interred as prisoners of war. Several stories reported on medals that were given to local men for bravery or exceptional acts of heroism in combat. The *Express-Courier* also reported on other home front activities such as the first successful air raid "black-out" drill in mid-December 1942. Another unique war story was published on August 18, 1943, when 80 soldiers who were in training at Colorado A & M joined with 40 Fort Collins young people plus 30 Italian prisoners-of-war to harvest the local bean crop! Starting in 1943, POW internment camps were built in this area. Over 4,000 local young men and women were serving in the armed forces, so there was a

In early 1944, as war casualties mounted, some Fort Collins residents proposed the creation of a veteran's war memorial for the grass median at LaPorte and College. The "War Dads" were able to raise funds and the "Honor Roll Monument" was dedicated on Memorial Day, May 30, 1944. It listed 3,000 who had served in the armed forces of the United States and included the names of 51 who had died up to that point in World War II. Fifty-seven men were also listed as missing or prisoners. A newer "Larimer County Veterans Memorial" was built in Edora Park, and dedicated on Pearl Harbor Day, December 7, 1989. The old monument was deactivated and demolished.

What kind of Fort Collins people volunteered or were drafted into the military service during the war? One was Joseph Alonzo Martinez, son of Lee and Eva Martinez. Alonzo graduated from Fort Collins High School in January, 1944, and was drafted into the Army in March. He was trained as an infantryman and joined the 84th Infantry Division on August 23, five days shy of his nineteenth birthday. The unit was shipped to the front lines in Europe in November 1944. He was killed by German machine gun fire in the Battle of the Bulge, in Beffe, Belgium, on January 3, 1945. He was interred in the U.S. Military Cemetery near Liege, Belgium. His remains were brought home to Fort Collins three years later and he was buried in Grandview Cemetery on December 13, 1947. Fort Collins' second American Legion Post was named for him, and the Alonzo Martinez Scholarship is still given each year in his honor. Another and more fortunate military man was Courtlyn "Court" Hotchkiss, who after the war, taught at the college for 32 years and served 14 years as a Larimer County Commissioner. Court served in the U.S. Army Air Force as a fighter pilot. He flew 53 successful missions over Europe, but was shot down in the spring of 1944 over occupied France. He managed to elude capture by the Germans and linked up with the French underground. They eventually got him to the coast and on a boat that took him to England. He had been listed as missing in action for six months.

Two former Aggies and Fort Collins High School classmates entered World War II around the same time. Martha Scott Trimble and Lewis "Corky" Walt were co-leaders in high school and college. Walt enlisted in the Marine Corps and quickly rose through the ranks to colonel. In the South Pacific, in the battle for Pelelu, he distinguished himself by leading his men to victory over the Japanese on what became known as "Walt's Ridge." He remained in the Marines, eventually becoming the Commandant of the entire Marine Corp. Trimble enlisted in the WAVES when that women's branch was created in 1942, becoming the first woman from Larimer County to be inducted into that service. Lieutenant Trimble taught aviation navigation to Navy pilots who were in training at Pensacola, Florida. After the war, she returned to the city and taught English at the college for many years.

Fort Collins High and Aggie's classmates, Lewis "Corky" Walt (above) and Martha S. Trimble (left), both officers in WWII. Trimble enlisted on December 12, 1942.

PHOTOGRAPH COURTESY OF THE LOCAL HISTORY ARCHIVE AT THE FORT COLLINS MUSEUM OF DISCOVERY.

There was one final war event in the area before war's end—the Japanese bombed part of Timnath! Two Japanese "balloon bombs" fell in a field on the Swets farm just south of Timnath in March 1945. One exploded on impact, creating a sizable crater in a plowed field, while the other did not detonate. The end of World War II brought jubilation to Fort Collins. The announcement that Japan had surrendered unconditionally came in mid-August 1945. Germany had surrendered earlier, in June. The newspaper on August 15 reported that local citizens jammed the downtown streets from 5:00 p.m. and on through the night. Life in town could begin to return to normal as the local men and women veterans began returning home.

The post-war years brought a new era of growth to the city. Many workers moved to town after Congress authorized $15,000,000 for the completion of the Colorado-Big Thompson Project, including money to build the 156,000 acre-foot Horsetooth Reservoir. The Bureau of Reclamation put up a small workers' housing village north of LaPorte Avenue and west of Shields Street, with thirty-five small prefab single family homes. It was called "Reclamation Village." Horsetooth Reservoir was completed in 1949, with water to fill it delivered in 1951. The first water was delivered to Fort Collins and the Poudre River later that same year. The area was now somewhat drought-proofed.

Post-war Colorado A & M was jolted by unexpected enrollment growth starting in January 1946, while the academic year, 1946-1947, virtually overloaded the college. Regular student enrollment had dropped to 701 during the 1943-1944 school term, not counting the military trainees, but jumped to 3,500 students in the fall of 1946, with 2,500 of those students being veterans. A "Vet Village" was built along West Laurel Street consisting mostly of war surplus Quonset Huts. Student housing was at a premium. Both the town and the college entered a period of rapid growth. Fort Collins' population, which had been reported at 12,251 after the 1940 census, was estimated to be 18,500 by 1948.

The city's municipal railway, the trolley streetcar system, purchased two additional cars in 1946 from Richmond, Virginia, partly in anticipation of growing ridership and partly for parts to maintain its fleet of streetcars. Shortly thereafter ridership began to decline as the post-war love of the automobile skyrocketed and many American families became two and three car households. By 1950 town growth away from the earlier core city and lower revenues, caused the city to license the Bussard Bus Line to serve the areas farther away from the streetcar tracks. On June 30, 1951, streetcar service was "temporarily" suspended for six months. Later this suspension was extended an additional year to see how the bus service would fare. In 1953 a vote of the people supported abandonment of the city-owned Fort Collins Municipal Railway. This was a long fall from 1947 when the *Saturday Evening Post* published a glowing account about the Fort Collins streetcar system in its December 6 magazine. The

"Some of My Best Friends are Street Cars" story called the city "...the smallest town in the U.S. to support a trolley system." The three-way "Y" at College and Mountain was dubbed "...an ingenious small town stunt." And the five cent fare was the lowest in the country, according to the *Post* story. The bus line continued for a couple more years after street car service was abandoned after J. D. Forney took over the bus operation, but low ridership doomed that effort. The city remained without public transportation until the city-run Transfort system went into service in 1974.

The final swansong of the forties was a horrendous blizzard that swept across the Great Plains in January 1949. New Year's Day had temperatures that approached seventy degrees and the forecast for Sunday, the 2nd was for "increasing cloudiness—possible snow flurries." Instead, heavy snow driven by winds in excess of sixty miles an hour hit northern Colorado and southern Wyoming. Holiday travelers were suddenly confronted by white-outs and large drifts and temperatures that dropped below zero. Sixty-five motorists were stranded between Wellington and Cheyenne on the old U.S. Highway 87, with many more trapped on U.S. 85 north of Greeley. Many heroic rescue efforts were made by local citizens and public servants. The Wellington American Legion hall became a refugee center as 125 stranded motorists were brought in from the storm. At Rockport, just south of the Wyoming line on the U.S. 85 highway, 465 travelers were jammed into a tavern and two stranded busses. Supplies in the hardest hit areas were quickly consumed. The sun broke through for a day, enabling trains to make their way to the most severely affected places and to help evacuate many of the stranded people. Another blizzard swept in on January 8, but it was not as intense. By February 19, six major blizzards and several less severe storms had ravaged the Great Plains. By late February, over 200,000 people had been isolated at various plains location by the series of storms and over 100 had died from weather-related causes. Thousands of head of livestock perished as a result of the storms and temperatures that dipped to as low as fifty below zero.

An air view showing "Vet Village" on West Laurel Street, on the northwest corner of the Aggie's campus, c. 1950.

CHAPTER 4

FORT COLLINS GROWS & GROWS

Pat Griffin, founder of Gas-A-Mat self-

pumping gas stations, on the right, c. 1950.

PHOTOGRAPH COURTESY OF THE LOCAL HISTORY
ARCHIVE AT THE FORT COLLINS MUSEUM OF DISCOVERY.

Fort Collins galloped into the second half of the twentieth century with an extended period of unprecedented growth. In 1950 the city covered 2.97 square miles. From 1925 up to 1950, there had been only four annexations, totaling eighteen acres. By comparison, 1950 to 1961 brought seventy-five annexations creating a city that covered over 6 square miles, and the pattern would continue. By 1980, Fort Collins city limits encompassed more than 21 square miles and the city was growing in all directions. The population grew from 14,937 in 1950 to almost 65,000 by 1980. The growth caused the face of Fort Collins to change tremendously. In 1954, citizens voted to change the make-up of the city council from three to five members with a city manager as the chief administrator. The vote also gave the council the power to appoint a mayor.

After the war, and as people were coming to the small college town, a new subdivision was platted in 1946 on the south edge of town, just north off of East Prospect. The Circle Drive development featured small single family homes; today they would be called "starter homes," along with a new concept—underground utilities. The city was one of the first towns in the U.S. to adopt this idea. At this time, the city limits basically ended at Prospect Road. College Avenue existed as a two lane road for its last half mile, from the Aggie's field house and Colorado Field to Prospect Road for several more years. This new subdivision foretold the coming rapid growth during the second half of the twentieth century. With growth, more houses and bigger business buildings became a necessity, as well as the need for larger churches and schools. First Methodist Church decided their 1908 downtown church was too small and built a new non-traditional, modern designed church at the corner of Stover and Elizabeth Streets in 1960. Five years later, St. Luke's Episcopal Church also deserted its quaint sandstone structure at the southeast corner of College and Oak Streets for a new building even further south on Stover Street. New housing developments would now come in rapid succession.

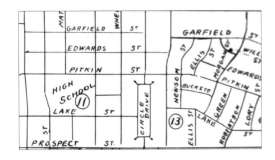

A big "stumble" in the growth pathway was the "shuttering" of the Great Western Sugar Factory on East Vine following the sugar beet campaign of 1953-1954. The company reported, in early 1955, that the plant would not reopen, and that local sugar beets would be processed from then on at the Loveland, Windsor, or Greeley factories. A diminishing demand for beet sugar, stiff competition from imported cane sugar, and falling prices paid to beet growers spelled the eventual demise of this important industry from Northern Colorado. One small industry that helped soften the blow from the loss of the sugar factory was something called "Gasamat." Local fuel supplier, Pat Griffin, developed a coin-operated gas pump in 1959. Its popularity quickly grew and over the next decade, the Fort Collins-based company expanded to ten more western states.

Above: Map of the 1946 Circle Drive Subdivision.
PHOTOGRAPH COURTESY OF THE LOCAL HISTORY ARCHIVE AT THE FORT COLLINS MUSEUM OF DISCOVERY.

Below: First Methodist Church, shown in 1910, was one of the first to move from their small downtown churches to larger, modern structures.
PHOTOGRAPH COURTESY OF JANE BASS POSTCARD COLLECTION.

On the city's west side south of Mulberry and west of Washington Street, two filings were made for annexation of proposed housing projects in 1948 and 1950. Called the Mantz Addition, after Carolyn Armstrong Mantz, who had sold the land to the developers, it surrounded Dunn Elementary, which opened in 1949, on the west and south, and fronted on Shields Street between Mulberry and Laurel Streets. Most of its homes were constructed between 1951 and 1959. Detached alley garages were now out of favor as were long deep lots. The new concept was for wider side-to-side and shallower lots. Attached one or two car garages with street access were now desired. New developments no longer had to stick to the rigid traditional grid system, so streets could be laid out with sweeping curves and even cul-de-sacs. South College Heights was platted in the summer of 1954, with its streets named after major colleges—Dartmouth, Rutgers, Stanford, etc. and was built out in the sixties. The Sheely additions, south of the college off West Prospect Road, was platted beginning in August 1953, and featured houses with some radical architectural designs—low flat roofs on very linear, modernistic homes. Nearby, just southwest of the college, Western Heights was laid out in 1957-1958. On the city's east side, University Acres, with streets named for former Aggie's presidents—Green, Ellis, Edwards, etc. was annexed into the city in 1957 and platted in 1961. Another east side subdivision, Indian Hills, laid out in the fall of 1958 south of Stuart Street, with its streets named for Native American tribes—Cherokee, Seminole, Navajo, etc. The city limits had now been pushed south to Drake Road, which was still a dirt road in the fifties. Congress passed the "Servicemen's Readjustment Act" known as the "G.I. Bill," in 1944, and three housing legislative acts between 1946 and 1949 established FHA loan programs for veterans with low or no down payments when they were buying a house, and offered thirty year mortgage loans with low interest rates. This was one big factor in pushing the home building industry to have more houses ready in the fifties, sixties, and seventies.

As the city's population was growing in the early fifties, there was a need for better recreational facilities. The local Elks Lodge, a long-time supporter of programs for young people, worked with the city government to get support for a fund-raising idea they were promoting. From the time of the creation of City Park, there had been a dock and diving platform for the swimming area in Sheldon Lake. The Elks wanted to raise money to build a modern swimming pool with clean filtered water. From 1952 to 1953, they raised $34,000 to build the City Park pool, with the city covering the rest of the $46,000 total cost. It was dedicated and put into use on August 17, 1953. The pool has undergone several changes and improvement in the intervening years. The upstairs of the 1921 City Park Pavilion building had been a roller rink and dance facility. It then became the teen hang-out, Club Tico, in 1948, an identity it kept until the early 1970s.

Changes in the face of local public education were also coming. A state law passed in the 1947, encouraged Colorado counties to consolidate their small districts into single large ones. In Larimer County there were 30 districts of various sizes. Small outlying communities were very protective when it came to their rural schools, which were often also centers for various social gatherings. Towns like LaPorte, Berthoud, Wellington, Waverly, and Timnath were very territorial about their K-12 schools and took pride in having their own high schools. A Larimer County School Reorganization Committee was formed in the mid-fifties and came up with a plan for six districts to be created throughout the county. It was met with considerable resistance and was rejected in September 1959. The newly elected County Superintendent of Schools, Margaret Miller, brought together the board presidents from all 30 districts and pointed out that an amendment to the reorganization act gave the Colorado Commissioner of Education the power to do the reorganization if a county failed to come up with a plan by January 1, 1960. County voters finally approved a new plan in the spring of 1960 and three districts were created—Poudre R-1, Thompson R-J2,

and Park R-3, each with their own school boards and superintendents. Fort Collins became the administrative headquarters for the Poudre R-1 District, which had brought together 21 small districts. David B. Lesher, the last superintendent of Fort Collins District #5, became the first superintendent of the new district. The second junior high in town was completed in 1961 and named for Lesher. The end of the 1964 school year was the final year for just one large high school in the city, Fort Collins High School, and the final year for high schools in the outlying towns as all high school students were to come to either the new Poudre High School or Fort Collins High School starting in September of that year. Since 1970, twenty-six new schools have been built—three new

high school buildings, five junior high school (now called middle schools), and the rest, elementary schools. On the fiftieth anniversary of reorganization in 2010, Poudre School District had an enrollment of 24,246 students

As businesses grew, larger facilities were needed, especially for a culture that was more and more automobile oriented. The face of downtown Fort Collins began to change radically. On July 1, 1950, most of Block 104 fronting on South College Avenue, surrounded by Magnolia, Mason and Mulberry and occupied by several elegant homes of early Fort Collins residents like the Welch-Evans House, was leveled to make way for a super market, Safeway, with a large on-site parking lot. Small neighborhood groceries were

Above: The Welch-Evans House near the northwest corner of College and Mulberry.

Below: Several stately old homes were demolished to make way for a Safeway supermarket in 1950.

**MORRIE'S
IN "N" OUT**

Beefburgers

1611 So. College   Phone HU 2-2222

*Above: Morrie's In "N" Out Drive-in,
at Prospect and College, c. 1950s.*

*Below: The beautiful 1908 First National
Bank Building at College and Mountain
Avenues was torn down when the business
was moved to the 200 block of Oak Street.*
PHOTOGRAPH COURTESY OF JANE BASS
POSTCARD COLLECTION.

giving way to these new large stores with their convenient assortment of goods—"one-stop shopping" was becoming the new catch phrase. First National Bank, a fixture in the downtown since 1881, needed more room in order to compete with other banks and for a drive-thru teller facility. Poudre Valley National Bank, across College from First National, had built the first Fort Collins' drive-up teller windows on the west side of its building in 1953 to meet one of these demands. First National was hemmed-in by other business blocks and needed to move in order to expand. Its new bank structure was built on the corner of Mason and Oak in 1961, with a drive-thru facility with several teller lanes eventually built on the block south of the new bank. The beautiful white colonnaded building built for Franklin Avery in 1908, at the southeast corner of Mountain and College, was razed. Motorists wanted easy ways to stay in their cars and still conduct everyday activities. One of the early drive-up windows in the city was built into the new city hall at the corner of LaPorte and Howes Streets. It opened in January 1958, so utility customers could stay in their cars and still pay their bills. The first drive-in restaurant as the city moved south of Prospect was Morrie's In "N" Out Beefburgers at the southwest corner of College and Prospect in the early fifties.

The downtown area had already lost two 1887 historic structures—the Franklin School and Larimer County Courthouse in 1957 when they were replaced by modern structures—one by a new courthouse and the other by Steele's Grocery. JCPenney Company tore down the beautiful and historic 1883 B. F. Hottel mansion in the 200 block of South College to build its low profile new downtown store in 1962. Long-established family-owned car dealers began to leave the downtown for larger showrooms surrounded by large display lots. Ghent Motors moved to the southwest corner of College and Drake, just outside the expanding city limits in 1965.

Colorado A & M was also on the move and college president, William Morgan, led the fight to get the state legislature to change the school's name. On May 1, 1957, A & M became Colorado State University. Enrollment jumped from 7,304 in the fall of 1962 to 15,361 at the beginning of the school year in 1968, the same year the 30,000 seat Hughes Stadium was built three miles west of the campus near the foothill's "A". Moby Gymnasium had been added to the campus two years before the stadium was constructed.

Forney Industries was a well-known local manufacture industry in the 1950s with its production of Forney Welders and welding equipment, as well as built-in home vacuum systems, wrought iron furniture, and the single engine airplane, "Forney Aircoupe." Beginning in 1956, the airplane was manufactured at Christman Field on the far west side of Fort Collins. Forney's later added a film division, a lumber yard, and Don-Art Printers, making it the largest single employer in the city for many years. During the 1960s, the city welcomed other light manufacturing industries such as Woodward Governor, who moved part of their production from Rockford, Illinois, to Fort Collins in the late fifties, building their present plant at Drake Road and Lemay Avenue in 1966. The homegrown industry, Aqua-Tec, the manufacturer of the Water Pik Oral Appliance, opened its doors in 1961. The company grew quickly, adding the production of shower massagers, and became part

of Teledyne Industries in 1967. The next year, First National Bank added its twelve-story tower in the 200 block of West Oak Street, and Home Federal Savings in the next block west added an eleven-story building to its bank.

Above: B. F. Hottel's magnificent 1883 home was razed to make way for a JCPenney store in 1962.

Left: J. D. Forney and his airplane, the "Forney Aircoupe," on the runway at Christman Field west of town.

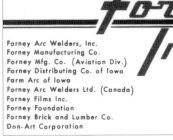

Forney Arc Welders, Inc.
Forney Manufacturing Co.
Forney Mfg. Co. (Aviation Div.)
Forney Distributing Co. of Iowa
Farm Arc of Iowa
Forney Arc Welders Ltd. (Canada)
Forney Films Inc.
Forney Foundation
Forney Brick and Lumber Co.
Don-Art Corporation

Forney Industries
Fort Collins, Colorado

A Letter from the President

THE FORT COLLINS AREA

volume one: the graphic past

FORT COLLINS TURNS
100 AND GROWS ON

*Above: Cover of one of two 1964
Centennial booklets.*

*Right: Birthday bulletin for Fort Collins
1964 Centennial.*

In the midst of all this expansion, in the summer of 1964, Fort Collins citizens paused to observe and celebrate the town's 100th birthday, the "Fort Collins Centennial Celebration." Several committees were formed to plan the year's activities. Virtually anybody who was anyone in the community found a role in planning for the big party! Kick-off activities began on May 30, Memorial Day, on the CSU campus with precision parachute jumps by the Golden Knights, a U.S. Army parachute team. U.S. Supreme Court Justice Byron L. White, a Wellington High School grad, gave the address, and the CSU Symphonic Band and the Community Chorus gave the premier performance of *Heritage*, a symphony written for the Centennial by Gregory Bueche. James R. Miller's work

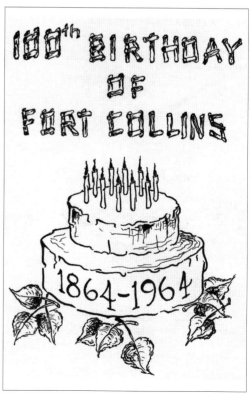

100th BIRTHDAY OF FORT COLLINS

1864-1964

The Fort Collins Epic was also presented. On July the Fourth, the city's traditional Independence Day Parade celebrated the Fort Collins Centennial, with many floats and performing groups emphasizing the town's birthday and heritage. There was "A Good Old Fashioned Band Concert" on the western edge of the college, performed by the U.S. Army band from the 5th Infantry Division stationed at Fort Carson. A beef and buffalo barbecue followed the concert, with a spectacular fireworks show that evening. Later in July, there were three evenings of performances of Pioneer Panorama, a play produced and directed by CSU English and theater professor, Ruth Jocelyn "R. J." Wattles. It starred many local residents as historical Fort Collins figures and told the story of Fort Collins' first century. The culminating activity of the Centennial was a big banquet in the CSU ballroom, recognizing members from pioneer families and giving special note to Livermore rancher, George Roberts, as the oldest of the "old timers" present at 101 years of age. His younger brother, Ernest, 97 years old, also attended. The brothers had settled at Livermore with their parents, Robert O. and Mary Roberts, in 1874, establishing the Roberts Ranch and Roberts Cattle Company.

Many local, county, and state dignitaries were recognized at the banquet as well as those who had worked to make the Centennial celebration a big success.

There were other celebration contests during the summer of 1964 like beard and sideburn growing contests, and historic displays in downtown business windows. Two Centennial booklets were printed and Centennial coins were minted as limited edition souvenirs. Additionally, several historic homes were marked with wooden commemorative signs. One of the highlights of the summer's events happened at the southeast corner of Mountain and College Avenues in July when the popular TV actor, Jack Benny, placed his handprint and signature in black cement in front of the Columbia Savings Bank. Handprints and signatures of Mayor Harvey Johnson and CSU President William Morgan flanked the actor's impression. Benny was an honorary vice president for MCA Entertainment, the owners of Columbia Savings and CBS Television, and the sponsors of his popular television show. He had been in Fort Collins two years before for the opening of that same Columbia Savings Bank. The Fort Collins' community could be justly proud of its Centennial celebration.

THE FORT COLLINS AREA

volume two:

at the centennial

Cover of the other 1964 Centennial booklet.

CENTENNIAL - BICENTENNIAL
HERITAGE COUNCIL

1876

1976

AVERY HOUSE

This beautiful Victorian house, built in 1879, belonged to Franklin C. Avery. Mr. Avery platted the original town in January, 1873. He made major contributions to the creation of a system of irrigation canals in Larimer County. The Avery family occupied this elegant sandstone home until 1962. This structure is listed on the National Register of Historic Places.

FORT COLLINS, COLORADO

Donated by Coterie Woman's Club, G.F.W.C.

Above: Several of these plaques were put on, or in front of, historic structures in honor of Colorado's Centennial and the U.S. Bicentennial.

Right: The original Fort Collins Water Works was one of the first structures given Fort Collins landmark protection.

A PRESERVATION ETHIC SLOWLY EMERGES

The destruction of the beautiful First National Bank, the elegant Hottel House and Welch-Evans House, along with Franklin School, the Larimer County Courthouse, and several other historic structures, led to an awakening for many Fort Collins citizens. They belatedly realized how much of their local heritage was being lost. A preservation ethic emerged and people pushed the city council to create some protection for other historic sites. On June 15, 1968, the council adopted an ordinance creating the Fort Collins Landmark Preservation Commission and spelling out its make-up, duties, and establishing the designation procedure. The ordinance outlined the restrictions placed on owners of designated landmarks in terms of alterations and demolition. The city council appointed the first commission members and the LPC's first landmark recommendation missed the mark slightly. In one of its first acts, the Landmarks Commission asked the council to designate city-owned land behind the power plant as the Old Fort Collins Site Historic District. This was done on November 13, 1969. The designated land was actually the old city dump, and the actual fort site was adjacent to the designated site. This slightly-off designation was rescinded several years later. The second place given landmark status was the original city-owned 1882-1883 Water Works and its surrounding structures on Overland Trail near LaPorte in late December 1971. The next designation was more complicated—The Avery House at 328 West Mountain Avenue. The Landmark Commission managed to get it on the National Register of Historic places in 1972, but was not able to give it the protection that local designation provided until after the city purchased the home for $76,000 in 1974. Two more structures were designated before the Landmark Preservation Commission became a committee of the Cultural Resources Board in 1975. A separate LPC did not re-emerge until the nineteen eighties.

Money to buy the Avery House came from an initiative passed by city voters in 1973, when Designing Tomorrow Today (DT2) was funded by a one cent sales tax with a seven year term. Over that time period, 16.1 million dollars was raised for capital improvement projects like the Lincoln Center, Transfort, and sewer lines for Alta Vista and Andersonville. The first Transfort busses, Mercedes-Benz minibuses, began operating on city streets on July 1, 1974.

The downtown public library was built around the old Pioneer Museum in the mid-1970s.

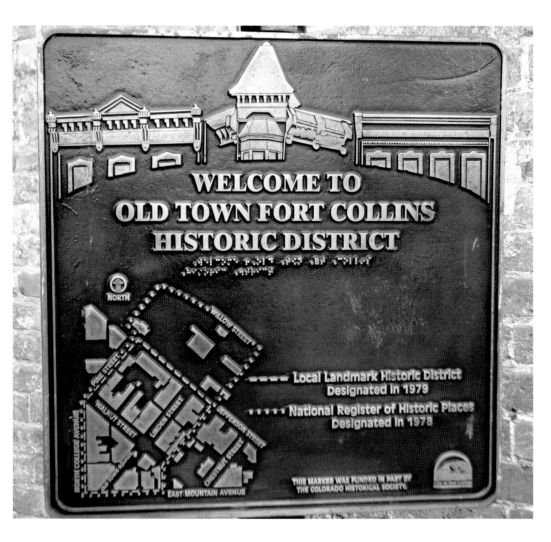

The Old Town Fort Collins triangle received
National Landmark status in 1978.

Some of the money also created a local Centennial-Bicentennial Commission in 1974 for the upcoming 100th birthday of Colorado's statehood and the United States' 200th birthday. One ambitious project, the reconstruction of the original Fort Collins Military Post, grew out of planning for the anticipated celebration of the two birthdays. The planned fort reconstruction and operation became cost-prohibitive, and the Heritage Committee of local CBC shifted its financial resources to a project to plaque several historic buildings. This project was completed with permanent plaques on, or in front of, twenty-four historic structures in the city by early 1977.

The mid-seventies saw several changes within the city. The large Foothill Fashion Mall on the south edge of the city was built in 1974 and the Larimer County Vocational and Technical Center opened in 1975. It later became part of the Front Range Community College system and is in a period of extensive additional construction in 2014. A new public library replaced the old Pioneer Museum, whose collection was moved across Lincoln Park into the 1903 Carnegie Library building, in 1975. The city's first branch library was built in cooperation with Front Range Community College at the corner of South Shields and Harmony Road in 1998. During the 1976 Centennial/Bicentennial year, Hewlett-Packard built its large manufacturing plant on East Harmony Road, the same year that Larimer County suffered its most destructive flood in history—the July 31 Big Thompson Canyon flood. Fortunately the Cache la Poudre only experienced minor flooding. The Fort Collins' Old Town area received designation as a National Historic area after it was placed on the National Register, August 2, 1978. Belatedly, it was also given local landmark district status a year and a half later in December 1979, which then placed strong local protections on the key buildings in the Old Town Historic District.

BRINGING THE DOWNTOWN BACK TO LIFE

A major effort to make the core downtown more appealing to both citizens and tourists began in the mid-seventies with a downtown redevelopment project. Decorative concrete islands were put in at the major intersections along College Avenue between Magnolia Street and LaPorte Avenue, with plantings in the medians and on either side of College Avenue. In the spring of 1977, in the middle of this project, there was a horrendous explosion in a flower shop on East Oak Street just off of College Avenue. It blew the back off of the Elks Lodge, which was housed in the historic 1908 YMCA building. The blast also damaged several other structures and shattered windows in a several block area. No specific cause for the explosion was ever found though there was talk that it may

have been intentionally caused by one of the business owners; but there was no proof of that theory. Repairs were made and the original YMCA building was encased in grey concrete, and the downtown project was finished in the spring of 1978

There was a re-discovery of how much of a treasure the Old Town area was, in the early nineteen-eighties. People began to see this fairly neglected and somewhat run-down area for its wealth of late nineteenth and early twentieth century buildings. The downtown College Avenue corridor was also perceived for its economic potential and redevelopment possibilities. The Downtown Development Authority (DDA) was formed in 1981 to begin looking at creative financing for restoration and redevelopment projects in downtown Fort Collins. The city had been recognized by *Money Magazine* in October 1980, as one of the best cities for people to

A tremendous explosion in April 1977, damaged several downtown buildings, like the 1908 YMCA building.

live in the United States. Eugene Mitchell, a local attorney turned developer, looked at the Old Town's potential, and at what Boulder had done with its Pearl Street Mall. He came up with an ambitious concept for a two block long pedestrian mall on Linden Street between Jefferson Street and Mountain Avenue. Economic realities of the time shrunk the project to one block between Walnut Street and Mountain Avenue. Mitchell brought in other Old Town property owners like Ray Dixon and Steve Ackerman to form Old Town Associates. Ground was broken for the "Old Town Square" project on December 15, 1983. Construction began early the following year and was completed in 1985.

Several other events marked the 1980s. The original Birney Car 21 streetcar underwent a seven year historic reconstruction, starting in 1977, by the Fort Collins Municipal Railway Society, Inc., with a controversial proposal to re-lay tracks along the original West Mountain right-of-way. Car 21 made its first run on 1,600 feet of newly laid track on historic, tree-lined Mountain Avenue in late December, 1984, as a test run for the community and the city council. It began limited weekend service the following spring, and has operated on a mile and two-thirds of track between the tennis courts in City Park and Howes Street for the past thirty years. The Edora Pool and Ice Arena received approval from city voters in May 1984, and construction was completed in the spring of 1987. Citizens also voted to ban smoking in enclosed public spaces in 1984 initiating a movement that eventually led to a vote that eliminated public smoking statewide. The Rawhide Electric Generating Plant came on line June 23, 1984. After a twelve year fight in Congress, seventy-five miles of the upper Poudre River were designated a national Wild and Scenic River by Congress. The Farm at Lee Martinez Park, part of the city's extensive park system opened on July 20, 1986. And voter approved annexation of land

Opposite, top: Gene Mitchell (second from right) joins Mayor Nancy Gray (far right) and city officials to break ground for the Old Town Square in late 1983.

Opposite, bottom: Old Town Square construction, 1984.

Below: Birney Car 21 alongside the old Pioneer Museum before undergoing renovation in the old streetcar barn at Cherry and Howes Streets.

Right: Inspiration Playground at Spring Canyon Park.

Below: Plaque at Inspiration Playground.

3 miles northeast of the city for a large Anheuser-Busch plant. The first Budweiser rolled off the bottling line in 1988. One big change in the face of the downtown was Walt Brown's ambitious plan to completely redo the space formerly occupied by the town's original Opera House, with the first three tenants moving in during the spring of 1990. The decade of the eighties truly foretold the growth and development that would follow over the next twenty-five years.

Citizens of Fort Collins passed a quarter cent sales tax initiative, Choices 95, in 1989 which contained a whole laundry list of municipal improvements and building projects. The north extension of Timberline from Hoffman Lane to Summit View/Vine Drive was one of the first parts of the project. Money became available for open space and trails, like adding 146 acres to the Cathy Fromme Prairie, in the southwest part of the city. Fort Collins had grown to 87,758 by 1990, and would add about 2,000 people each succeeding year, reaching 99,728 by 1995. The July 1991, *Colorado Business Magazine* rated the city among the ten fastest growing job markets in the U.S. and one of the top thirty best places to retire in the nation. To serve this growing senior citizen population, Choices 95 had included

building a new Senior Center off of South Shields Street, which was dedicated and opened in December 1995. Three new city parks were also developed: Rogers Park, Eastside Neighborhood Park, and the first part of what would eventually become the large Spring Canyon Park, which now includes the fully handicapped-accessible Inspiration Playground, the Fort Collins Veterans Plaza and a dog park.

Above: The Anheuser-Busch Plant northeast of Fort Collins.

Left: Flood Memorial at Spring Creek Park.

The last decade of the twentieth century also saw a big push to attract high tech and small, clean manufacturing businesses to the city. The Harmony Corridor became the focus for many of these businesses with Hewlett Packard leading the way with a 350,000 foot expansion to its plant completed in early 1990. The *Colorado Business Magazine* for July 1991 in an detailed article, "Fort Collins: A Lifestyle for Economic Vitality," reported that the city already had 25 high tech research and development companies, as well as 3,800 small goods and services businesses. There were almost 150 restaurants, giving the city an astounding ratio of one restaurant for every 600 residents! Besides the many parks and open spaces, there were five golf courses—three of which were city-owned and operated and two privately owned courses. An extensive system of biking and hiking trails was spread throughout the city. Fort Collins' reputation as an outdoor recreation community was growing.

The twentieth century drew to a close with a major disaster, the Spring Creek Flood, in the summer of 1997. As much as 14 inches of rain fell in a twenty-four hour period near the foothills in the southwestern part of Fort Collins, turning little Spring Creek into a raging torrent of water. When the water backed up at the Burlington Northern railroad grade just south of Prospect Road, the water pressure forced some large concrete plugs to blow out under the railroad grade. The rushing water submerged a mobile home park on the east side of the tracks and four people drowned when they could not reach higher ground. One other person died when she tried to rescue her dog from the rising waters of the creek. Many homes and businesses sustained damage as irrigation ditches filled and overflowed. Several buildings on the CSU campus suffered severe flood damage including the Lory Student Center and the Morgan Library. In several campus locations, irreplaceable books and journals were lost and some professors lost a lifetime of work and research as water filled their offices up to the ceiling. Repairs took months and were very costly since most people discovered that their policies did not have flood coverage. So what would the new millennium bring?

Above: Floodwaters, July 29, 1997, on the Colorado State University campus.

Right: Flood monument marking the 1997 Spring Creek Flood.

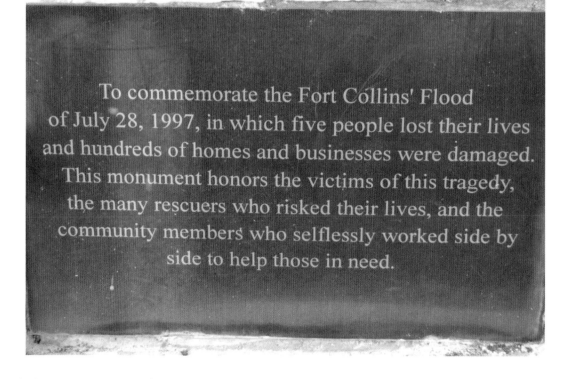

To commemorate the Fort Collins' Flood of July 28, 1997, in which five people lost their lives and hundreds of homes and businesses were damaged. This monument honors the victims of this tragedy, the many rescuers who risked their lives, and the community members who selflessly worked side by side to help those in need.

CHAPTER 5

INTO THE TWENTY-FIRST CENTURY

The end of December 1999, brought a world-wide panic—Y2K. Many feared the turning of the calendar at midnight on December 31 would cause the complete failure of almost all electronic devices like cell phones, computers, and traffic controls. There were long lines at filling stations and grocery stores as people stocked up for the anticipated "shut-downs." Virtually nothing of the sort happened and people awoke to discover their computers had not crashed and were showing January 1, 2000. Life moved into the new century without a stumble, and Fort Collins looked at its many opportunities for growing its economy.

Aerial view of Fort Collins.

PHOTOGRAPH COURTESY OF RYAN BURKE,
PHOTOGRAPHER FOR THE FORT COLLINS CONVENTION
AND VISITORS BUREAU/VISIT FORT COLLINS

Modern Fort Collins businesses.

PHOTOGRAPH COURTESY OF RYAN BURKE,
PHOTOGRAPHER FOR THE FORT COLLINS CONVENTION
AND VISITORS BUREAU/VISIT FORT COLLINS.

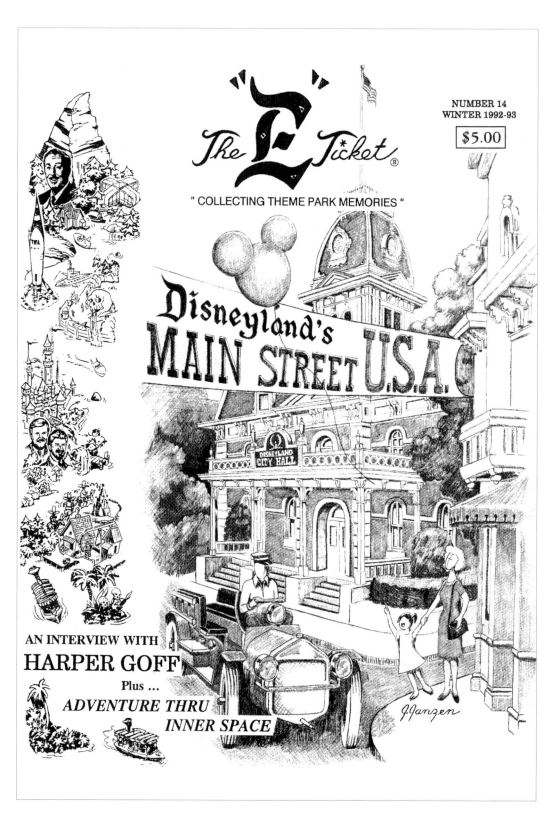

Disneyland's Main Street. Some historic Fort Collins buildings inspired it.

One vital segment of the market is the brewing industry; with several brew pubs, two craft breweries, a half dozen or so small breweries (the number keeps growing) and a large Anheuser-Busch plant. Fort Collins also has two cider bars and a couple of distilleries. The Fort Collins Convention and Visitors Bureau, also known as "Visit Fort Collins," promotes the city as the "Napa Valley of Beer." The local brewing industry is not a new phenomenon; there was a brewery in LaPorte in the 1860s. One Overland Trail traveler, at that time, was thrilled to discover that place. He noted it was run by two "Germans" and he was able to buy "one pint of beer for 25 cents, paper money."

Other than home brewers, and the fact that the town was "dry" until 1969 except for a few 3.2 beer bars that started in the thirties, Fort Collins brewery history does not truly begin until 1989. That year saw the opening of the first brew pub, CooperSmith's Pub & Brewing, on the historic Old Town Square, and the first micro-brewery, O'Dell Brewing Co. started by Doug and Wynn O'Dell. It began in an old downtown grain elevator before moving to its present Lincoln Avenue location. These were followed two years later by New Belgium Brewing, which began in in the basement of the husband and wife team of Jeff Lebesch and Kim Jordan's home in 1991 before moving to the old UPRR freight depot on Linden Street in 1992 and to its present 500 Linden Street location in December 1995. In the new century, New Belgium grew rapidly, making the transition from micro-brewery, one that sells less than 15,000 barrels a year, to the title of craft brewery. With its production of 764,264 barrels of beer in 2012, the company became the largest craft brewery in Colorado and the third largest in the United States. Its popular "Fat Tire" beer can be purchased thirty-one other states and the District of Columbia. The city's third largest craft beer producer, Fort Collins Brewery, moved in to its new plant on Lincoln Avenue in 2011, completing the so-called Fort Collins "Beer Triangle." It added a restaurant, Gravity 1020, a year later. All the breweries offer tasting and tours, and are a tremendous boost to area tourism. The city hosts the Colorado Brewers Festival that is billed as "Colorado's Largest and Oldest Outdoor Beer Festival" in late June every summer.

Fort Collins has always been a tourist friendly town, but the draw has grown during the new century as people all over the country and in targeted foreign markets have been made aware of the city's many year-round and seasonal offerings—good dining locations, the breweries, the beautiful Poudre Canyon with its camping, fishing, and white water rafting, and the myriad of bike trails, natural areas, golf courses, and open spaces, in addition to its central Northern Colorado location. Among the many features that tourists come looking for are the historic buildings that inspired Disneyland's Main Street. Harper Goff, a local high school graduate who took up a career in art and worked in the California movie industry as a set designer, met Walt Disney in London in 1951, when each of them, both model railroad buffs, reached for a same model train engine. During their conversation that followed, Disney learned of Harper Goff's artistic talent and offered him a job helping to design part of his new entertainment park, Disneyland. As the plans began to take shape for "Main Street, USA," Goff asked Disney if he could incorporate design elements from some historic buildings in Fort Collins. After seeing photos of the Fort Collins' buildings, Disney agreed. The town hall on "Main Street" shows this best, incorporating elements of the original 1887 Larimer County Court House (see photographs on pages 36 and 40). Six other Fort Collins' structures lent design elements to other "Main Street" buildings, so Fort Collins can justly boast that the town is truly "the basis for Main Street, Disneyland!"

Another element that is tourism-related, which outdoor enthusiasts find, are the many hiking and biking trails and the large number of natural areas and open spaces. Both the city and county have done a phenomenal job of using citizen-initiated tax money to acquire open space land, with Larimer County's Red Mountain Open Space and the City's Soapstone Prairie Natural Area being two of the premier acquisitions of this century. Regional cooperation on the Poudre River hiking and biking trail, which will eventually run from the fish hatchery at Bellvue nearly 40 miles down to the confluence of the Poudre with the South Platte River, is creating another key recreation component. The last few miles of needed trail right-of-way land will be purchased in the next few years. Fort Collins currently has 50 parks made up of six large community parks and 44 smaller neighborhood and pocket parks; almost 30 miles of hiking and biking trails; the Gardens on Spring Creek, an eighteen acre community botanic garden; four whitewater rafting companies; and many outdoor opportunities for locals as well as for visitors, making

City Manager Darin Atteberry speaking
at the kick-off of the Fort Collins new
MAX bus route, May 10, 2014.
PHOTOGRAPH COURTESY OF WADE TROXELL,
CITY COUNCIL MEMBER.

Fort Collins a very outdoor-oriented city. The Colorado Ice, an arena football team; the Colorado Eagles, a semi-professional ice hockey team; and the Fort Collins Foxes baseball team, as well as the Colorado State University and local high school athletic teams, provide spectators with diverse opportunities for competition sports viewing. Cultural attractions include many art galleries and studios, two long-term performing arts companies, Bas Bleu and Open Stage, and various music groups, like the Fort Collins Symphony and the Larimer Chorale, most of which are housed in the newly-remodeled Lincoln Center Performing Arts Center.

The push to make Fort Collins a more viable economic community has created inevitable conflicts as citizens and entrepreneurs struggle to find the optimum degree of growth and development. While there is a good deal of pride in well-respected home grown and long-term businesses, there are conflicts over affordable housing and transportation issues. The new MAX transit route, that began service in May 2014, creates a north-south bus route which connects to the rest of the city's Transfort routes. The proliferations of large apartment buildings worry some local citizens as Fort Collins seems to be literally growing "up!"

And yet most people will point with pride to Woodward, the aerospace and energy systems company's decision to move its world headquarters to Fort Collins and to build its complex of buildings on the old Link-N-Greens golf course site near the downtown.

OtterBox, a 1998 start-up company, has had a phenomenal growth story in the first fourteen years of this century. Seeing a need to protect new and much more expensive cell phones, or as they are now called "mobile devices," Curt Richardson developed attractive cases to protect them. Starting small out on Link Lane, the company moved twice to locations in the center of Old Town, before building and moving into its new world headquarters building on Meldrum Street. Still growing, from less than 100 employees in the early days of the company to over 1,000 today, OtterBox broke ground for a new five-story building at Meldrum and Magnolia Streets in the spring of 2013, adding to what is being called the OtterBox campus near the Lincoln Center. OtterBox has captured fifty percent of the protective cases for Smartphones and iPads and continues to seek other areas in this growing market. Founder Richardson, views Fort Collins as a perfect match for his company. In a recent *Coloradoan* interview, he verbalized his reasons for expanding in the downtown,

> I get really excited when I talk about Woodward on the other side of Old Town, Otter on this side and Pat Stryker's Bohemian Cos. in the middle. It's a great combination of really those three big entities right here in Old Town. It will have a lot of impact. Old Town will grow and spread out a bit, which I think is a good thing.

When you add in the number of other high tech companies and manufacturing industries that have moved into Fort Collins since the beginning of this new millennium, along with long-term companies like Water Pik, which celebrated fifty years of business in Fort Collins in 2012, and Advanced Energy, the city has experienced an almost unbelievable

Above: The site of Woodward's new international headquarters, with Coy Farm barn and milk house preserved.

Below: Water Pik, one of Fort Collins homegrown industries.

Above: The Colorado State University Engines and Energy Conversions Lab, in the original Municipal Power Plant, expanded with a large, architecturally sympathetic addition in 2014.

Right: This construction was taking place in the Downtown River District in 2014.

economic growth so far in this century. The forty-two year old Foothills Mall, which languished during the early part of this century, currently undergoing a major rehabilitation and expansion project along with the repurposing and additions to The Square shopping center, are real stimulators to the so-called "mid-town" Fort Collins as they get under way in 2014. When finished in 2015, they will showcase stores like Trader Joe's, Sierra Trading Post, and a ten-screen Cinemark Theatre in addition to other commercial space. Other parts of the city are also experiencing growth. The new life-style mall, Front Range Village, brought a Super Target, Lowe's, Babies"R"Us®, the Council Tree Library, and numerous other shops and restaurants together in one open-air mall is making southeast Fort Collins an major economic draw.

Not to be out-done, downtown Fort Collins has experienced an economic rebirth recently.

The Old Town Square is approaching its thirtieth birthday and is need of some rehabilitation work. Peggy Lyle, assistant director of the Downtown Business Association, described this work in an interview quoted in a recent Fort Collins *Coloradoan* story,

> The infrastructure of the Old Town Square is 'well loved' and in need of updating. Fort Collins loves and uses it so much, it is like a well-worn teddy bear. ...The DBA is excited to help the Downtown Development Authority re-polish this gem.

Renovations will be done during 2015 and include demolishing the Bike Library kiosk and expanding the stage area to the north. With the number of beautifully restored historic buildings in the Old Town, upgrading the Old Town Square will add much to the ambiance of that area of historic Fort Collins.

The Poudre River Library District's Council Tree Library in the Front Range Village lifestyle mall.

One final forward-looking effort for the city is the one that created a "River District" for the downtown segment of the Poudre in 2008. Planned projects include historic signage along Linden Street north of Jefferson Street, converting the Feeder Supply building into a pub-style restaurant with a new apartment building just north of the 1902 structure, and improvements along the riverscape. This section of Linden Street has recently undergone a major upgrade north to the bridge over the Poudre. Projects in the District already underway are the Legacy Senior Residences set to open in 2014; the recently completed 65,000 square foot expansion of the original 1930s municipal power plant, now the home of the CSU Engines and Energy Conversions Laboratory; and the Encompass Technologies' mixed use building north of one of the city's longest-term and very popular Mexican restaurants, the El Burrito, or Sam's, as it is known to locals. All of this activity is taking place on the spot which was the birthplace of the Fort Collins Military Post site of 150 years ago.

Fort Collins at the base of the Rockies.

This all brings us back to what makes Fort Collins a unique Sesquicentennial city—managed growth, a variety of recreational and cultural opportunities, a pleasant geographic location, and a diverse citizenry. Perhaps Water Pik's CEO Richard Bisson best described our city in a January 1, 2014, *Coloradoan* story that says this very nicely,

When you look around the country, (Fort Collins) has reasonably priced homes, excellent public schools, and a government that stays out of your way and asks 'how can we help.' ...you see a lot of entrepreneurial firms coming here all because this is a great place to play as well as work.

This truly describes "Fortunate Fort Collins!"

"VISIT FORT COLLINS!"

Above: The El Burrito Restaurant, a long-time fixture in Old Town Fort Collins, sits on the original Fort site, the birthplace of Fort Collins 150 years ago.

Left: Postcard greeting from early Fort Collins, Colorado.

PHOTOGRAPH COURTESY OF JANE BASS POSTCARD COLLECTION.

BIBLIOGRAPHY

More to read about the Fort Collins area:

Ahlbrandt, Arlene, *Annie, The Railroad Dog*, 1998

Ahlbrandt, Arlene, *Lady Moon and Her Animal Friends*, 1999

Ahlbrandt, Arlene, *Memories of the War Years*, 1993

Ahlbrandt, Arlene, *101 Memorable Men of Northern Colorado*, 2002

Ahlbrandt, Arlene, *Unforgettable Women of Northern Colorado*, 1997

Avery, Edgar D., *Diary, 1890.* Transcribed by Jane Bass

Bliss, Elyse Deffke, with Alice Dickerson, *Apples in the Mummy's Eye*, 1994

Brinks, Rose, *History of the Bingham Hill Cemetery*, 1988

Burnett, Frank, *Golden Memories of Colorado*, 1965

Case, Stanley R., *The Poudre: A Photo History*, 1995

Clark, Francis, *Early Sawmills in Larimer County*, 1992

Clark, Francis, *Early Settlers Along the Little South Fork of the Cache la Poudre*, 2001

Coffin, Roy A., *Northern Colorado's First Settlers*, 1937

Duncan, C. A., *Memories of Early Days in the Cache la Poudre Valley*, N.D.

Fleming, Barbara, *Legendary Locals of Fort Collins*, 2013

Fleming, Barbara and Malcolm E. McNeill, *The Miller Photographs*, 2009

Fleming, Barbara and Malcolm E. McNeill, *Fort Collins Then and Now*, 2010

Fry, Norman, *Cache la Poudre: The River*, 1954

Gates, Zethyl, *Mariano Medina: Colorado's Mountain Man*, 1981

Gray, John S., *Cavalry and Coaches: the Story of Camp and Fort Collins*, 1978

Greenamyre, Katherine, *Let Me Take You Back With Me,* 1991

Hansen, James E., *Democracy's College in the Centennial State*, 1977

Hoerlein, Mary Ann, *Who is J. D. Forney*, N.D.

Jessen, Kenneth, *Railroads of Northern Colorado*, 1982

Livermore Women's Club, *Among These Hills*, 1995

McNeill, Malcolm E., *The Automobile Comes to Fort Collins*, 2013

Morgan, Gary, *Sugar Tramp: Colorado's Great Western Railway*, 1975

Mumey, Nolie, *The Saga of Auntie Stone and Her Cabin*, 1964

Noel, Thomas J. and Ron D. Sladek, *Fort Collins and Larimer County: An Illustrated History*, 2003

Nortier, Molly and Michael Smith, *From Buckets to Basins*, 1982

Parrish, Shirley, *The Epic of Larimer County*, 1959

Peterson, Guy, *Fort Collins: The Post, The Town*, 1972

Pike, Robert, *Home of the Champions: The History of Fort Collins High School, 1889-1989*, 1994

Sarchet, Fancher, *Murder and Mirth*, 1956

Schell, Stephen C., *Following John C. Fremont Through Northern Colorado, 1843*, 2010

Sundberg, Wayne C., *Fort Collins First Water Works*, 2004

Sundberg, Wayne C., *Historic Fort Collins*, 1975

Swanson, Evadine B., *Fort Collins Yesterdays*, 1975

Thomas, Adam, *Hang Your Wagon to a Star: Hispanics in Fort Collins, 1900–2000*, 2003

Thomas, Adam, *Work Renders Life Sweet: Germans From Russia in Fort Collins, 1900–2000*, 2003

Tresner, Charlene, *Streets of Fort Collins*, Revised Edition, 2007

Trimble, Martha Scott, *One-Hundred-Five Years with St. Luke's Episcopal Church, 1875-1980*, 2000

Walker, Phil, *Visions Along the Poudre Valley*, 1995

Watrous, Ansel, *The History of Larimer County, Colorado*, 1911

White, Phil, *Memories of Growing Up in Fort Collins*, 2013

ARTICLES

Bucco, Edith, "Founded on Rock: Stout Stone Industry," *Colorado Magazine*, Fall 1974

Gray, John S., senior editor, "The Poudre River" Magazine, 1976

Peyton, E. S. and R. A. Moorman, "The Last of the Birneys," *American Railway Journal*, 1966

Fort Collins Birney Car 21 loading at City Park.

SHARING THE HERITAGE

Historic profiles of businesses, organizations, and families that have contributed to the development and economic base of Fort Collins

Festivities in Old Town Square by the fountain.

QUALITY OF LIFE

Healthcare providers, foundations, universities, and other institutions that contribute to the quality of life in Fort Collins

POUDRE VALLEY
HEALTH SYSTEM

Above: The original hospital opened in 1925. Seventeen major additions were completed during the next nine decades. In 2014, PVH prepared to tear down the original building to make room for an addition that allowed for expansion of the emergency room and other medical services.

Below: Cardiologist Dr. Gary Luckasen, shown below in the early 1990s, was a leader in developing the regional heart program at Poudre Valley Hospital. The main part of the program was transferred to Medical Center of the Rockies after the Loveland hospital opened in 2007, but PVH continued to provide various levels of cardiac care.

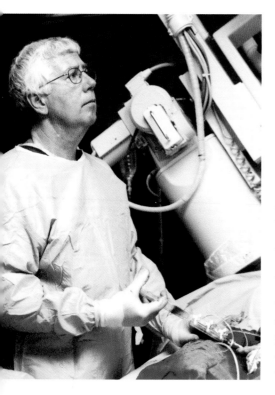

Amid a small grove of cottonwood trees, surrounded by fields of corn and sugar beets, Larimer County Hospital was built and opened in 1925 in a rural area a mile southeast of what later became known as Old Town Fort Collins.

During the next nine decades, the hospital at 1024 South Lemay steadily grew in size and services. It was renamed Poudre Valley Hospital. It became a national leader in providing quality patient care. It continued to expand on the twenty-six acre site and, when it eventually became landlocked by neighborhoods and businesses, it developed Harmony Campus five miles to the southeast for outpatient services while the main campus on Lemay focused on inpatient care.

The original three-story, red brick hospital was constructed with a large verandah and tall white pillars on the west side entrance. A four unit apartment house, known as the contagious ward, or Pest House, was built about 200 feet east of the hospital to house patients who suffered from contagious illnesses. The construction cost of the hospital and Pest House was $181,001, paid by a thirty year county bond issue. The hospital's total capacity was forty patients.

Forty acres of adjacent farmland were used to raise vegetables and livestock—hogs, sheep and chickens—to feed patients. In the fall, local citizens held agricultural fairs and horseraces. People volunteered to pick and can vegetables and fruits so patients had food during the winter.

Patients could open their windows for air on steamy summer afternoons and chat with folks passing by outside or watch cows grazing nearby. The physician staff had twenty-two doctors who practiced in the area. The county's home for the poor and elderly was also located on the hospital grounds.

"When one speaks of a county hospital and a county poor farm, it conjures up images of impoverished catacombs," recalled an early administrator, J. R. Peterson. "But this was not that kind of place at all. This was a beautiful place."

The hospital did not grow during its first two decades due to the Great Depression and World War II. Most people were so financially strapped they could not afford hospital care. During this time, though, Colorado established a pension plan for elderly citizens, eliminating the need for the county poor and old folks home. It was torn down. The farming operation slowly went by the wayside, too, and was gone by the late 1940s. The Pest House, unused for decades, was razed to make room for the construction of a hospital wing in the early 1990s.

Then came the post-World War II boom. "This was a period that saw recovery from the Great Depression and the turmoil of the war years, as well as new advances in medical drugs and hospital care techniques," Peterson remembered. "We also had an accelerated growth of the population in our area. Military personnel returned from the war. The college (now Colorado State University) had a dramatic increase in enrollment. All of this had an impact on the hospital."

Northern Colorado's rapid population increase prompted hospital expansion in the 1950s, 1960s and early 1970s—at a total cost of about $6 million, paid by bond issues approved by public votes. By 1973 the hospital's square footage had increased from 64,022 to 168,822. Bed capacity rose to 218. New services such as radiology, pathology and lab were added.

The hospital's most significant advance came in 1960 when local voters overwhelmingly approved a ballot issue that created Poudre Valley Hospital District, enabling the annual collection of a two-mill levy on property taxes. The revenue was used to keep abreast of technology and expand services.

G. Wayne Ballah and other community members laid the groundwork for the district in the 1950s when they started the Larimer County Hospital Improvement Association. The association's purpose was to raise money for Larimer County Hospital and a small Loveland hospital that later became McKee Medical Center.

At the time, the two hospitals were owned by Larimer County, and the three county commissioners were split over how much funding should go to each hospital.

"It became obvious that the county commissioners weren't going to put another dime into our hospital," Ballah recalled in a 1996 interview shortly before his ninety-third birthday and only weeks before his death. "So we (Larimer County Hospital Improvement Association) decided to raise $100,000 or $200,000, or whatever was needed. But the amount kept going up until we realized we just didn't have the ability to raise much more."

So the new hospital district board proposed a deal with the county. The district would buy the hospital and land and pay for it as property tax revenue came in. This would require a large amount of faith on the part of county officials because the mill levy would not start bringing in revenue until the following year.

Public hearings were held. The only opposition came from residents in Loveland, which would not be part of the new district and would, in essence, lose a county hospital if the deal went through.

"I'll never forget the last public hearing we had," Ballah said, chuckling in anticipation of the anecdote he was about to tell. "There were people from Loveland there, and Bill Michaels (another district board member) explained to them what we wanted to do—buy the hospital for $300,000 even though we didn't yet have the (mill levy) money to pay for it.

"Bill turned to the group and said, 'All we're doing is asking you to trust us.' Then he said, 'You will, won't you?'

"A lady from Loveland jumped up and shouted, 'Hell, no, we won't trust you!'"

But, as it turned out, county officials did have trust. The county sold the hospital building and land to the hospital district for $300,000, paid in $100,000 annual installments over three years.

During the next three decades, PVH increased services and developed regional centers for cardiac, neurological and orthopedic care. By the 1980s, the hospital was the leading source of healthcare for residents in northeastern Colorado, western Kansas and Nebraska, as well as southern Wyoming.

In the early 1990s, PVH underwent a $20 million expansion to increase the size of the emergency room and expand pediatric, nursery and women's care. This was the seventeenth major addition. Meanwhile, the hospital district, with an eye toward future needs, purchased ninety-six acres in 1992 along the rural Harmony Road in southeast Fort Collins.

A major turning point for the hospital occurred in the early 1990s. By then, every president since FDR had tried but failed to reform healthcare. In the early 1990s, President Bill Clinton assigned his wife, Hillary Clinton, to lead a task force to develop a plan to rein in healthcare costs. A vigorous national debate ensued. Hillary's efforts were buried under tsunamis of opposition from insurance companies and the healthcare industry, as well as the capital's contentious political climate.

The Poudre Valley Hospital District's governing board realized the national debate was a forerunner of significant changes to come in the hospital industry. So the board conducted an extensive study about the future of healthcare. The study found that many hospitals were on the road to bankruptcy and were selling themselves to national hospital chains. Once that happened, the bottom line—rather than the quality of patient care—became what mattered most at the hospitals.

Above: By 2000, the twenty-six acre Poudre Valley Hospital site was landlocked by neighborhoods and businesses. So the Harmony Campus was built to accommodate outpatient care while the hospital focused mainly on inpatient care. Lemay Avenue is toward the top of the photograph.

Below: Pulmonologist Dr. Diana Breyer and Rulon Stacey, president and CEO, talk with a nurse during a rounding on a patient care unit. An outside firm conducts an annual employee satisfaction survey for Poudre Valley Hospital. From 2008 to 2012, survey results showed that employee satisfaction was among the highest in the nation, largely due to close communication among employees, physicians, volunteers, and administrators.

The PVH District board determined the best strategy for maintaining a high level of quality care was to keep healthcare locally controlled. A companion strategy called for ensuring the hospital's financial stability by partnering with other organizations.

However, there was a huge roadblock. Nonprofit hospitals like PVH that received revenue from public property taxes were forbidden under Colorado law from entering into ventures with private companies. As a result, the hospital board created a non-profit corporation, Poudre Valley Health Care, Inc., more commonly called Poudre Valley Health System, that would receive no property tax revenue.

The district board developed a plan that would grant PVHS a fifty year lease to operate the hospital and its land. In exchange, the district would retain the annual property tax revenue, which had grown to $2.1 million. In addition, the district would receive millions of dollars in rental fees from PVHS. The hospital district, which eventually changed its name to Health District of Northern Larimer County, would use the revenue to provide healthcare to people with lower incomes.

At 8:33 p.m. on May 1, 1994, the signing of a tall stack of legal documents by representatives of the hospital district board and PVHS was completed in a small office in the hospital's original building.

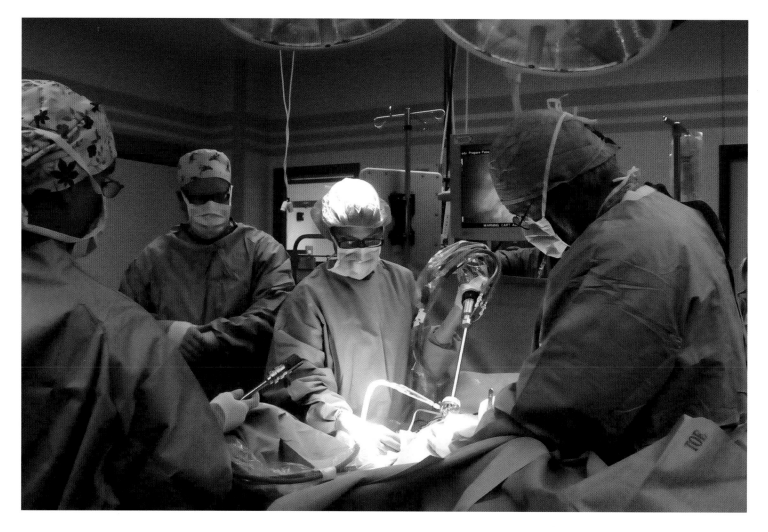

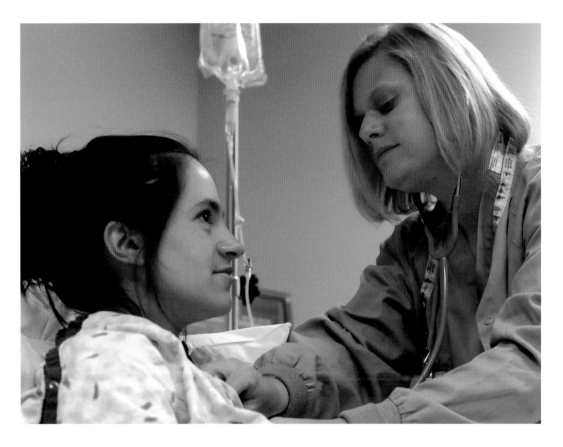

"Well, that's it," calmly said Bob Addleman, president of the district board and one of the architects of the plan. "What we've done is much the same as was done three decades ago when the hospital district was created. We've created a structure that will position us for the future."

With the new corporate structure in place, the PVHS board hired Rulon Stacey to be the health system's president and CEO. Stacey was an up-and-coming administrator who gained valuable management experience at a large urban hospital in Chicago and rural experience at a small hospital in Leadville, Colorado. *Modern Healthcare* magazine named Stacey one of the nation's twelve best executives under the age of forty.

Under Stacey's leadership, PVHS boldly raced forth on a course of unprecedented growth. The first major initiative was to build Harmony Campus on the ninety-six acres purchased by Poudre Valley Hospital District in 1992. The campus, which opened in 2000, was developed so PVH could offer outpatient services there and local physicians could purchase space to relocate their medical clinics there. In 2014, PVH opened a regional cancer center on Harmony Campus to bring all diagnostic, care and recovery services together under one roof. By then, the campus was about forty percent developed, leaving plenty of acreage for future needs.

After the turn of the century, the need for more healthcare services became urgent as the population boom continued beyond all expectations in northern Colorado. The populations of Larimer and Weld Counties grew sixteen and thirty percent, respectively, from the 2000 to 2010 federal censuses.

So the health system built a hospital along Interstate 25 in Loveland—right in the epicenter of the region's population growth. In 2007, Medical Center of the Rockies opened as a full-service hospital and became the regional center for trauma and cardiac care.

As the health system moved forward with the proverbial bricks and mortar of expansion, the PVH staff, as well as MCR employees, many of whom transferred there from PVH, developed a culture and tradition of providing high-quality patient care. Between 2004 and 2013, PVH was recognized eight times as one of the nation's 100 top hospitals by an independent organization that tracked patient outcomes in the healthcare industry.

Right: Neonatologist Dr. Daniel Satterwhite and neonatal nurse practitioner Carol Wallman examine an infant in the Neonatal Intensive Care Unit at PVH. The Fort Collins NICU is the only one of its kind between Denver, Colorado and Billings, Montana. The physicians and nurses routinely care for sick babies as well as those born as early as twenty-eight weeks gestation. Forty weeks gestation is considered full term.

Below: Kevin Unger, president and CEO of PVH and Medical Center of the Rockies, rounds with medical technologist Shari Claus at the Harmony Campus Lab in southeast Fort Collins. There are three labs in Fort Collins and a blood donation center to serve the community.

In 2008, PVHS, with PVH as its flagship hospital, was the only health system to receive the Malcolm Baldrige National Quality Award, an award given annually by Congress to the nation's top-performing organizations.

A decade into the twenty-first century, PVH was impacted once again by national healthcare debate. In 2010, Congress passed healthcare reform—the Affordable Care Act—designed to contain healthcare costs and make coverage more available for Americans. Nicknamed Obamacare after President Barack Obama, the legislation resulted in a national trend that saw hospitals and health systems partnering together so they could provide care to larger populations of people.

Stacey took a leadership role in forging a new nonprofit partnership, University of Colorado Health. UCHealth consisted of PVHS hospitals and services, including the 280 bed PVH; 136 bed Medical Center of the Rockies; University of Colorado Hospital, Aurora, Colorado; and Memorial Health System in Colorado Springs. The partnership created a 14,000 employee health system along Colorado's Front Range, broadening the availability of general and specialized medicine for patients.

"It's all about improving the quality of care for our patients," Stacey said when legal papers for the new partnership were signed in 2012. "With our combined strength, we will be able to raise the bar for quality healthcare in Colorado."

In 2014, as the City of Fort Collins celebrated its 150th anniversary, PVH was far into an extensive plan to create new opportunities for patient care. The northwest side of the hospital along Lemay Avenue—the original hospital building from 1925—was prepared for demolition. A two-story building to accommodate an expansion of the emergency room and other services will be built in its place.

In 2000, PVH was designated as a Magnet Hospital for Nursing Care, the nation's eighteenth hospital to receive the recognition considered the gold standard for nursing care. By 2014 only 400 of the nation's 5,000 hospitals were designated as Magnet Hospitals. By then, PVH had already been designated four consecutive times, a feat only ten other hospitals accomplished.

As the hospital poised itself in 2014 for the future, the staff remained committed to quality, said Kevin Unger, president and CEO of PVH and MCR. The affable Unger, who was born in 1969 at PVH, began working for the health system in 2001 as vice president of planning and strategic development. "PVH employees have continued to build upon their culture and tradition of quality," he pointed out.

"My family and I feel fortunate that we have such an excellent hospital in our community," he continued. "As an employee I am continually impressed with how hard nurses and other staff members work to improve their skills and bring in new ideas and work processes to ensure that patient care remains among the nation's best."

This history was written by Gary Kimsey, who worked twenty-three years in public relations and marketing for Poudre Valley Hospital, Poudre Valley Health System and subsequently University of Colorado Health before retiring in 2014. This history is largely based on one that Kimsey wrote in 1997 after interviewing early hospital administrators and clinicians, most of whom have since passed away. Kimsey was editor of the employee newsletter and intranet, and he did firsthand reporting on the more recent events mentioned in the history.

Above: In 2014, Poudre Valley Hospital opened a state-of-the-art cancer center on the Harmony Campus in southeastern Fort Collins. The cancer center was designed to have all services—from diagnosis to recovery—in one location. This was a revolutionary concept in cancer care in the U.S., wherein most communities' cancer patients have to travel from one location to another to get treatment. Having all services under one roof helps to decrease the stress on a cancer patient.

Left: Radiation oncologist Dr. Joshua Petit was instrumental in bringing the world's most advanced cancer treatment to Poudre Valley Hospital in 2012. The TrueBeam STx (shown in the photograph) can be used to treat virtually any type of cancer in any location on the body. The ultra-precise technology can treat more complex and more advanced cancers than older linear accelerator technologies. The TrueBeam was located on the Harmony Campus and became an important service of the cancer center there.

*In 2011, a joint operating agreement between Poudre Valley Health System and University of Colorado Hospital was signed creating University of Colorado Health. In 2012, Memorial Health System in Colorado Springs joined University of Colorado Health.

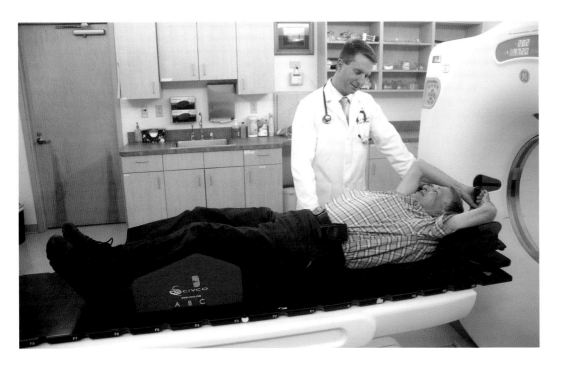

QUALITY OF LIFE

POUDRE SCHOOL DISTRICT

Above: Auntie Stone's cabin, 1866, site of the first classroom in Fort Collins.

Below: A. H. Dunn, Superintendent of District 5.

EARLY HISTORY OF EDUCATION IN NORTHERN COLORADO*	
1866	Elizabeth Parke Keays began teaching her son and another student in a bedroom of her "Auntie Stone's" log cabin on the Fort Collins Military Post. After more students came, classes moved into an abandoned fort commissary building. District 5 was organized with two men serving on the first school board.
1879	Growth created a need for a larger school. A bond issue of $7,500 was approved to build a two-story, four-room brick and stone school. The Remington Street School opened in the fall of 1879.
1880	Kindergarten was adopted by District 5, creating K-8 education in Fort Collins.
1887	A second school, Franklin School, was built at the southwest corner of Mountain Avenue and Howes Street after a $19,500 bond issue passed. The board hired the first district superintendent, Edward G. Lyle, for an annual salary of $1,400.
1889-1891	A four-year high school program was adopted and added to the K-8 program at the Franklin School. Approximately forty students enrolled in the new high school program. The first high school class, made up of four young women and one young man, graduated in 1891.
1900-1910	The population grew from 3,053 to 8,210. A three-story school was built in 1903 on Meldrum Street for high school students and third through seventh grade students. Two elementary schools, one on Laurel and one on La Porte, were built 1906-07.
1915-1921	Additions were added to the high school on the south side (1915) and north side (1921). Twin elementary schools, Washington on the west side of town and Lincoln on the east, were constructed in 1919.
1923	A $330,000 bond issue was approved in 1923 to build a new Fort Collins High School, completed in 1925. The first high school then became a junior high.
1947-1959	The Colorado Legislature passed legislation in 1947 encouraging districts to consolidate into larger, efficient districts. A committee, representing the thirty districts in Larimer County, took on the controversial consolidation issue in the 1950s.
1960	Voters approved dividing the county into three districts: Thompson R-2J, Park R-3 and Poudre R-1. Poudre School District R-1 was born on July 1, 1960, consolidating twenty-one reorganized districts.
Information listed is from the PSD Fiftieth Anniversary History Booklet written by Wayne C. Sundberg.	

Poudre School District would not be what it is today without the people who have put their hearts into educating the children of our community. One might say that education in northern Colorado began when a young widow moved west, made a home on the Fort Collins Military Post and began teaching in a small log cabin.

When Elizabeth Parke Keays came to live with her elderly aunt Elizabeth Stone in spring 1866, she began teaching her ten year old son, Wilbur, and another child, Harry Cooper, in the upstairs bedroom of "Auntie" Stone's cabin. And thus, the history of education in Fort Collins began.

It was almost 100 years later when Poudre School District R-1 was officially born on July 1, 1960, after voters approved consolidating smaller school districts into larger, more efficient districts in Larimer County. The new Poudre School District R-1 covered roughly 66 percent of the county, encompassing 21 reorganized districts with about 6,000 students, 249 classrooms and 264 teachers.

Now in 2014, PSD educates more than 28,000 students in fifty school buildings. But it is the people—teachers, principals, staff and community members—who have most influenced the history of one of Colorado's strongest high-performing school districts.

PSD HONORS LOCAL EDUCATORS*

To honor the contributions of those who have made a difference, PSD has made a tradition of naming elementary and middle schools after influential local educators. This continues a tradition that began earlier in the district's history.

In 1949 the school board decided to honor the elder statesman of Fort Collins education, A. H. Dunn, who led the district, known then as District 5, through a time of growth and change. Dunn served 37 years from 1893–1930, first as a high school principal for 19 years, followed by 18 years as superintendent. A new elementary school on Mulberry Street was named Dunn Elementary School (now an IB World School).

Harris Bilingual Elementary, built in 1919, honors Mame R. Harris, a longtime teacher and principal in town. Putnam Elementary School of Science opened in 1956 and was named after A. H. Putnam, an exemplary school custodian.

Lesher Middle School, an International Baccalaureate World School, opened in 1960 and is named after David B. Lesher, the last superintendent of District 5 and the first superintendent of the new Poudre School District R-1. Blevins Middle School opened in 1968 and is named for Theodore Roosevelt Blevins, a PSD educator and coach who was posthumously awarded the Silver Star for "gallantry in action" during World War I.

Boltz Middle School, built in 1973, was named after I. K. Boltz, Fort Collins High School principal from 1940-1943 and PSD superintendent from 1962-1971. After his retirement, Boltz became the executive director of the Federal Relations Commission, serving as a liaison between the federal government and Colorado public education.

Traut Core Knowledge Elementary, opened in 1993 and is named for both Lena and Evelyn Traut, who taught in PSD for eighty-two combined years. More recently, Bethke Elementary opened in 2008 and honors longtime Timnath educator Paul Bethke, who worked locally and at the state level to make public schools better.

Currently, possible namesakes for new schools are nominated by the public and reviewed by a community/staff committee, who refer top choices to the Board of Education.

Other PSD schools, the approximate year they opened and their namesakes:

- Bacon Elementary (2003) is named for Bob Bacon, a PSD teacher for 30 years, a Board of Education member for 8 years, and a state legislator for more than 8 years.
- Bauder Elementary (1969) is named after longtime PSD music teacher, Katharyn Bauder.
- Beattie Elementary (1972) is named after community leader, athlete, and educator Dan Beattie.

Above: Lesher Junior High School, 1960.

Below: Evelyn Traut reading to students at Traut Core Knowledge Elementary School, March 2014.

Above: Original Fort Collins High School
(center) with additions to the left and right.

Below: Cache La Poudre School, District 60
before consolidation.

Opposite, top: Fossil Ridge High School,
opened 2004.

Opposite, bottom: Rocky Mountain High
School graduates, 2013.

- Bennett Elementary, an IB World School (1963) is named for Merle Bennett, the founder of PSD's kindergarten program.
- Eyestone Elementary (1973) is named after past Wellington mayor Robert E. Eyestone, former teacher, principal and superintendent.
- Irish Elementary (1968) is named for Jean Powell Irish, former teacher and principal in PSD for more than thirty years.
- Johnson Elementary (1988) is named for two lifelong Fort Collins educators Mary and Curtis Johnson.
- Kinard Core Knowledge Middle School (2006) is named for longtime PSD educator Hal Kinard.
- Kruse Elementary (1992) honors Ray Kruse who served as a teacher, coach, athletic director and principal.
- Linton Elementary (1989) is named after Wayne and Shirley Linton, two dedicated educators. Shirley taught first grade at LaPorte Avenue School starting in 1951 and later taught kindergarten until retiring in 1985. Wayne began his career at Lincoln Junior High in 1950 and opened Blevins Junior High as principal in 1968.
- Livermore Elementary (original school built in 1871), is named after Adolphus Livernash and Stephan Moore, two early settlers to the area.
- Lopez, a "Leader in Me," Elementary school (1986) is named after William Lopez, the first Mexican-American educator in PSD, former Fort Collins City Council Member, and Larimer County Commissioner.
- McGraw Elementary, an IB World School (1992) honors PSD educator Beryl "Brownie" McGraw.
- O'Dea Core Knowledge Elementary (1963) is named for PSD teacher and principal Margaret O'Dea.
- Olander School for Project-Based Learning (1990) is named for Emil "Lefty" and Eleanor Olander, both dedicated educators who served youth for fifty-eight years collectively.
- Preston Middle School (1993) is named for the Ben Preston family who made significant contributions to education in the community.
- Rice Elementary (2007), located on the south edge of Wellington, honors Edgar Rice, Jr., an educator, administrator, and resident of the Wellington area.
- Riffenburgh Elementary (1968) is named for Waldo Riffenburgh, former president of the PSD Board of Education.
- Shepardson STEM Elementary (1978) honors Margaret C. Shepardson whose forty-year teaching career began in 1923.
- Tavelli Elementary (1968) is named for PSD teacher Anna Tavelli.
- Webber Middle School (1990) is named for Don Webber, PSD teacher, coach, principal and superintendent.
- Werner Elementary (1987) is named after Gail Werner, who served as a teacher, principal, elementary schools' and reading coordinator during her twenty-one years working in PSD.
- Zach Core Knowledge Elementary (2002) is named after Robert and Grace Zach, two English teachers and department chairs who were curriculum builders for over twenty years.

In contrast to school namesakes, many older PSD schools carry the name of prominent landmarks or locations to illustrate the rich history of northern Colorado. Red Feather Lakes (1980) and Stove Prairie (1896) Elementary schools, are named after their locations, as well as Timnath Elementary (1900), Laurel School of Arts and Technology Elementary (1906) and Wellington Middle School (1964).

Cache La Poudre School (about 1913) was named after French explorers who settled in the area. Cache la Poudre means "cache of

powder" and refers to where trappers stashed supplies in the foothills. The school eventually separated into two schools CLP Elementary and CLP Middle School.

Lincoln Middle School, an IB World School, (became solely a junior high in 1925) was named after President Abraham Lincoln, an important figure in Fort Collins because he signed the bill that allowed land-grant colleges like Colorado State University to be formed.

Poudre High School (1963) is named after the Poudre River while Fossil Ridge High School (2004) is named after the low ridge in front of the foothills to the west and southwest of Fort Collins. Fort Collins High School (1889) is more than 120 years old and retains its original name. Rocky Mountain High School (1973) is named after the mountains, and was inspired by the John Denver song, *Rocky Mountain High*.

In recent years, several non-traditional schools have formed, including Centennial High School, Polaris Expeditionary Learning School, Lab School for Creative Learning, Poudre Community Academy, and the PSD Global Academy.

PSD TODAY

Mission: Educate…every child, every day.

Vision: Poudre School District exists to support and inspire every child to think, to learn, to care and to graduate prepared to be successful in a changing world.

PSD covers more than 1,800 square miles in northern Colorado. The district offers a wide spectrum of programs including early childhood and school offerings like International Baccalaureate, Core Knowledge, Bilingual/Dual Language Immersion, Hybrid/Online, Expeditionary Learning, STEM and more!

PSD students consistently perform higher than students statewide on standardized tests and frequently attend prestigious universities and colleges. PSD continues to focus on student achievement, excellent instructional practices, safe and engaging learning environments, sustainability and wellness.

OUR STUDENTS

Student Enrollment: 28,439

- Asian: 3.06 percent
- Black/African American: 1.37 percent
- Hispanic/Latino: 17.93 percent
- Native American: 0.53 percent
- Native Hawaiian/Pacific Islander: 0.13 percent
- White: 74.31 percent
- Two or More: 3.15 percent

OUR SCHOOLS

- 28 elementary schools
- 8 middle schools
- 4 comprehensive high schools
- 6 option (100 percent choice) schools
- 2 alternative high schools
- 3 charter schools

OUR STAFF

- Total Staff: 3,615
- Certified: 1,917
- Classified: 1,587
- Administrators: 111
- Total teachers: 1,436
- Average teaching experience in PSD: 11.72 years

* Many of the historical facts about school namesakes were taken from the PSD Fiftieth Anniversary History Booklet written by Wayne C. Sundberg.

BANNER HEALTH

Below: Banner Health began serving Fort Collins area patients in 2006 with the opening of Fossil Creek Family Practice, now known as Banner Health Clinic specializing in Family Medicine, on Carpenter Road.

Bottom: The Banner Health Center in Fort Collins , located at 702 West Drake, Suite A, is staffed with primary care physicians and specialists to serve patients of all ages.

Banner Health has provided health care services in Fort Collins since 2001. However, the history of our local hospitals and medical practices in Northern Colorado goes back much farther.

Banner Health, with headquarters in Arizona, operates twenty-five acute care hospitals, the Banner Medical Group, outpatient surgery centers and an array of other services across seven states. Our almost 39,000 employees have helped us become recognized as one of the top health systems in the country and have enabled us to develop an international reputation for quality medical research in areas like Alzheimer's disease and Parkinson's.

On the Front Range of Northern Colorado, Banner Health employs nearly 5,000 people, operates dozens of Banner Health Centers and Clinics, and manages three hospitals: North Colorado Medical Center in Greeley, McKee Medical Center in Loveland and Banner Fort Collins Medical Center (scheduled to open in April 2015). Banner Health also operates East Morgan County Hospital in Brush and Sterling Regional MedCenter in Sterling.

Banner Fort Collins Medical Center will be a full-service medical center providing emergency care, surgical services, inpatient care, labor and delivery, medical imaging, and laboratory services. It will be equipped with an advanced electronic medical record system and iCare ICU technology, which provides an additional layer of monitoring for intensive care patients. In addition, the campus will house an outpatient Banner Health Center where patients can meet with medical specialists.

The hospital is part of Banner's expanding presence in the city that began in 2001 with the opening of Fossil Creek Family Practice on Carpenter Road. Now known as Banner Health Clinic specializing in Family Medicine, the clinic is one of a handful of Banner Health Centers and Clinics in Fort Collins that employ providers from the Banner Medical Group. The providers who staff these facilities represent a variety of medical specialties and provide care to patients of all ages.

As a system, Banner Health's mission is to make a difference in people's lives through excellent patient care. That mission holds true for staff, physicians and volunteers at each of our hospitals, clinics, laboratories, pharmacies and medical imaging centers. Our Fort Collins patients, along with all of our patients, benefit from coordinated care between all facilities and specialists who are committed to quality outcomes and an excellent patient experience. Working with our employed Banner Medical Group physicians and aligned independent practitioners, we offer residents leading heart care with services provided through the CardioVascular Institute of North Colorado, comprehensive cancer care through the McKee Cancer Center and NCMC's Cancer Institute, burn and wound care through the Western States Burn Center at NCMC, neurosurgery, urology, orthopedics, gastroenterology, pulmonology, general surgery, allergy, behavioral health care, family medicine, internal medicine, women's health, and more.

All Banner Health providers and facilities adhere to the same Banner Health mission to make a difference in people's lives through excellent patient care. As a nonprofit organization, Banner Health reinvests every dollar it earns back into our system. This means quality health care for residents, quality jobs for our employees and a commitment to each of the communities we serve, including Fort Collins.

Banner Health's beginning dates back to the September 1, 1999, merger of nonprofits Samaritan Health System and Lutheran Health Systems.

Samaritan Health System was formed in 1911 and provided clinical excellence in California and Arizona, primarily in the metro Phoenix market. Lutheran Health Systems had a long-standing history dating from 1938 as a respected health care provider in rural communities located across Western and Midwestern states. Lutheran's Colorado operations included North Colorado Medical Center, McKee Medical Center, Sterling Regional MedCenter and East Morgan County Hospital in Brush.

North Colorado Medical Center is the largest of those facilities. Its history dates back to 1902 when the first hospital was built in Weld County at Island Grove Park for the isolation of the contagiously ill and the care of the county indigent. The Greeley Hospital was opened in 1904 as the first general and acute care hospital for the general population of the community and county. This two-story building located at Sixteenth Street and Eleventh Avenue was the most modern, up-to-date, well-planned facility of its kind for that time. This building housed thirty beds, and one equipped operating room for surgical cases and maternity work.

By 1942, Weld County Hospital was in need of reorganization and officials realized that a new building would be needed for more X-ray equipment, beds, laboratory areas, and space for ancillary services. On March 8, 1945, a 15.8 acre site at the southeast corner of the Green Farm (Sixteenth Street and Sixteenth Avenue) was purchased for the new facility and on November 9, 1952, a new 220-bed, $3.25 million facility opened.

In 1982 the hospital changed its name to North Colorado Medical Center and, in 1995, NCMC was leased to Lutheran Health Systems. In 1999 the newly-formed Banner Health took over operations of the hospital.

Today, NCMC is a fully-accredited, private, nonprofit facility licensed to operate 378 beds. It serves as a regional medical center with community-based and specialty services in a service area including southern Wyoming, western Nebraska, western Kansas and northeastern Colorado. North Colorado Medical Center professionals are nationally recognized for excellence in many programs such as burn and trauma care. Designated as a Level II Trauma Center, the highest in Northern Colorado, NCMC has provided a medical air transport service to the region since the early 1980s and now has three helicopters available for patient transport. State-of-the-art technology offers extra monitoring of

Above: Banner Health Fort Collins Medical Center will open in April 2015 as a full-service medical center providing emergency care, surgical services, inpatient care, labor and delivery, medical imaging and laboratory services.

Below: North Colorado Med Evac operates three air medical transport helicopters serving residents of Northern Colorado, southern Wyoming and western Nebraska.

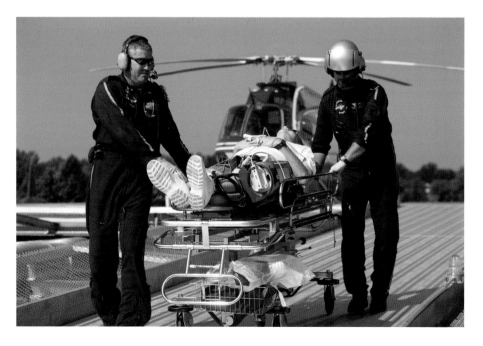

Above: Banner Health Centers can take care of your primary health care needs. The centers offer same and next-day appointments and convenient evening hours.

Below: Maurice Lyons, DO, (left) and Todd Bruce, PA-C, are part of the CardioVascular Institute of North Colorado, providing heart/thoracic and vascular services across the region.

NCMC patients in intensive care units, minimally-invasive surgery and an intelligent OB program, designed to reduce the chances of complications during labor and delivery.

Our other Front Range hospital, McKee Medical Center, opened in 1976, but it was not the first hospital to serve the Loveland community.

The first hospital in Loveland was Sutherland Hospital established in 1896 by W. P. Sutherland, MD, in his home on Sixth and Grant. His screened-in porch was turned into an operating room. When Dr. Sutherland passed away in 1917, a group of physicians leased and maintained the hospital until 1929. In 1929, William Gasser, MD, established a ten to fourteen bed hospital known as Loveland Hospital. This hospital was in existence until 1947. From 1947 to 1951 Loveland had no local hospital.

Through much work between the city of Loveland, the Elks Club and area chambers of commerce, Lutheran Health Systems (then Lutheran Hospitals and Homes Society) was selected to participate in building a new facility in Loveland. The forty-two bed, 35,300 square foot hospital opened November 25, 1951, at Douglas and Eighth Street. Over the next several decades, the hospital provided services to an ever-expanding population.

During this time, local farmer Thomas McKee was a patient in the aging, crowded hospital. He recognized a need and donated 29.5 acres of his farm for a new health care facility. In 1973, Lutheran Hospitals and Homes Society agreed to build a new facility on the property donated by McKee.

In 1976, McKee Medical Center opened for business with eighty beds at 94,355 square feet, and began operations shortly before a massive Big Thompson River flood in July killed 144 people. During the aftermath of the flood, McKee received hundreds of patients and the new facility proved to be the town's greatest asset.

McKee Medical Center has 115 licensed beds at 421,972 square feet, and boasts a variety of services including Cardiovascular, Level III Trauma, Emergency Services, Robotic Surgery, Clinical Laboratory, Nutrition Services, Medical Imaging, Digital Mammography, Wellness Services, Women's Services, and a comprehensive Cancer Center. Like NCMC, Banner Fort Collins Medical Center and other Banner Health hospitals, McKee used advanced technology to provide additional monitoring to patients in the Intensive Care Unit and the Intelligent OB program.

Both McKee and NCMC were recognized in 2014 as two of America's 100 Best Hospitals™ as measured by *Healthgrades*, the leading online resource for comprehensive information about physicians and hospitals.

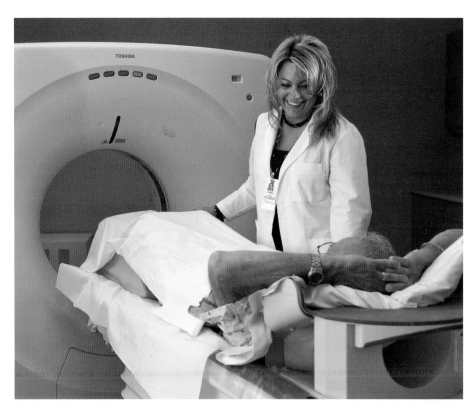

As the health care industry continues its transformation in the wake of The Affordable Care Act of 2010, Banner Health continues to be defined by its mission and dedication to the communities we serve. Whether we are providing patient care in our hospitals, in our medical practices, or in our patients' homes, we will continue to serve Northern Colorado with outstanding patient care that is comprehensive, coordinated and convenient.

Above: Cyndy Dingae, a Banner Health MRI and CT technologist, assists patients with their medical imaging needs.

Below: Amanda Chambers, PACS specialist, prepares medical imaging equipment during a trauma drill. Banner Health offers the latest in technology to benefit patients.

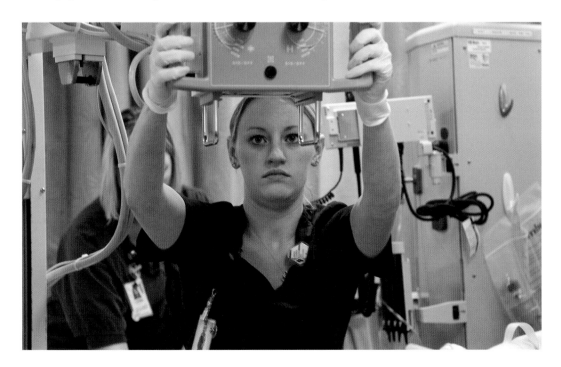

COLORADO STATE UNIVERSITY

Above: Horse and buggy traffic passes Old Main in 1881. As the second building constructed on the Colorado Agricultural College campus, Old Main was a hub of student life.

Below: Military science students pose for an Air Corps photograph at Christensen Field in 1943. Throughout World War II, Colorado A&M bolstered national defense by hosting military training groups.

With nearly 31,000 students and 1,600 faculty members on a busy, bustling campus, today's Colorado State University bears little resemblance to the tiny agricultural college established in Fort Collins 144 years ago.

According to James C. Hansen, Colorado State University professor emeritus of history, CSU originated in 1870 when the territorial legislature established an agricultural college at Fort Collins. The school qualified for endowment under federal legislation, which provided land grants to academic institutions offering instruction in agriculture and the mechanic arts.

Robert Dazell deeded thirty acres of land for a college site in 1871 and, in 1872; the Larimer County Land Improvement Company contributed another eighty acres. But it was not until 1874 that the Territorial Legislative Assembly allocated $1,000 to aid in constructing college buildings. Even that modest sum required college trustees to match the amount. Several months later, a sixteen by twenty-four foot red brick building was constructed, demonstrating local support for the new school, which was named Agricultural College of Colorado.

Nearly a decade passed before classes began in Fort Collins but on September 1, 1879, President Elijah Evan Edwards and a two member faculty welcomed the new institution's first five students. Edwards wasted little time initiating the college's first outreach to the agricultural community, presenting the first school-sponsored farmers institutions at Fort Collins.

Research, teaching, and outreach were all key college programs when Charles A. Lory began his thirty-one year tenure as president in 1909. A former ditch rider whose family had homesteaded in Colorado, Lory imbued the school with a commitment to practical education and service to the state. During his presidency, enrollment grew from 217 to 2,048, and the college developed into a well-rounded technical institution. By 1940, degrees were available in agriculture, engineering, home economics, veterinary medicine, forestry, vocational education, agricultural economics and rural sociology.

The calamity of the Great Depression posed exceptional challenges for the school as Lory led efforts to mobilize outreach support for the state's hard-hit rural areas.

American involvement in World War II threw normal college routines into disarray. Enrollments plummeted as students and faculty left for military service. Although the college remained open because of President Roy Green's success in bringing military training programs to the campus, national defense, rather than collegiate goals, prevailed. Research and extension efforts strongly emphasized agricultural output.

The school, now known as Colorado A&M, faced a new set of challenges when the war ended in 1945 and soldiers flocked to colleges for an education paid for by the G.I. Bill. More than a thousand students attended the college at the end of the war, and about 1,600 were enrolled by the spring of 1946,

two-thirds of them veterans in need of housing. The cheapest and quickest housing the school could provide was a tiny community of military-surplus Quonset huts set up at the corners of West Laurel and Shields Streets. Students established a trailer court beside Veterans Village in the fall of 1946 when 3,500 students crammed into the school's now inadequate classroom space.

William E. Morgan, who became president in 1949, led the school's emergence as a modern educational institution. A prudent planner, he foresaw the need for major campus expansion, identified areas of excellence, and encouraged their development.

Colorado A&M shed its image as a narrow technical college and became a university in appearance and name during the 1950s. The college awarded its first Ph.D. degree in 1955 and, two years later, the school's name was changed to Colorado State University. Curricular improvements in the liberal arts, library acquisitions, and international programs gave legitimacy to the title of 'university'.

Despite its agrarian roots and predominantly conservative attitudes, CSU became the scene of intense student activism during the turbulent 1960s and early 1970s. Racism and campus regulations for women were among the early targets of student activists. The civil rights movement on campus picked up momentum and visibility during this period.

CSU entered the 1980s rated as a Class I Research University by the Carnegie Foundation for the Advancement of Education, with a new Veterinary Teaching Hospital and several other 'firsts' ranging from climatology to solar energy. These accomplishments included the first cat to receive a bone marrow transplant to correct a rare disease, the first endowed professorship to provide leadership in computer-assisted engineering, and a $25 million grant to conduct research and provide graduate education for water problems in Egypt.

The 1990s brought additional research and scholarly recognition to CSU, along with a renewed emphasis on undergraduate teaching and outreach arms of the university's land-grant mission. At his inauguration ceremony in 1991, President Albert Yates called for the university to "Strike a balance between teaching and research that enriches both while not diminishing either."

Today, Colorado State University, under the leadership of President Tony Frank, operates the 586 acre main campus in Fort Collins, in addition to a foothills campus, an agricultural campus and the Pingree Park Mountain Campus. About 31,000 students attend CSU, including nearly 27,000 on-campus, resident-instruction students. The school employs 6,400, including 1,600 faculty members, and is Fort Collins' largest employer.

Above: Students study outside Morgan Library in 1967. Construction of the library and other new learning facilities was an important step in Colorado A&M's transition to a fully accredited university in the early 1970s.

Below: A doctoral student conducts tuberculosis research in 2013 in CSU's Biomedical Engineering labs. The University houses the nation's largest tuberculosis research group.

COLUMBINE HEALTH SYSTEMS

In 1970, Bob Wilson joined a construction crew working on an addition to the Columbine Care Center on Parker Street in Fort Collins. Bob discovered that he really enjoyed interacting with the residents and took a job as maintenance man for the facility. However, the facility soon fell into bankruptcy and those handling the receivership hired Bob to become administrator of the failing facility.

Bob borrowed a suit coat and cut his hair and went to work as the administrator. Within six months, Bob had begun to turn the facility around and was able to gather together enough money to purchase the facility. The rest, as they say, is history.

Starting with one 120 bed nursing home in 1971, Columbine Health Systems now includes 486 nursing home beds in 5 facilities, in 3 communities, spread over 2 counties. In addition, Columbine operates 189 assisted living apartments and 275 independent living apartments. Columbine cares for about 150 home care clients and currently looks after 30 non-medical home care clients and 20 infusion clients.

From his friend Terry Drahota, who built many of his facilities over the years, to his banker, Tom Gleason, Bob credits a number of individuals for Columbine's success, including Barry Fancher, who has worked with Bob since 1978, Jean Neidringhaus, who was director of nursing at Columbine Care Center East and became administrator for Columbine Care Center West, and Dr. Charles Collopy, a good friend who gave Bob much support.

Bob's family was also very active in the organization's success. Lloyd Wilson, Bob's dad, helped with the accounting and his mom, Stella Wilson, helped in dozens of ways, including sewing curtains for the resident rooms.

The facility, Columbine Care Center, began with forty-eight beds, then remodeled and expanded to a total of 120 beds. There were only thirty-five employees in the early days, most of them women from nearby farms who came into town to work at the nursing home.

Today, Columbine Health Systems operates 3 independent living facilities, 3 assisted living facilities and 5 skilled nursing facilities in Fort Collins, Loveland and Windsor. Also serving those communities are Columbine Medical Equipment, Columbine Poudre Home Care, Bloom at Home (which provides non-medical home care), Poudre Infusion Therapy, Centre Pharmacy, and the Lifestyle Centre Health Club. Fleet Transportation Services and the Columbine Distribution Centre serve the residents and facilities.

Columbine skilled nursing facilities are located at 940 Worthington Circle, 815 Centre Avenue, 4824 South Lemay Avenue, Fort Collins; and 1475 Main Street, Windsor. Independent living facilities providing

gracious living for mature adults are located at 909 Centre Avenue, 900 Worthington Circle, Fort Collins; and 1515 West 28th Street, Loveland. Assisted living facilities that balance daily assistance with independence are located at 900 Centre Avenue, Fort Collins; 1422 West 29th Street, Loveland; and 1475 Main Street, Windsor. The headquarters/management office is located on the Fort Collins campus at Drake/Shields.

Columbine employs nearly 1,400 people who care for 1,150 people each day. Most of the clients have lived, worked or retired to the area, or moved to the area so their children could more easily look after them. Many were moved to the area by their family because they knew the care provided by Columbine was superior to where they lived previously.

Bob likes to tell the story of finding his Grandmother's hall tree in his brother's barn in Iowa. The hall tree was all in pieces but he took it to an older gentleman, Andy Anderson, for repair. After a few weeks, Andy returned the hall tree in perfect condition. A few months later, Andy and his son appeared at the front door of Columbine Care Center with his suitcase. Andy turned to his son and said, "I'm in the right place. I repaired that hall tree."

Bob has served as president of the Colorado Health Care Association for twelve years and feels this has provided unique insights that have assisted in the growth of Columbine Health Systems. Traveling back and forth to Washington, D.C., as a member of the Board of the American Health Care Association and as president of the Independent Owners of nursing homes has allowed him to meet with industry leaders and stay abreast of the emerging trends in the business.

One of Bob's goals is to introduce young people to Gerontology. He worked with Brad Sheaffor in the Social Work Department at Colorado State University in the early 1970s to provide internship opportunities for students at Columbine Care Center. Today, Bob sponsors a $30,000 scholarship at CSU for the gerontology program and student scholarships. In addition, Columbine hosts student interns in human development, CNA, LPN and RN programs, social work, exercise sports science, pharmacy, pre-OT, and pre-med each semester.

Northern Colorado has been very supportive of Columbine Health Systems over the years and this generosity is repaid through many contributions to numerous organizations and individuals in the community.

Looking to the future, plans are in the works to expand further east of I-25 to serve Johnstown and Millken to the south and Windsor to the east. Columbine has purchased nine acres to the east of the Medical Centre Building and Columbine Commons for two-story independent living and patio homes with two-car garages.

HEALTH DISTRICT OF NORTHERN LARIMER COUNTY

🏕

Right: The Family Dental Clinic provides a full range of services to residents unable to afford the full cost of care.

Below: The Health District is helping people understand new health insurance options.

The Health District of Northern Larimer County was the first of its kind when it was founded more than fifty years ago. Today, in many ways, it is still one of a kind.

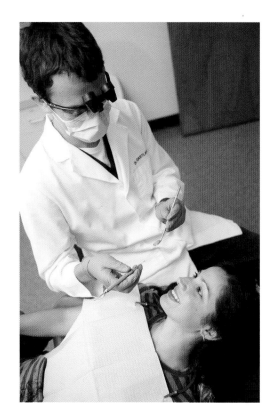

The Fort Collins-based Health District is a public agency whose mission is to create a healthier community. It provides dental care, mental health, prescription assistance and health promotion services to residents in the northern two-thirds of Larimer County. In addition, it also works to create healthy change by fostering collaboration among area organizations, advocating for policy change, assessing local health needs and bringing outside funding into the community.

Governed by a publicly elected board of directors, the Health District is similar to other special districts created to fund essential local services such as fire protection. It was established by voters in 1960 to address growing healthcare needs in Fort Collins. The local hospital was overcrowded and underfunded. In response, area residents created the state's first tax-funded hospital district.

The Health District took over the hospital in 1962, renaming it Poudre Valley Hospital. For more than thirty years, it owned, operated, expanded and modernized the facility. By the 1990s, however, a shifting healthcare landscape prompted the Health District to re-examine its primary mission.

In 1994 the Health District turned over operation of Poudre Valley Hospital to a new local, private, not-for-profit entity under a long-term lease arrangement. This enabled the hospital to pursue business strategies that would strengthen its financial standing for the future. Meanwhile, the arrangement freed the Health District to focus on other pressing healthcare needs unique to the community.

Before drawing up new plans for the future, the Health District looked carefully at what the community needed. The process included a comprehensive written survey of area residents, as well as feedback gathered from across the community. The Health District has repeated this process every three years, developing a detailed and valuable picture of the community's healthcare needs.

In 1996 the Health District launched several services aimed at filling local gaps in care. As the community has changed over the years, the Health District has changed alongside it—adding, ending or modifying programs and services in response to evolving needs. Today, the Health District engages in a broad range of activities that promote a healthy community through several different approaches.

Cost can be a barrier to health care, so the Health District provides certain targeted services with sliding fees, putting good health within reach of more district residents

with low incomes. Nearly a quarter of local residents skip taking their medication because of cost. The Health District's Prescription Assistance program helps many of these people obtain the medicine they need to stay healthy.

Dental care is sometimes overlooked, yet oral health impacts a person's overall physical health and economic potential. Unfortunately, thousands of Larimer County residents lack access to even basic dental care. The Health District's Family Dental Clinic helps meet the need by providing acute, preventive and restorative care on a sliding fee to qualifying children and adults. In addition, the Health District's Dental Connections program helps link even more residents in need of affordable care with services provided by local private dentists.

Through the years, the Health District has been a leader in broadening local access to mental health services. People struggling with depression, anxiety or substance abuse often do not know where to turn for help or are unable to afford counseling once they do. Connections, a collaboration with Touchstone Health Partners, provides free information and referrals for mental health and substance abuse care, including low-cost counseling. A separate program places mental health and substance abuse professionals in two Fort Collins medical clinics.

Cost and convenience also can be barriers to receiving preventive care. For those needing an effective and affordable way to quit smoking,

the Health District offers its Step Free from Tobacco program. For those concerned about risk of heart disease, there are quick, low-cost cholesterol and blood pressure screenings each week at convenient locations throughout Fort Collins. Both services are open to district residents of all incomes.

The Health District also rallies the community to solve challenging healthcare issues too large for any one organization to tackle. It does this by advocating for policies and legislation that impact the health of district residents, as well as seeking additional sources of private and public funding for programs. The Health District has been particularly effective at coordinating large-scale collaborative projects that spark community-wide change, such as the Community Mental Health and Substance Abuse Partnership that is helping ensure more people have access to appropriate and timely care.

When the new healthcare law created opportunities for more Americans to get affordable health insurance, the Health District swung into action, launching its newest program in 2013: Larimer Health Connect, which provides free, in-person assistance to individuals, families and small businesses to help them understand their options and enroll in health coverage.

As it has for more than fifty years, the Health District seeks innovative solutions to problems that challenge our community's potential for good health, making it a public agency as unique as the city it calls home.

Above: The office at 202 Bristlecone Drive is one of two Health District facilities in north Fort Collins.

Below: Low-cost cholesterol and blood pressure tests are offered weekly throughout Fort Collins.

COMMUNITY FOUNDATION OF NORTHERN COLORADO

Above: A few of the founding trustees and spouses. Back row, left to right: Buford Plemmons, Ray Chamberlain, Bob Everitt and Charles Patchen. Front row, left to right: Emily Patchen, Margaret and Donald Webber.

Opposite, top: Ribbon Cutting Ceremony, left to right, Mike Dellenbach, Wynne Odell, Doug Hutchinson, Steve Hagberg and Dave Edwards.

Opposite, center: Community Foundation executives, left to right, Executive Director Kaye Arnold 1982–1986, Executive Director Diane Hogerty 1986–2002, and President Ray Caraway 2003–present.

Opposite, bottom: Hach Community Room Dedication, left to right, Bruce and Muriel Hach with Foundation President Ray Caraway. The Community Foundation renamed its board room the Hach Community Room in recognition of the Hach Family's leadership. This room is available free of charge as meeting space for nonprofits.

The Community Foundation of Northern Colorado is a public charity that manages and administers hundreds of charitable funds and millions of dollars in assets. Donations to the funds are tax deductible and grants from the funds are distributed to 501c3 agencies, schools, and churches.

When the Community Foundation was founded in 1975 by twenty-one community leaders, Fort Collins was a small college town on the verge of major growth. A citizen's planning group was organized to identify projects needed by a growing city and the group developed a list that included a new library, a new performing arts center, parks, an indoor swimming pool, the Poudre Walkway Trails, and city offices. Voters approved a one-cent sales tax to help pay for the projects.

Following the citizen's planning group's work, an initiative called Designing Tomorrow Today (DT2) was created and given the challenge of raising funds for the projects recommended. One of the suggested projects was to turn the Lincoln Junior High School building into what is now known as the Lincoln Center. In an effort to organize the fundraising, Mayor Carson contacted a Poudre School District Administrator, Buford Plemmons, and suggested the creation of a community foundation.

Additionally, a local resident, Olive Ludlow, had left a $25,000 bequest for a purpose that was somewhat unclear, and it seemed a community foundation would be an appropriate repository to receive the gift. And so, the Community Foundation of Northern Colorado was born.

After construction of the Lincoln Center was completed, it was decided that the Foundation could still be used as a means of holding funds for nonprofit organizations and other special projects. At first the organization was known as the Fort Collins Community Foundation, but the name was later changed to Community Foundation of Northern Colorado as the service area expanded.

A part-time Executive Director Kaye Arnold was hired in 1982 to administer the collection and disbursement of funds from the Foundation to nonprofits and to aid in the formation of new organizations. In 1986, Diane Hogerty was selected as the first full-time executive director; this positioned the Foundation to grow its fundraising efforts and community impact.

Ray Caraway became president of the Foundation in January 2003. At that time, the organization's assets totaled more than $14 million. That same year, Caraway led the Cornerstone Campaign, which raised $1.6 million from board members and a small number of philanthropic leaders to provide an infusion of operating capital to jump-start the organization's growth and provide a solid foundation for carrying out its donor services role.

Following the Cornerstone Campaign, the organization's assets increased from $14 million in 2003 to $80 million at the close of 2013. This growth enhanced the Foundation's donor services role and grew its community leadership role. The Foundation served as the fiscal sponsor for organizations such as Book Trust, Project Smile, CHAMP, and others. The Foundation was also able to launch community projects such as UniverCity Connections, Inspiration Playground, Veterans Plaza of Northern Colorado, and the expansion of the Rialto Theater in Loveland. The campaign also enabled the organization to build a new office at 4745 Wheaton Drive in south Fort Collins, a facility that provides meeting space to numerous local nonprofits.

To date, the Foundation has distributed more than $50 million in grants and programs to a large number of charitable organizations. The Community Foundation of Northern Colorado is now the largest community foundation in the state, outside of Denver, and is similar in size to statewide community foundations serving Wyoming, Nebraska and Montana.

In recent years, the Foundation played a vital role in responding to community tragedies by connecting charitable organizations with the resources they need most for rebuilding. The Foundation collected and distributed $1.94 million to support Larimer County's recovery from the 2013 flood. In 2012 the Community Foundation was involved with disbursing more than $600,000 to aid in wildfire recovery efforts; this amount includes grants made from the Foundation's SERVE 6.8 Fund, Make It Rain Fund, High Park Fire Restoration Fund, and numerous donor advised funds, in addition to grants made from the Colorado Fire Relief Fund based on recommendations from a local grant making committee.

After a decade of rapid growth, the Foundation is now in a position to do even more for the region. The Catalyst Campaign, an ambitious effort to provide resources to help the organization enhance its capacity building and community leadership roles, was launched in 2013. Thanks to the extraordinary leadership from current and former board members, the Foundation is creating an even greater impact in Northern Colorado.

The Community Foundation's role within the community is now three-pronged. Its donor services role includes the stewardship of more than 360 individual charitable funds, managing four investment pools, issuing gift annuities, managing charitable trusts, and overseeing special assets such as real estate, water rights, and even a small manufacturing firm. Its capacity building role includes managing endowment funds for forty-six local

nonprofits, and its community leadership role brings people and resources together in support of important local issues.

For more information about the Community Foundation of Northern Colorado, please visit www.NoCoFoundation.org.

FORT COLLINS COUNTRY CLUB

Fort Collins was beginning to grow into a major city in 1959 when the founders of Fort Collins Country Club recognized the need for a family-oriented Country Club offering golf, swimming, tennis and other social and recreational programs.

Two sites were considered as the location for the new club; a farm owned by State Senator Ed Whitaker, and the land currently occupied by the Fort Collins Foothills Mall. The Whitaker Farm site was chosen because it included a generous supply of water, a resource that continues to be an asset to the Club today.

Whitaker sold the land to the founders for $85,000 and the Whitaker Farm House served as the original Clubhouse. A second structure was used to house the first superintendent of the golf course and the barn became the first Pro Shop.

Robert 'Spike' Baker, William Allen, Jack Harvey and William Galyardt are credited with developing the mission and promoting the financing program that insured success of the new club. Don Chapin formulated a business plan and his many contacts in the community helped turn the plans into reality.

To raise the capital needed to develop the Country Club, each of the original founders invested $1,000 and had to find one other family with $1,000 to invest. In turn, each of these new candidates was expected to find one additional family to invest in the venture. The plan resulted in 279 original bondholders.

Work on the first nine holes of the golf course began under the direction of Henry Hughes, the club's first golf course architect. Fred Foss, who had farmed the Whitaker Farm for many years, was hired to build the course and become the first golf course superintendent.

The course and club opened officially in the winter of 1959 and dues were only $12 per month. The Club got its first liquor license in 1960 and began Clubhouse service in the old Whitaker Farm House.

To fulfill the vision of a family-oriented club, construction soon began on a pool and tennis courts. The first pool was located about where the current Clubhouse sits and the pool's bathhouse was used by golfers as a locker room. Six tennis courts were constructed on the site of the existing pool.

By 1962 the Club had 170 members and Ray Bostich, a former member of the CSU golf team, became the first golf pro and served until his retirement in 1992.

Recognizing the need to expand the golf course to eighteen holes, the Board laid out thirty-eight building lots along the north and east sides of the club property and installed water, sewer and telephone lines. Depending on location, the lots sold from $3,800 to $5,500. Construction of the second nine holes began in 1967 and the expanded course opened a year later.

Foss retired in 1980 and was succeeded by Bob Montabone, who directed a number of improvements, including installation of a fully automatic irrigation system.

The Club began to employ professional club managers in the late 1970s. Among them was Randy Fisher, who oversaw the largest expansion of membership and infrastructure in the Club's history. The old Whitaker Farm House no longer met the member's needs and in the mid-1980s the Board had to decide whether to make major renovations to the old farm house or build a new Clubhouse.

Once again, a development project was undertaken to raise funds for a new Clubhouse. Lots were mapped out on what is now Cottonwood Point Drive and Cottonwood Grove. The sale of these choice lots supplied most of the funds needed to construct a new Clubhouse, pool and bathhouse, the four existing east Tennis Courts and a new Tennis Pavilion. The Whitaker Farm House was last used in 1986 and replaced with the existing Clubhouse in 1987.

The improvements helped spark a major growth spurt and golfing membership rose to more than 400 in 1989. To accommodate the growth, the main dining room was expanded in 1990 and the west patio became indoor space. The south patio was added to accommodate seasonal outdoor dining needs.

To compete with new golf clubs, a redesign of the course by Dye Designs began in 1994. To cope with the Club's growing pains, Norman Nuwash was recruited to become the first CEO and General Manager in 1995. In 2007 the Fort Collins Country Club opened a new Spa facility in the lower level of the main Clubhouse.

The Fort Collins Country Club now has more than 600 members, the most in its history, and employs nearly a hundred people. Scott Szymoniak serves as general manager.

A $6 million renovation that began in 2014 will include new amenities to help the Club maintain its reputation as the area's premier country club. These improvements will include three indoor tennis courts, a fitness facility and new casual dining facilities.

FRONT RANGE CENTER FOR BRAIN & SPINE SURGERY

TOP: PHOTOGRAPH COURTESY OF TONY ARDUINO.

Above: Left to right, Dr. Timothy Wirt, Dr. Donn Turner and Dr. Douglas Beard.

Front Range Center for Brain & Spine Surgery is a full-service practice dedicated to spine and brain surgery. Founded in 1978, the Center has become the regional leader in surgical and non-surgical treatment of spinal and intracranial pathology and treatment of problems concerning the peripheral nerves.

Dr. James Warson, the founding neurosurgeon, recalls that he was leaving a practice in Lexington, Kentucky, when Dr. Syd Smith, a local neurologist, asked him to consider locating in Fort Collins.

Dr. Warson found there was no CAT scanner in the area, so he had to do diagnostic studies such as arteriograms by himself. "If I needed a CAT scan performed, the patient had to go to Boulder or Cheyenne. One patient got caught in a blizzard and wasn't found until two days later," he says.

"We had a steady stream of emergency patients from Wyoming, and later from Nebraska and Kansas," Dr. Warson continues. "These patients never missed a follow-up appointment. I'd like to think it was because of the quality of their care, although I suspect Fort Collins' shopping and restaurants may have played a part."

Dr. Timothy Wirt, who joined the practice only two years after it was established, remembers the days when patients had to travel long distances for treatment and feels the acquisition of sophisticated technology such as CT and MR scanning has helped Front Range become the region's leader for spine and brain surgery and treatment. "The neuro team director, Kay Miller, RN, and I visited churches and reached out to local businesses to raise the capital for our first CT scanner at Poudre Valley Hospital," Dr. Wirt recalls.

Front Range was the first neurosurgery practice in Fort Collins and, over time, diversified to include orthopaedic spine surgery. The practice has supported Poudre Valley Hospital for thirty-five years by providing neurosurgical trauma care as well as elective neurosurgical and orthopaedic spine care.

The physicians at Front Range are:

Dr. Wirt joined the Center in 1980 after completing his surgical internship and his neurosurgical residency at Vanderbilt University Hospital. He earned his M.D. degree from the University of Michigan. Dr. Wirt became a certified member of the American Board of Neurological Surgery in 1982 and a fellow of the American College of Surgeons in 1984.

Dr. Turner, who joined the practice in 1984, received his M.D. degree from Washington University School of Medicine in St. Louis, and completed his neurosurgical residency at the University of Iowa. Dr. Turner was certified by the American Board of Neurological Surgery in 1986 and became a fellow of the American College of Surgeons in 1988.

Dr. Beard, a native of Fort Collins, completed his medical studies at Creighton University in Omaha. He fulfilled his orthopaedic residency at the University of Nebraska Medical Center in 1991, followed by spine surgery fellowships at Tulane University and Northwestern University School of Medicine. He is certified by the American Board of Orthopaedic Surgery.

SURGERY CENTER OF FORT COLLINS, LLC

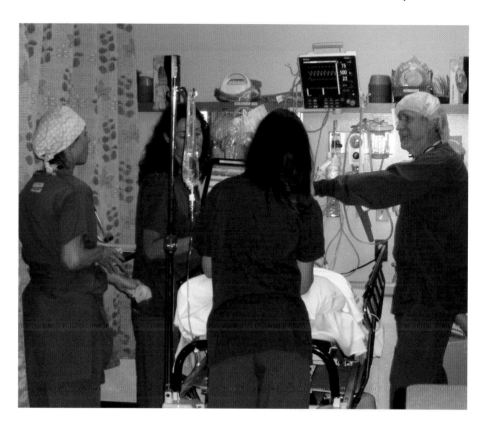

The Surgery Center of Fort Collins, located at 1100 East Prospect Road, provides ambulatory surgical services including colonoscopy, ear/nose/throat, general surgery, gynecology, infertility, neurosurgery, orthopedics, pain management, plastic surgery and podiatry.

The Surgery Center (SCFC) was founded in June 2000, by a group of independent, single-specialty surgeons who acquired a seventy-five percent interest in a facility that was initially opened in 1990 by HealthSouth. That facility experienced a lack of growth and the founders of SCFC approached HealthSouth with an offer to assume controlling interest and facility management. Surgical Care Affiliates, a subsidiary of HealthSouth, retained a twenty-five percent interest in the facility.

Surgeons and administrators from Fort Collins Women's Clinic, Front Range Center for Brain and Spine Surgery, Fort Collins Surgical Associates and Northern Colorado Anesthesia Professionals provided the impetus for developing SCFC.

In 2005, Poudre Valley Hospital acquired a twenty-six percent interest in SCFC during a time when the hospital was seeking to align and partner with local physicians in healthcare facilities. Currently—and for the foreseeable future—physicians will retain a 49 percent interest, Poudre Valley Hospital a 26 percent interest, and SCA a 25 percent interest.

Surgeons at SCFC are board certified and must undergo a rigorous review of their credentials prior to being granted the privilege of performing surgery at the center. The anesthesia staff includes highly qualified board certified physicians from Northern Colorado Anesthesia Professionals, the region's premier anesthesia group. The clinical staff includes well-trained RNs, Surgical Technicians, CNAs, Radiology Technologists and others who provide care and support services for patients.

Twenty-three physicians now have an ownership interest in SCFC, and another ten operate at the facility. The staff totals thirty-nine. SCFC performed 2,800 surgeries in 2013, with patients referred from independent surgeon practices in Northern Colorado, Southeast Wyoming, Southwest Nebraska and Western Kansas. Patient volumes have remained steady for several years and are increasing with the addition of colonoscopy services. Other technologies and services of value to surgeons and their patients are also being developed.

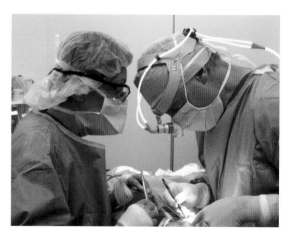

Ambulatory surgery centers such as SCFC have proven to be highly cost-effective, efficient, high quality and exceptional outcome sites of service for patients and insurance carriers, including governmental insurance. Given the value proposition of surgery centers, increasing numbers of surgeries will be done safely, effectively and cost-efficiently in this environment.

SCFC is very involved in community activities and offers an annual 'free surgery' day. In addition, charitable contributions are made annually to the Poudre Valley Hospital Foundation.

For more information about the Surgery Center of Fort Collins, check the website at www.surgerycenterftcollins.com.

A STEP AHEAD FOOT & ANKLE CENTER

Left to right: Dr. Robert C. Schulte,
Dr. Michael J. Burns and
Dr. Chad M. Knutsen.

Below: Dr. Kate Johnson.

The foundations of A Step Ahead Foot & Ankle Center started in the 1970s when Dr. William Trewartha moved his practice of podiatric medicine and surgery to Fort Collins from the Denver area. Dr. Michael Burns moved to Fort Collins in 1982 and practiced with Dr. Trewartha part-time while he commuted to finish some research at the Temple University College of Podiatric Medicine in Philadelphia. Dr. Burns subsequently operated separate practices in both Fort Collins and Loveland.

Dr. Robert Schulte and Dr. Chad Knutsen bought the practice and Fort Collins Foot & Ankle Clinic became A Step Ahead Foot & Ankle Center in 2001 when Dr Trewartha retired. Within a year, Dr. Burns joined them as well.

Dr. Schulte and Dr. Knutsen then purchased Dr. Baum's practice in Loveland, currently located at 3850 North Grant Avenue. The two offices are only ten miles apart and patients may choose to visit either office. The Fort Collins office is still located at the original location in the Spring Creek Office Park and is a survivor of the 1997 flood.

Dr. Schulte grew up on the eastern plains of Colorado and graduated from the Scholl College of Podiatric Medicine. He then completed a two year surgical residency at Loretto Hospital and Hugar Surgery Center in Chicago.

Dr. Knutsen, a native of eastern Iowa, graduated from the Scholl College of Podiatric Medicine and completed a one year internship and two year surgical residency at Mercy Hospital and Medical Center in Chicago.

Dr. Burns graduated from the California College of Podiatric Medicine. He served as chairman of the Department of Podiatric Orthopedics and the director of the Gait Study Center at the Temple University College of Podiatric Medicine. He is a past president of the American Board of Podiatric Surgery.

A podiatrist is a licensed physician and surgeon, specializing in the examination, diagnosis, and treatment—both medically and surgically—of foot and ankle conditions. A Step Ahead is fortunate to have three highly qualified podiatrists on staff, and a fourth one, Dr. Kate Johnson joined the practice in 2014.

A Step Ahead Foot & Ankle Center has had a number of long-time employees, including Jacque Warren who has been with our company for over sixteen years and Jack Burgin the practice administrator who worked for the doctors from 1997 until his retirement in 2012. Lola Anderson, who semi-retired in 2013, literally came with the practice when purchased from Dr Baum.

Among the many organizations supported by the practice are the Phantom 4 Miler, which benefits animal health groups; Hope Lives; the Pink BOA 501K for cancer research; Mudbrigade, to benefit first responders; Flying Pig, which aids families who have children with disabilities; Storm Academy, to benefit kid's soccer; and Realities for Children, which benefits many agencies in the area. A Step Ahead is also a long-time member of the Fort Collins and Loveland Chambers of Commerce and the Better Business Bureau.

For nearly a century, The Eye Center of Northern Colorado, P.C., has offered compassionate and comprehensive medical, surgical and optical care to achieve the best vision possible for each of its patients.

The Eye Center has operated under its current name since 1991 but the practice enjoys a rich heritage that began in 1916 when W. F. Brownell, MD, began helping patients with eye care from an office in downtown Fort Collins.

In 1932, George Garrison, MD, joined Dr. Brownell in the practice and later married Dr. Brownell's daughter. During World War II, Dr. Brownell remained in Fort Collins to serve the community, while Dr. Garrison served in the armed forces. Dr. Garrison returned to Fort Collins to rejoin the practice following the war, a pattern that has been repeated many times as Eye Center doctors have gone out in the world to help others, and then returned home because of their commitment to the community.

The practice continued to serve the community in the decades following the war, attracting the best and brightest doctors by encouraging a culture of collaboration and team work.

Laser vision correction was first FDA approved in 1995 and shortly thereafter, The Eye Center introduced this revolutionary approach to the region. A year later, doctors from The Eye Center and those from Poudre Valley Ophthalmology joined forces to offer a higher level of care for all of northern Colorado, Wyoming, and western Nebraska. Together, they were able to have the best technology, the most skilled and caring doctors, and the most specialized and highly trained staff.

The Eye Centers commitment to quality is seen through the many improvements in eye care it has introduced to the region over the years. The Eye Center was the first to place ocular implants in Fort Collins and the first to introduce refractive surgery and complex cornea, retina, strabismus, orbital and glaucoma surgery in northern Colorado.

The Eye Center of Northern Colorado now operates three locations in Fort Collins and Loveland. Satellite clinics are located in Cheyenne, Laramie, Rawlings, Fort Morgan, Wellington and Arvada. The practice includes a team of fourteen ophthalmologists and optometrists who have performed more than 60,000 cataract and refractive surgical procedures and more than 25,000 cataract procedures. The practice provides custom LASIK eye surgery, using Custom Wavefront Diagnostics, an IntraLase Laser and an Alcon Allegretto Laser. It is the only practice in Colorado to offer cataract surgery using the bladeless LenSx® Laser.

The doctors and staff at The Eye Center are deeply involved in the community and are active in such organizations as Realities for Children, A Child's Dream, Foothills Gateway, Project Homeless, Lions Clubs and Ensight Skills Center. In addition to supporting the local community, many of the physicians at The Eye Center are involved in international eye surgery mission work.

For more information about The Eye Center of Northern Colorado, check their website at www.eyecenternoco.com.

THE EYE CENTER OF NORTHERN COLORADO, P.C.

Above: Image of laser room is in our state-of-the-art LASIK facility that was built in 2013.

Below: Our main office shortly after construction in 1997.

ORTHOPAEDIC & SPINE CENTER OF THE ROCKIES

The Orthopaedic & Spine Center of the Rockies has served the people of Fort Collins—as well as Colorado, Wyoming and western Nebraska—since 1969. The physicians and staff strive to provide the very best medical and surgical care, based on patient involvement and education.

OCR provides comprehensive orthopaedic, spine, sports medicine, sports concussion and podiatry services. It also offers a surgery center, a recovery center for short-term overnight stays, therapy, digital X-rays and MRI, and cast/splint/brace services.

The practice was organized in 1969 under the name of Fort Collins Orthopedic Associates. The founders were Dr. Charles Collopy, Dr. Robert Johnson, Dr. Benedict Magsamen and Dr. Douglas Murray. The four physicians had come to Fort Collins separately in the 1960s and formed a partnership after a few years in practice. The doctors were among the first orthopaedic specialists in the region and helped pioneer the development of that specialty here.

"One of the factors that helped us excel was the development of a clinic with doctors who focus on the various orthopedic specialties," comments Dr. Johnson. "We have specialists in hand, spine, joint replacement, foot-ankle, trauma, sports medicine surgery, and other disciplines."

The practice became the Orthopaedic Center of the Rockies in 1990 when the facilities were moved to the current location on East Prospect Road in Fort Collins. The building included a therapy department with pools and a surgery center. The facility was expanded in 1998 with the addition of a third operating room and a ten-bed recovery center.

OCR opened its first Loveland office in 1985, and moved in 2009 to its current facility at 3470 East Fifteenth Street.

In 2009 the group's partners changed the name to Orthopaedic & Spine Center of the Rockies to emphasize the practice's services for people with back and neck conditions and injuries.

OCR has expanded to 281 employees, including twenty-five doctors, in recent years. Thirteen of the twenty-five doctors have joined the staff since 2005, adding their expertise in such specialties as spine, diabetic foot-wound care, sports medicine, and sports concussions.

OCR provides sports medicine services for Colorado State University, the Colorado Eagles, Colorado Ice, and local high schools, as well as about forty rodeos each year.

The doctors and employees enjoy making community involvement a priority. These efforts include a "Jeans Dollars" fund. Employees contribute three dollars when they wear denim on Friday. The doctors match the employees' donations, which are given to a local charity each month.

The founders left to right:
Dr. Ben Magsamen, Dr. Charles Collopy,
Dr. Robert Johnson, and Dr. Doug Murray.

ASSOCIATES IN FAMILY MEDICINE, PC

Associates in Family Medicine is a local family practice with eight clinic locations and more than fifty medical providers in northern Colorado. AFM delivers high quality, compassionate and convenient care to people of all ages, throughout the entire life span. The physicians and providers at AFM are dedicated to providing the very best healthcare for every member of the family.

AFM was founded in 1962 by Donald Wells, M.D. After completing a three month rotation in Fort Collins as part of the General Practice Residency Program at Colorado University Denver, Dr. Wells decided to open his own solo practice directly across from the Poudre Valley Hospital.

Although other doctors advised him to locate downtown so that farmers could visit the office when they came to town to shop, Dr. Wells established his one-man practice in a brand new building across from the hospital. In those days, the typical cost for an office call was around $3, but given Dr. Well's advanced training, his patients were willing to pay $4 and the practice was busy right from the start.

The 1970s saw a strong movement toward the concept of managed care and health management organizations (HMOs) and Dr. Wells and his associates decided to pursue a local HMO, Choice Care.

In the early 1980s, a 'managed care' organization, Peak Health, approached AFM about establishing a network in northern Colorado. Believing in the managed care philosophy, AFM was one of the first groups of providers to sign with Peak Health. As a result, AFM's practice grew rapidly and additional physicians were hired to help care for patients. The practice also expanded to other locations during this period.

Eventually, AFM and other local independent healthcare providers joined forces and organized United Physicians of Northern Colorado (NPNC), designed to ensure that patients had an option for quality healthcare at a reasonable cost. At its peak, UPNC had more than 18,000 enrollees and was very successful.

Dr. Wells eventually stepped down from the CEO position at AFM to become the medical director for UPNC, at which time Marvin Lein was at the helm of AFM's administrative operations before AFM's current CEO, Dr. James Sprowell, assumed the role in 2006.

AFM now operates eight full-service clinics and employs 225 people, including more than 50 medical health professionals, 32 of whom are physicians. Last year in 2013, AFM had more than 132,000 patient visits.

Going forward, Associates in Family Medicine plans to build upon the legacy of its founders and a history of success that has always been based on a foundation of embracing innovation to deliver exceptional, convenient healthcare at offices in your neighborhood.

Above: Associates in Family Medicine Clinic and Urgent Care at South Shields Street and West Horsetooth Road.

Below: Dr. Donald Wells, founder of Associates in Family Medicine.

Allura Skin, Laser & Wellness Clinic

Above: The four original employees of Allura: Virginia, Becky, Yvonne and Mina have now grown to thirty-one employees.

Below: Left to right, The owners, Dr. Rebecca (Becky) de la Torre and Yvonne Hampson, R.N., with the first esthetician to join the company, Bobbie Marriott. The photograph was taken at the fifth year anniversary.

Allura Skin, Laser & Wellness Clinic is one of the largest and fastest growing companies in the skin care industry. In five quick years, Allura soared to the top two percent of skin and laser clinics nationwide. Allura is a medical spa specializing in a blend of aesthetics and science using the full spectrum of the most effective, non-invasive cosmetic treatments and medical wellness, while maintaining the highest standards of quality, service and excellence.

Dr. Rebecca de la Torre, the founder of Allura, started as a family physician in Loveland. In 1999, while still in family practice, she trained in aesthetic lasers and injectables. In 2004, she became the medical director and created a "full service" clinic that included facial lasers. With this increased workload, she hired two nurses: Yvonne Hampson, R.N. in 2004 and Mina Muirhead, R.N. in 2005.

With the financial investment in the growing aesthetic practice, Dr. de la Torre decided to practice fulltime in the aesthetic industry. Originally intending to purchase the laser clinic where she worked, she opted instead to open her own clinic.

Given a two week notice to move, Dr. de la Torre sought help from family and staff who agreed to move with her to the new clinic. Four days later, Allura had a name, a logo and an office space. Two weeks later, in October 2008, they officially opened the doors to Allura Skin & Laser Clinic in Fort Collins. Four months later, they opened their second clinic in Loveland/Johnstown. Within a year, the staff had grown from four to seventeen.

Allura has always been a family business. Dr. de la Torre's sister, JoAnn Willis, did the IT and Cris de la Torre helped with legal issues. With the clinics growing at such a fast pace, they hired Yvonne's husband, Jackson Self, to handle the daily operations.

In 2011, Dr. de la Torre decided it was time to add a partner who was dedicated to Allura, was not afraid to work extra hours and do all the little things a business owner does; and most importantly, someone she could trust. That person was Yvonne. Yvonne became a partner in 2011 and has proven to be invaluable as a provider, a friend and partner.

As Allura has grown, so have our services. We added permanent make-up and body contouring. BioIdentical Hormone replacement using pellets for both men and women was added in 2010 giving us a true "wellness" side to the clinic and our name was changed to Allura Skin, Laser & Wellness Clinic.

In 2012, Allura was named the fifth fastest growing company in Northern Colorado, growing at a pace of twenty-five percent the first three years. That growth continues today. Allura currently has thirty-one staff members. Allura is a community focused company donating services and money to over thirty organizations. "We're grateful to our previous and current staff working at Allura, as well as to our clients who place their trust in us. Finally, we're grateful to the owners, Becky and Yvonne, for the long, hard days they've worked to make Allura such a great success story."

The Women's Clinic of Northern Colorado, P.C., formerly The Fort Collins Women's Clinic, is an OB/GYN medical practice with locations in Fort Collins and Loveland.

As one of the longest continuous operating obstetrics practices in Northern Colorado, the clinic is responsible for the delivery of thousands of babies every year. We know both the joy and apprehension of bringing new lives into the world, and understand the importance of the relationship between an expectant mother and her obstetrician or midwife. We look forward to being beside our patients at each step along the journey toward a happy delivery.

The Women's Clinic of Northern Colorado, P.C., specializes in women's primary healthcare, including routine annual exams, abnormal Pap smear treatment, family planning and diagnosis and treatment of infertility. The clinic also specializes in care for the needs of menopausal women, including prevention and treatment of osteoporosis, hormone replacement therapy, surgical repair of urinary incontinence and abnormal bleeding. All of the clinic physicians specialize in gynecologic surgery.

At the Women's Clinic, you will find the latest technologies and a welcoming environment. Among the many services provided by the clinic are bone density scanning, full-field digital mammography, ultrasound, genetic counseling, and robot assisted surgery. Classes are provided for breastfeeding, childbirth prep, infant and child CPR, sibling prep, new Dad prep, Mom and Baby Yoga, and prenatal Yoga.

The clinic, then known as The Fort Collins Women's Clinic, first opened in 1965 in a location at 1080 East Elizabeth Street.

The clinic has been a pioneer in providing such services as the area's first OB/GYN with a fellowship in high risk pregnancy management. In the early 1980s, the clinic was the first to integrate Certified Midwifery into a physician's office, and the area's first female OB/GYN was hired in 1985. In the late 1990s, the clinic started a Free Mammo day to provide free mammograms and breast exams to women without health insurance, a tradition that continues today. In 2013 the clinic hired the area's first full time Board Certified Perinatologist to better manage high risk pregnancies.

The Women's Clinic of Northern Colorado, P.C., now offers two convenient office locations, allowing it to serve more communities in Northern Colorado. The main office is located at 1107 South Lemay in Fort Collins. With the opening of the Loveland office in 2010, the clinic brings a full complement of women's health services to the women of Loveland and the surrounding communities of Berthoud, Greeley, Eaton, Evans, Ault, Windsor and Johnstown. Available services in Loveland now include mammography, bone density scanning, ultrasonography and more. The Loveland office is in the North Medical Office Building at the Medical Center of the Rockies, off I-25 and Highway 34.

The Women's Clinic of Northern Colorado, P.C., has recently improved its website, www.fcwc.com, allowing patients to conveniently pay their bills, print receipts, and print forms prior to their visits. In addition, there are quick links to other useful sites for women.

THE WOMEN'S CLINIC OF NORTHERN COLORADO, P.C.

FORT COLLINS YOUTH CLINIC

Fort Collins Youth Clinic has grown with Fort Collins for half a century, providing highly professional, skillful and compassionate care for infants, children and young adults. The Youth Clinic has cared for generations of area youth and takes pride in its role as both a partner and a resource to parents in their children's development.

The Youth Clinic began when a young pediatrician, Dr. Don Beard, was looking for a place to begin his practice. Dr. Beard had grown up in Wyoming and was interested in a location with a more enjoyable climate. When he heard of a potential opening in nearby Fort Collins, he decided to check out the possibilities with Dr. Ray Hanson, a local obstetrician.

"I had to meet with Dr. Hanson at his home, because he was recovering from the mumps," Dr. Beard recalls. "I asked if he thought Fort Collins could use a pediatrician and he replied, 'Can you start tomorrow?'"

Dr. Beard saw a great opportunity to serve the growing city and Fort Collins Youth Clinic was established on July 1, 1964. The name 'Youth Clinic' was selected because the practice was organized to serve the needs of children from infancy through adolescence. The first office was located across from the Poudre Valley Hospital, an area that is now a parking lot.

Joining Dr. Beard in founding the new Youth Clinic over the first few years were Tom Wera, MD, James McGinnis, MD, and Max Elliott, MD.

The Youth Clinic has grown to three locations and provides a central resource for all childcare needs. As a comprehensive pediatric medical home, the pediatricians and staff emphasize the importance of routine well-care check-ups and parents are encouraged to participate in all areas of their child's care.

As a medical home, the Youth Clinic cares for children when they are sick—or well—and helps the entire family stay healthy. The staff helps coordinate care and sets goals for a child's growth and development. Parents are kept informed and doctors are available to answer any questions about tests or treatments. The clinic also works with parents and other care providers to coordinate patient care. To better serve their patients, the professionals of the Youth Clinic are available seven days a week.

The Youth Clinic currently serves 18,500 patients with a staff of eighty-five. The staff includes 10 pediatricians, 7 pediatric physician assistants, and 30 nurses. In addition to the clinical staff, the clinic has a pediatric psychologist, pediatric speech and language pathologist, occupational therapist and a registered dietician.

The Fort Collins Youth Clinic operates two locations in Fort Collins: 1214 Oak Park Drive and 1200 East Elizabeth Street. The Loveland clinic is at 2500 Rocky Mountain Avenue.

Additional information on Fort Collins Youth Clinic may be found at www.youthclinic.com.

FRONT RANGE COMMUNITY COLLEGE

Front Range Community College, the largest community college in Colorado, has one major focus: student success. FRCC enrolls more than 29,000 students annually at four sites and online. About 3,000 students transfer each year to four-year institutions, from Colorado State University to Colorado School of Mines. About 5,000 people working in Northern Colorado are trained each year by FRCC's Corporate Solutions division, and thousands take advantage of continuing education classes.

Front Range began in 1968 in Adams County as part of Community College of Denver. In 1972 the Larimer County Voc-Tech Center was established through the efforts of the Poudre School District in Fort Collins, Thompson School District in Loveland and Park School District in Estes Park.

As the result of a new Colorado law, the Larimer Voc-Tech Center merged with Front Range Community College in 1988, creating the Larimer Campus. Even today, more than 400 Larimer County high school students attend classes in eight career/technical programs and have the option of earning college credits as well as high school credits.

A new agreement in 1995 made the state of Colorado fifty percent owner of the whole campus, with an increasing ownership share for each new dollar of state capital investment. This agreement opened the way for new construction on the campus. Three new buildings opened in 1998: Harmony Library, a 31,000 square foot joint-use library with the City of Fort Collins (and today with the Poudre River Public Library District); Challenger Point, a 22,000 square foot building housing science labs, classrooms, a lecture hall and office space; and the Longs Peak Student Center, a 20,000 square foot student-funded building with dining hall, conference rooms, bookstore, fitness center and office area for student activities and clubs.

Sunlight Peak, a new science laboratory building, opened in 2010, with Challenger Point reconfigured for mathematics and other classes. In 2014 ground was broken for a new building for Automotive Technology, Electo-Mechanical and Energy Technology, and Welding Technology.

The Larimer Campus opened with 1,300 students in 1988, and enrollment has grown steadily to the current enrollment of 9,700. Total college enrollment at all sites is now more than 29,000. The school's current operating budget totals more than $130 million for all sites.

The Larimer Campus also includes locations in Loveland, Stargazer Village, Fossil Ridge High School and on Prospect Road in Fort Collins. Other FRCC sites are in Brighton, Longmont, Westminster and online.

An economic impact analysis in 2012 revealed that Front Range Community College's annual impact on its service area totals $412.5 million.

Above: Front Range Community College Larimer Campus in 1987.

Below: Front Range Community College Larimer Campus in 2013.

FORT COLLINS

Top, left: Shoppers in Fort Collins enjoy the convenience of a small town with all the amenities of a larger city.

Top, right: Fort Collins hikers enjoy nearby Horsetooth Reservoir.

Below: Bicycling is a way of life in Fort Collins.

Sixty miles north of Denver, Fort Collins is the largest city in Northern Colorado. It is home to Colorado State University (CSU), with 27,000 students, several large high-tech employers, and leading businesses in the microbrew industry.

Nestled at the base of the Rocky Mountains and along the banks of the Cache la Poudre River, Fort Collins offers exciting recreational opportunities, unique cultural offerings, and is a regional center for employment and shopping. We boast the convenience of a small town with all the amenities of a larger city.

Our residents are well educated, engaged in their community and passionate about their area amenities. The high quality of life enjoyed by residents, businesses and visitors is a result of the community's focus on the environment, enthusiasm for health and the outdoors, a strong educational system, extensive park and open space systems, and a strong bicycle culture.

In 1864, Fort Collins was founded as a military fort along the Colorado branch of the Overland Trail, and was commonly referred to as "Camp Collins." The post was given the name in honor of Lieutenant Colonel William O. Collins, the popular commander of Ohio Cavalry troops whose headquarters were at Fort Laramie. Fort Collins was incorporated as a town in 1873.

In its early days, Fort Collins was a hub for agricultural production, and gained prominence for sugar beet manufacturing. Today, Fort Collins is home to leaders in clean energy, bioscience, computer software and hardware development, and water innovation. Colorado State University is also an international leader in the development of sustainable technologies and alternative energy sources.

With a moderate, four-season climate boasting 300 days of sunshine each year, Fort Collins is an ideal place to play. The city maintains more than 600 acres of parks, 40,000 acres of natural areas, thirty miles of off-street hiking and biking trails, three golf courses, and more.

Bicycling is a way of life in Fort Collins. The city offers more than 280 miles of bike lanes, thirty miles of trails, and a bike library. It has been designated a Platinum Bicycle Friendly Community by the League of American Bicyclists.

Downtown Fort Collins is a shining example of Fort Collins' commitment to preserving our past while developing a vibrant economy. Throughout the year, live music and entertainment, as well as great local dining, can be found throughout the historic Downtown district. As the heart of the community, it plays host to numerous festivals and special events throughout the year, and even served as inspiration for Disneyland's Main Street U.S.A.

Fort Collins also offers a wealth of cultural amenities. The community is home to several local theater troupes, a ballet company, an opera company, a symphony, and more. The Lincoln Center performing arts complex hosts first-class professional performances by these local entities as well as national touring groups. The Fort Collins Museum of Discovery creates meaningful opportunities for people of all ages to learn, reflect and have fun through hands-on and collections-based experiences in music, science and local history.

Fort Collins regularly tops best-of lists throughout the country. In recent years we have been named America's Most Satisfied City (*Time* magazine), among the Best Towns in America (*Outside* magazine), a 2012 Tree City USA (The Arbor Day Foundation), among the Best Places for Business and Careers (*Forbes* magazine), the Top Downtown in the Country (Livability.com), and the Best Place to Live in America (*Money* magazine).

When the Fort Collins Public Library was first organized more than a century ago, demand for books was so high that adults could check out only two volumes at a time, and only one could be fiction. Teachers, however, could check out as many as ten books.

Today, the Library District houses 400,000 items in its three buildings and patrons download more than 141,000 eBooks annually, along with digital audio and films.

The library had its beginning in 1884, when a 'free reading room' was opened next door to the town fire department on Walnut Street. Demand for books became so great that about fifty citizens gathered in 1899 and began a search for a room to house the books. The minutes of the committee, handwritten by Mary Killgore, report that, "A delightful surprise awaited the members of the executive committee when they assembled in the new library rooms on Mountain Avenue. Two pleasant, carpeted rooms equipped with tables, chairs, pictures, magazines and 500 books bound in cases, greeted the members."

On January 14, 1900, the Fort Collins Public Library and Free Reading room officially became the sixth public library in Colorado. Six months later, however, the library committee learned the rooms it had been renting were no longer available and the books were moved to-and-from several locations over the next three years.

At the time, wealthy philanthropist Andrew Carnegie was awarding grants to communities throughout the nation wishing to build libraries. Carnegie agreed to provide $10,000 for construction of a library building, and a site in Lincoln Park was selected for the facility. Carnegie provided an additional $2,500 toward construction three years later.

The Carnegie Library, with a collection of 2,770 books, opened in the summer of 1904. The library remained at the original location until 1975 when the Old Town Library was constructed. Elfreda Stebbins became the first librarian and served until 1931. The former Carnegie Library is still owned by the city and housed a museum until 2013.

Fort Collins voters approved construction of a new library building in 1975 and a site was selected in Lincoln Park, near the old Carnegie Library.

The Poudre River Public Library District was created in 2006 in response to a growing community need for library services. The District now includes three locations. Old Town Library at 201 Peterson Street; Harmony Library, a joint venture with Front Range Community College, at 4616 South Shields Street; and Council Tree Library at 2733 Council Tree Avenue in the Front Range Village retail development. The Administrative Center is located at 301 East Olive Street. Early and digital literacy classes are conducted at partner organizations by the Outreach Service staff.

The Poudre River Public Library District, with 150 employees, now serves more than 140,000 cardholders and covers a 1,800 square mile region in northern Larimer County. More than 3,000 people visit the libraries each day and more than 3 million items are checked out each year.

POUDRE RIVER PUBLIC LIBRARY DISTRICT

UNITED WAY OF LARIMER COUNTY

Below: Map of Camp Collins.

The United Way of Larimer County Community Services building at 424 Pine Street was built in 1986 to serve as a home for local human service organizations. The construction of the building was possible through community collaboration between the City of Fort Collins, which owns the land, and a number of community entities, including nonprofits and private donors. Today, the building houses United Way of Larimer County and Teaching Tree Early Childhood Learning Center, an early childhood development facility. The building sits on the site of Camp Collins, which moved to this location from its original location in La Porte in 1864. The current site shares a park-like setting with the Northside Aztlan Community Center and is situated along the beautiful Poudre River.

United Way has its roots in Denver when the Charity Organization Society (COS) formed in 1887 to meet the compelling needs arising from the boom and bust cycle of mining in Colorado. Over the years, the COS became the War Chests, then the Community Chests and, finally, the United Way.

The Fort Collins Area United Way and United Way of Loveland, Berthoud, and Estes Park were formed and started serving the county in 1958. The two United Ways came together in 2003 to become United Way of Larimer County. Over the decades, United Way has served the community in both resources invested and in adding value to the community to change and save lives throughout Larimer County. In 2014, United Way invested approximately 8.5 million dollars to support the changing needs of our community as well as to support flood relief to those affected by the floods of 2013. Over the last fifty-six years, United Way has evolved as community needs have changed. Today, United Way of Larimer County is committed to reducing poverty by fifty percent by the year 2025 by focusing on moving families from poverty to prosperity in three broad areas: health, income, and education.

United Way of Larimer County has always focused on serving the most vulnerable populations in our community. After the closure of the only day services center for the homeless, United Way of Larimer County partnered with community organizations and stakeholders to build the Sister Mary Alice Murphy Center for Hope (Center for Hope), located in Fort Collins, which opened in 2008. The Center for Hope serves homeless and near homeless individuals and families and is a one-stop center with over thirty partners providing a vast array of services to over 100 guests per day.

United Way of Larimer County is proud to partner with the City of Fort Collins as the community moves into the next 150 years of growth and prosperity for all.

Profile donated by Johnston Enterprises, Inc., dba Interstate Battery of the Rockies.

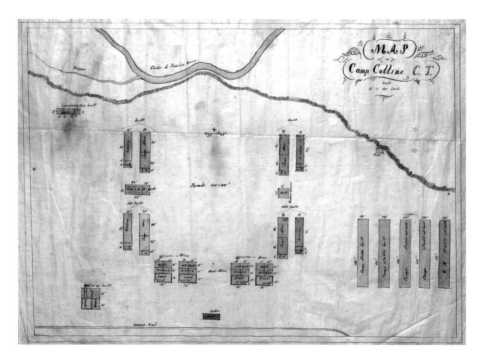

Roberts Ranch, May 2007.

Outdoor dining in Historic Old Town Fort Collins.

THE MARKETPLACE

Fort Collins's retail and

commercial establishments offer

an impressive variety of choices

FORT COLLINS COMFORT INN

Whether traveling for business or pleasure, the Comfort Inn Hotel in Fort Collins is your home away from home when visiting the Northern Colorado area.

Conveniently located off I-25, the Comfort Inn is only minutes from downtown Fort Collins, Colorado State University and NORCO Soccer. Other nearby attractions include the New Belgium Brewery, the Anheuser-Busch Brewery where the famous Clydesdales are trained, Aggie Theater, Lincoln Center and Budweiser Events Center at The Ranch.

Frequent guests of the Comfort Inn range from medical guests, to sports teams, to work crews, to vacationing families. The property features both long-term oriented guests and short-term visitors. Room rates are very competitive.

The mission of the hotel is to provide the best staff service, while offering the most comprehensive and cleanest hotel facilities and striving to provide a comfortable, friendly experience for every guest.

The hotel was constructed in 2002 and purchased in 2007 by Dariusz and Zosia Czyszczon who had moved to Northern Colorado, after owning and operating several hotels in the Pueblo/Colorado Springs area for the previous sixteen years. Upon purchasing the Comfort Inn, they immediately began turning the hotel into one of the highest ranking of its type, achieving the Gold Award from Choice Hotels in 2010.

Since purchasing the property, both Dariusz and Zosia have worked extremely hard to maintain a family-run business with the finest facilities and oversee the day-to-day operations of the property. The hotel was renovated several times between 2007 and 2014. A major renovation and upgrade occurred soon after the new owners purchased the hotel, and included the installation of granite counter tops in all rooms and the common areas. Subsequent renovations have consisted of replacing all the previous beds and bedding sets, updating the carpeting in the rooms and hallways, painting all the rooms and replacing all outdated furniture.

A. J. Ritchie, the front desk manager from 2009 to 2012, was instrumental in helping the property earn the Gold Award for brand standards in 2010. The current Desk Manager, Tim Kefalas, is working hand-in-hand with Dariusz and Zosia to achieve Platinum status, which includes only the top five percent of Choice Hotels.

The Comfort Inn provides sixty-two guest rooms, all appointed with irons, ironing boards, hairdryers, flat screened televisions with cable, and free wireless high-speed Internet access. Extra-large suites include sofa sleeper, microwaves, refrigerators, coffeemakers and speaker phones. All guests have access to an indoor heated pool and hot tub and well equipped exercise room. Business travelers may easily access the business center, meeting room and copy and fax machines. Laundry facilities are located on-site to meet the needs of executive and extended-stay guests.

Guests enjoy a morning breakfast full of hot and delicious options, making breakfast at the Comfort Inn the perfect way to start your day. The free hot breakfast includes eggs, sausage, biscuits and gravy, yogurt, fresh fruit, cereal and more—including a choice of hot waffle flavors.

The hotel employs 8 housekeepers, 4 front desk staff, 1 maintenance specialist and 1 front desk manager. Dariusz and Zosia act as both owners and general manager and head of housekeeping respectively.

The owners and employees of Fort Collins Comfort Inn are dedicated to the community. In June 2012, when the High Park wildfire hit the mountains above Fort Collins, the Comfort Inn provided rooms for both evacuees and FEMA workers as they fought to contain the fire throughout a turbulent month. Dariusz currently serves on the board

of directors for both the Fort Collins Business Bureau and Fort Collins Hotel Association. He also actively volunteers his time and property for Boys and Girls Club and Outdoor Buddies, a group that works with the disabled community.

The general business plan for Comfort Inn is to receive and maintain platinum status for the property. The sales focus will then transition more towards corporate guests and accounts to encourage more professional and business travelers as guests.

The Fort Collins Comfort Inn is located at 601 Frontage Road. For more information about the hotel, check the website at http://www.comfortinn.com/hotel-fortcollins-colorado-CO109.

POUDRE PET & FEED SUPPLY, INC.

Animal lovers in Northern Colorado have learned they cannot beat the service and product selection offered by Poudre Pet & Feed Supply in Fort Collins. With its deep commitment to service, the Poudre Pet & Feed stores provide an old-fashioned 'hometown feed store' atmosphere where clerks know their products and are eager to serve their customers.

The company began in 1988 when Karen Horak and Karen Morris purchased an existing business that had been around since the 1950s. Under their direction, the company has grown by leaps and bounds. "We had about $10,000 in inventory when we began, now it's more than a million dollars," Horak points out.

Initially, Poudre Pet & Feed was located in a small building on Howes Street, on the north side of Fort Collins. As customer demand increased, a store was opened at 6204 South College. In 1999 the north store was moved from the Howes location to its current location at 622 North College Avenue, at the corner of College and Vine, just north of Old Town. A third location was opened in October of 2011 at 2601 South Lemay Avenue at the corner of Drake and Lemay, next to Sprouts. The fourth store—located at 2100 West Drake Road on the corner of Drake and Taft Hill—opened in March of 2012. To serve the customer base in the Loveland area, a store was opened at 2400 North Lincoln Avenue in Loveland in June of 2014.

"As the city grew, the agriculture part of our business declined and we shifted to more emphasis on pets, particularly dogs and cats," explains Horak. "The stores still serve the 'hobby farms' but the focus is on domestic pets."

Poudre Pet & Feed carries more than fifty brands of dog and cat foods, as well as food for birds, small mammals, reptiles and fish. Food for horses, poultry and livestock is also available. There is also an extensive selection of pet bedding, cages and crates, grooming supplies and other accessories.

Poudre Pet & Feed even offers self-service dog wash facilities at its east and west locations. The facilities provide raised tubs and grooming stands, warm water, easy access stairs, no-slip mats, dog dryers, aprons, and brushes.

With a knowledgeable, caring staff, prices that even the big chains cannot match and friendly, hometown service, Poudre Pet & Feed has found a winning combination. "No matter what you need, you can find it here with a smile at Poudre Pet & Feed Supply. We have a feed for every need," says Horak.

The company is proud to offer many locally-made and green options for pets. There is an emphasis on pet food that is nutritionally sound and holistic, without a lot of additives.

The store's forty plus employees are highly trained and attend regular classes to stay abreast of latest developments in pet nutrition. This allows the staff to suggest just the right food for any particular pet.

Poudre Pet & Feed is very visible within the community and works closely with and supports a number of local organizations such as NOCO Nature Festival, Larimer Humane Society, Animal House Rescue and Grooming, Fort Collins Cat Rescue, Denkai Animal Sanctuary, Rocky Mountain Raptor Program, Be Local Northern Colorado, 4 Paws Pet Pantry and Fort Collins Area Chamber of Commerce.

Poudre Pet & Feed now has its own Mobile App. Visit the Google play store on Android or the app store on iPhone to download it. A number of great features and special coupons are available for those who download the app. Poudre Pet & Feed offers Senior Discount Day the first Wednesday of each month and free delivery on Thursdays.

To learn more about Poudre Pet & Feed Supply—and receive coupons and senior discounts—please visit their website at www.poudrefeed.com.

Left: A picture of our west location. This was taken right after it opened, and we are very excited to be in this new locations!

Right: A picture of the toy aisle at our south store. As you can see we have a broad selection of toys. We always try to keep up with the newest and greatest toys.

WILBUR'S TOTAL BEVERAGE

Above: Left to right, Dennis Dinsmore,
Jeff Matson and Mat Dinsmore.

Wilbur's Total Beverage is Fort Collins number one destination for liquor, wine and beer. With its large selection of wine and spirits and a convenient location, Wilbur's focuses on providing an outstanding product line and customer-friendly service.

Wilbur's got its start in October 2000 when Dennis Dinsmore; his son, Matthew; and Janet Robinson purchased a struggling beverage store with the goal of providing the community with the friendly, professional treatment they would enjoy when looking for adult beverages. They were joined in the venture by Andy Thomas of Denver after the move to the current store in 2004.

At the time, Dennis had been laid off after eighteen years in a corporate position and Mat was working toward his business degree at Colorado State University. Dennis and Mat had always dreamed of working together and when the opportunity presented itself, Mat sold a company he was operating so he would be free to work with his dad. At the time, Mat was just short of his twenty-first birthday, but was allowed to work the 'back of the house' and the cooler until his birthday. The business skills he learned at CSU helped the new company toward its goal of becoming a major retailer in Northern Colorado.

Key players in the early days of Wilbur's Total Beverage were office manager Pam Bell, beer buyer and department manager Jeff Matson, and wine consultants and buyers Joe Henry and Steve Stadler, all of whom still apply their skills at Wilbur's today.

Wilbur's had seven employees when it opened in 2000 and all worked hard to achieve the company's goals. Wilbur's now employs approximately forty-eight full, part-time and owner-employees and all work just as hard, if not harder.

"We have been blessed with a very constant core of managers and still retain all of the original six," comments Dennis. "Some left for short periods, but then returned. Every year, we feel the pinch of having some of our college 'kids' leave after three to five years of learning to know each other. We have also seen about a dozen of our employees find bigger, more lucrative jobs in our industry.

"We always form a bond with those who work well with us and make the promise that we will never stand in their way of progressing to better jobs. In fact, we help wherever possible, asking only that they honor a strong work ethic while working at Wilbur's. This philosophy has served us well," Dennis continues.

From its location on College Avenue between Drake and Prospect Streets, Wilbur's offers the finest selection of fine wines and spirits in the area. Wilbur's takes the intimidation out of wine shopping by helping customers find wines and spirits that are perfect for their specific occasions. Weekly wine tastings provide an opportunity for customers to sample different varieties and increase their appreciation of wine.

Wilbur's also offers the most extensive selection of domestic, micro and imported beers available in the region. The store features a barware/gift selection encompassing local and Colorado breweries, glassware, wine service, decanters, openers and many other items.

"Our commitment to the community has always been paramount to what we intend to do," explains Dennis. "The role of supporting and protecting the community has always been out front of anything we do. This includes strictly enforcing the checking of IDs to prevent alcohol from getting into the underage population, education about the dangers of binge drinking, and support for such organizations as Team Fort Collins, an advocacy group to prevent underage drinking."

Wilbur's also supports its own 'Wilbur's Fighting Breast Cancer' fund at Poudre Valley Medical Center, which helps women get immediate appointments and catch problems before they can become deadly. Wilbur's has also raised more than $120,000 to help Pathways Hospice provide their much needed service to the community. In addition, Wilbur's supports such local service groups as Rotary, Santa Cops, Kiwanis, Sustainable Living, Rist Canyon Volunteer Fire Department, Sertoma, Poudre

Valley Hospital, Children's Heart Foundation, Foothills Gateway and more than a hundred other charitable events and organizations.

Wilbur's Total Beverage received two prestigious national awards in 2013, being selected as a regional Brown Forman Retailer of the Year and Market Watch Retailer of the Year. "Both Matthew and I were thrilled and honored to be selected for these awards," says Dennis. "We feel that anytime a local business is honored on a national scale, it reflects on the entire community."

Dennis retired from the business in June 2014 but left it in the capable hands of Matthew and the crew he enjoyed working with for fourteen years.

To learn more about Wilbur's Total Beverage, visit www.wilburstotalbeverage.com.

VISIT FORT COLLINS CONVENTION AND VISITORS BUREAU

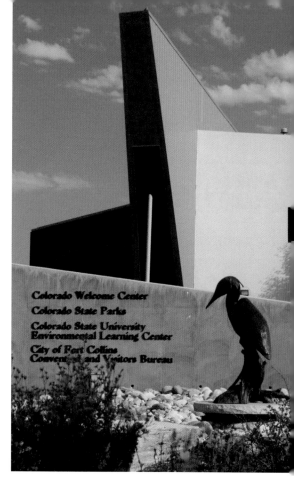

On February 21, 1984, the Fort Collins City Council took a grand step forward to market and enhance the city as a meeting and leisure destination. That was the date the city passed a three percent lodging tax to promote Fort Collins and began the process of starting the Fort Collins Convention and Visitors Bureau. Community leaders such as Susan Kirkpatrick, Karen Weitkunat and Mike Poppenweimer served on the first board of directors and hired Deane Drury as the first executive director.

The first location of the CVB and Visitor Center was in the historic Seckner Building. When the state was considering locations for a Colorado Welcome Center, a group of visionaries came together to fund and build the Coors Pavilion in Fort Collins at I-25 and Prospect. Donations and support from Coors Brewing Company, Stryker Short Foundation, John Q. Hammonds Hotels and Resorts, K & M Company, Colorado State Forest Service, Volunteers for Outdoor Colorado, Great Outdoors Colorado Trust, the City of Fort Collins, the Fort Collins Convention and Visitors Bureau and Colorado State Parks enabled this joint use facility owned by Colorado State University to become a reality. The Colorado Welcome Center opened to the public on July 5, 2000, and now serves to welcome visitors to Colorado State Parks, Colorado State University and the City of Fort Collins.

For a number of years the CVB operated out of the Welcome Center and had a satellite Visitor Center in Old Town Square in the center of downtown. As the organization grew, the need to be downtown, connect with the community and offer better visitor service led the CVB to move to its current location at 19 Old Town Square. Being in the heart of downtown has become an ideal location.

The Fort Collins Convention and Visitor Bureau is a Destination Marketing Organization, common to most communities. However, in recent years DMOs have sought to rebrand themselves in a way more relevant to the traveling public and the meeting and convention industry. So, in 2013, the CVB adopted a new name...Visit Fort Collins.

Tourism is a critical part of the local economy. A 2011 study conducted by Dr. Harvey Cutler and Dr. Martin Shields of Colorado State University reveals that tourism produces $120 million in economic activity and $11.3 million in city tax revenue. Visit Fort Collins is directly responsible for about twenty-five percent of that total, and proudly leads the hospitality industry in this great community.

Fort Collins has long had an aspiring, forward-focused nature, which has helped it become one of America's most livable communities. The business community, working through the Fort Collins Area Chamber of Commerce, has had a key role in making that so.

Since its founding in the early 1900s, the Chamber has helped transform Fort Collins from an agricultural township into a thriving city of 156,000. The community serves as the corporate headquarters for Woodward and OtterBox, has a vibrant downtown based primarily on locally-owned businesses, enjoys a robust entrepreneurial climate centered around the Rocky Mountain Innosphere and Colorado State University Ventures and has a strong high tech sector anchored by Hewlett-Packard.

At the center of community life is Colorado State University, one of the country's finest public research universities.

The Fort Collins Area Chamber of Commerce has 1,100 business and professional members that range in size from sole proprietors to the area's largest employers. These firms employ more than 60,000 people and provide immeasurable benefit to the area through the taxes they pay, their volunteer work and charitable donations and the services and goods they make available.

The Chamber serves these firms and the broader community in numerous ways by working on a strong business climate through lobbying and political action, promoting the community to people outside the area, providing information and marketing avenues to connect businesses with customers and building community and regional leadership capacity through leadership development programs.

The Chamber's work plan is adjusted somewhat each year to meet changing needs and opportunities, but annually the Chamber delivers:

- nearly 12,000 customer referrals to member companies,
- approximately 220 business and professional development marketing and educational events,
- over twenty major advocacy and signature events, and
- sixty graduates of leadership development programs.

A key focus of the Chamber is on the retention and expansion of primary employers in Fort Collins. In modern parlance, 'primary employers' are companies that sell most of their services or products outside the local market. Such companies are extremely important sources of community income. Expansions of Avago, Hewlett-Packard, OtterBox and Woodward are recent examples.

At the heart of all this is a guiding philosophy of Chamber leaders that a robust economy and wonderful quality of life are inextricably bound together. In essence, a strong economy pays for the community's great quality of life amenities, which in turn make the community attractive to talented people and companies.

The Chamber's ability to serve the region and its businesses rests upon a high standard of operational excellence. The Fort Collins Area Chamber of Commerce is Colorado's only 5-Star Accredited chamber of commerce.

FORT COLLINS AREA CHAMBER OF COMMERCE

BEST WESTERN UNIVERSITY INN

For a night, weekend, or even longer, you will find that Best Western University Inn is the ideal place to stay when visiting Fort Collins. To promote responsibility with contagious enjoyment while leading our industry in genuine hospitality is what the Inn hopes to achieve with its guests, whether you are here for business or for pleasure.

Located across the street from Colorado State University, this small and charming Inn offers easy access to the CSU Center for the Arts, government offices, Poudre Valley Hospital and medical centers, as well as a wide array of dining, entertainment and shopping in historic Old Town Fort Collins.

The Best Western offers seventy comfortable sleeping rooms that are 100 percent non-smoking. For the business traveler, rooms with a king bed—and select rooms with two beds—offer an efficient work desk area. All rooms include wireless high-speed Internet and pillow-top beds, and all standard room amenities including mini-fridges. For special getaways, Best Western provides a deluxe poolside room and spacious two-room suites, which include one-and-a-half baths, wet bar, living room and two flat screen televisions. You will also find exercise and laundry facilities on site.

Other features include a complimentary continental breakfast, large indoor pool and hot tub, and fitness room. The Inn also provides a 1,200 square feet meeting room, perfect for small meetings, workshops, reunions and informal gatherings.

If you are traveling with a pet, pet friendly rooms are available.

The Best Western is close to many local microbreweries including New Belgium, Odell, Fort Collins Brewery, Funkwerks, Pateros Creek, Equinox, Coopersmiths and Big Horn Brewery. The regional Anheuser-Busch Brewing facility, home to the famous Clydesdale horses, is only a few miles away. The annual Colorado Brewers' Festival the last weekend of June draws visitors from throughout the nation.

Outdoor enthusiasts can enjoy boating, biking, and hiking at beautiful Horsetooth Mountain and Reservoir just minutes away. You can take a day trip to raft, fish, or take in the spectacular views on the scenic Poudre River, or enjoy Estes Park and Rocky Mountain National Park. The Inn offers free bicycle rentals and the Fort Collins Bike Library is located on the property.

All Best Western hotels are independently owned and Best Western University Inn is locally owned and operated. A sister property is located in Loveland—Best Western Plus Crossroads Inn & Conference Center, approximately twenty minutes from Fort Collins.

The management and employees of Best Western help support a number of community organizations, including the Canyon Concert Ballet, Fort Collins Symphony, RAMFAM, Colorado State University, Fort Collins Innkeepers Association, Downtown Business Association and the Fort Collins Chamber of Commerce.

The Best Western University Inn, located at 914 South College Avenue, is large enough to serve but small enough to care. Guests are encouraged to book early for great savings and availabilities during special events at the University.

For additional information, check the website at www.bwui.com.

Honesty, integrity and value have been the guiding principles behind the success of Fort Collins Muffler & Automotive Repair.

The shop was opened by Jim and Martha 'Marty' Dwyer in 1976 and started out as an exclusive muffler shop with only four bays. Over the years, the company purchased additional property adjoining its original location on South College Avenue and has expanded to twelve bays. This has allowed Fort Collins Muffler & Automotive Repair to evolve into a full-service bumper-to-bumper repair shop.

Throughout its thirty-eight year history, Jim and Marty have been dedicated to providing the best possible service with outstanding products and a highly qualified staff.

Fort Collins Muffler & Automotive Repair include everything from air conditioner service to wheel balancing, as well as mufflers. The company also sells and installs tires. The company is an AAA approved facility and prides itself in selling customers only what they need at the price they are quoted.

Fort Collins Muffler & Auto Repair provides customers with many services not normally expected at a 'muffler shop'. This includes twenty-four hour emergency towing, complimentary brake and exhaust inspections, pickup and delivery of vehicles and a complimentary shuttle service. Customers may drop off their vehicles for repair after hours by simply locking their car and dropping the keys and a repair form through the front office door slot.

FORT COLLINS MUFFLER & AUTOMOTIVE REPAIR

Left and above: Jim Dwyer.

The company's eighteen employees are highly trained and technicians are ASE certified with a combined total of more than 135 years experience. Each employee is service-focused with the safety of you and your family in mind. Fort Collins Muffler & Automotive Repair now services more than 6,000 cars each year.

Another principle that has guided the company over the years is a strong emphasis on community service. Management and employees have a strong belief in giving back to the community and Jim was instrumental in working with the city to obtain Fort Collins first sheet of ice, known as EPIC, for hockey and ice skating. The family's passion for hockey includes the five sons—Jimmy, Kevin, Brian, Chris and Dennis—all of who are avid hockey fans and were local players at EPIC.

The company supports Fort Collins Youth Hockey, CSU Men's and Women's Hockey, Northern Colorado Youth Hockey and Fort Collins Adult Hockey. In addition, the firm supports Fort Collins baseball leagues, Fort Collins Stars softball, Buckaroo softball, Fort Collins High School, Turning Point Center for Youth and Family Development, and Realities for Children.

Fort Collins Muffler & Automotive Repair is determined to remain the community's "One Stop Shop" for all its customer's car needs by selling only the services needed at the best possible price.

THE CRAIG C. CAMPBELL INSURANCE AGENCY, INC.

Top: The previous building on the same location from 1973 to 2008.

Above: The current building as constructed in 2009.

The Craig C. Campbell Insurance Agency, Inc., is in the business of protecting and growing assets for its clients, and believes in a creed that reads, "World Class Customer Service is Our Culture." The agency represents Farmers Insurance and offers auto, home, life, business and other forms of insurance, as well as financial services.

The agency began in 1966 when Eugene Benedict added insurance to the existing Benedict-Siebel Real Estate Agency. The agency moved from South College Avenue to 262 East Mountain Avenue in 1973 when Eugene joined with Farmers District Manager Jim Bowser and agent Kelly Wolfe to construct the Old Town Fort Collins Building on Mountain Avenue.

In 1990, Craig Campbell, Benedict's son-in-law, opened his Farmers Insurance Agency in the building and the agency name became The Benedict and Campbell Insurance Agency. The two Farmers agents developed a business continuation plan over the next decade to minimize customer disruption when Benedict retired. That plan was executed when Benedict retired in 2001 and the agency name was changed to The Craig C. Campbell Insurance Agency in 2004.

The firm grew from 2,000 polices in 1990 to 5,200 policies in 2001. Currently, the agency has 6,000 policies. The agency employs eight persons.

In 2009, Campbell and his wife, Janet, participated in the development of the Mitchell Block Building at the same location on East Mountain Avenue. The agency now operates from the same first floor location as in the original building.

Campbell and his employees are involved in a number of community and charitable activities, including the Fort Collins Breakfast Rotary Club and the Overland Sertoma Club. The agency has been a member of the Chamber of Commerce and Campbell has served on the board of directors. When the Salt Lake City Olympic torch passed through the city in 2002, the agency hosted coffee and rolls for customers, fans, and security officers. The agency location remains at the center of the Old Town festivals including Bohemian Nights.

As part of its Mission Statement, The Craig C. Campbell Insurance Agency emphasizes its belief that "World Class Customer Service is our Culture" and promises to "offer our clients advice regarding protection and growth, insurance products for protection, and financial services products to assist clients grow their assets. We value and behave with honesty and integrity regarding clients, representative companies, and each other."

For additional information about The Craig C. Campbell Insurance Agency, check the website at www.farmersagent.com/ccampbell1.

DELLENBACH MOTORS

For nearly fifty years, "Do the right thing. Exceed expectations. Make a Difference" have been the words Dellenbach Motors operate by every day. Whether selling new or used cars and trucks, or service, parts and body shop repairs.

In 1965, R. W. Dellenbach, along with his wife, Patricia and their large family of eleven children moved to Fort Collins to purchase the Chevrolet franchise. R. W. was already experienced in the automotive business, beginning in North Platte, Nebraska, as a service manager, a parts manager in Pueblo, and then eventually purchasing the Chevrolet dealership in Fort Lupton.

Originally, Poudre Valley Motors was located on North College Avenue. As the business began to expand it was clear a larger location was necessary. After a few years, the dealership built a new facility at its current location on South College Avenue in 1971 with the anticipation that Fort Collins was growing south. The new location also brought a new name—Dellenbach Chevrolet.

In 1996 the Dellenbach family purchased the Cadillac, Oldsmobile and Subaru franchises, which were located one block south. Once again the business had outgrown its current space and the former Round the Corner Restaurant, Long John Silvers, NAPA Auto Parts and First Bank Properties became the new Subaru, Cadillac and Fleet/Commercial locations. Dellenbach Motors was now operating four franchises and occupying a majority of one full city block in Midtown Fort Collins.

The most prestigious honor a new car dealer can receive is the "Time Dealer of the Year" award. In 1986, R. W. received the honor because of his commitment to both customers and employees.

While growing up, most of R.W. and Patricia's eleven children worked at the dealership in some capacity in every department. R. W. passed away in 2008 and to this day, seven of the Dellenbach children and ten grandchildren have continued their careers within the dealership. It is truly a family-owned and operated business that has the same values and ethics that it started with so many years ago. Alongside the family, there are over 120 full-time employees.

It was not a coincidence that R. W. and Patricia moved to Fort Collins all those years ago. They realized it was a close-knit community with good schools and the perfect place to raise their family. The Dellenbach family has a history of giving back to the Fort Collins community in numerous ways. For more than twenty-five years Dellenbach Motors has partnered with the United Way of Larimer County by donating a car to help with the fundraising effort by raising awareness of the needs in our community. There is a long list of organizations, including Pathways Hospice, the new Cancer Center, and Discovery Museum—to name a few—that have the support of the Dellenbach family.

Best Rental, Inc.

Best Event Rentals

After years of experience in the landscaping and building maintenance business, Ron Nebelsick was certain he wanted to own his own business. "I always liked having the right tool or equipment to do the job and it was important that it worked properly," he explains. Ron believed he could provide that sort of service to others who wanted the right tool for their job. Best Rental was established in 1982 when Ron and his wife, Pat, purchased $70,000 worth of rental inventory and opened their first location at 6314 South College.

Although he was not aware of it, Ron opened in the middle of a recession, and it was September, the beginning of the slow season for construction-related business. Business was slow at first and Pat ran the store during the day while Ron worked for another company, installing solar systems. After working all day, he would go to the store and service anything that had been rented during the day while Pat went home to prepare dinner for their five young children.

In the early days, the business struggled financially and Ron was working seven days a week. Two things kept him going: his faith that God would lead him to where he was supposed to go, and the strength of his family. He also remembered that his grandparents had survived and raised their family during the Great Depression of the 1930s and he was determined to survive as well. It took six years in business before the store had grown to the point that Ron and Pat could hire their first full-time employee.

After the start on South College, Best Rental moved several times. After four years, Best Rental moved to Drake Crossing, then, in 1994, moved to South Mason Street. In 2001, Best Rental moved to a larger building and added some party rental items. The final move—in 2010—was to the present location at 1540 Riverside Avenue. Each move allowed opportunity for growth. Best Event Rentals, which carries a wide variety of party rental needs, was organized as a separate business in 2012 and moved to a separate building next door.

The commitment of many great employees, tremendous customer support and the help of his family contributed to the growth and success of Best Rental. Over the years, all of the five kids and several grandkids have worked at Best Rental. Son Aaron Nebelsick started during high school, continued through college, and now manages the equipment store. Daughter Tricia Steinbock worked in the equipment side, helped grow the party inventory, and now runs Best Event Rentals.

The success of Best Rental and Best Event Rentals has allowed Ron and Pat to support local nonprofits: Alpha Center, Open Door Mission, Relay for Life, March of Dimes, and to fulfill personal missions work through Timberline Church. They have traveled to Mexico, Guatemala, Sri Lanka and Haiti to help communities recover from tsunamis and earthquakes.

We want to thank all of our present and past employees and the great customers we have worked with over the years, and have become some of our friends.

- Ron and Pat Nebelsick and family.

BEST WESTERN TRANSMISSION, INC.

Best Western Transmission specializes in solving all drivetrain needs, including automatic and manual transmissions, differentials, transfer cases and driveline electronics. At Best Western, honesty and integrity are the top values, and customer satisfaction is the top priority.

In an industry that is sometimes considered 'fly-by-night,' Best Western Transmission has been locally owned since 1976. The business actually began about a year earlier when Russ Flowers was working at a gas station in Denver and a friend, Chuck Coble, was working at a nearby auto shop. Although they had little money, the two decided to go into business for themselves. For more than a year, they worked out of a small garage with few tools and no equipment, but plenty of 'know-how' and experience. The business was relocated to Fort Collins where their knowledge of transmission work led to the organization of Best Western Transmission in April 1976.

Russ recalls that he learned all aspects of the business from the ground up. He and Chuck lived in a camper trailer during the week, commuted to Denver on the weekends, and worked hard to earn the trust of his customers. "We built this business from bare bones," Russ comments.

After three years, Russ bought out his partner and became the sole owner of Best Western Transmission. The company has expanded over the years and now operates from three locations: 1810 South College Avenue in Fort Collins and two locations in Colorado Springs. The company employs about fifteen persons.

By emphasizing quality service and customer satisfaction, Best Western Transmission has earned a reputation for being the very best transmission shop in town. Customers often voice their appreciation for the honesty and integrity shown by Best Western, as well as the willingness to go way beyond the call of duty to help a motorist in need.

Russ recalls one customer who had the transmission in his motor home overhauled before leaving for Montana. Because of an 'enhancement,' the transmission failed during the trip and the motorist called for help. Russ loaded his car with tools, left during a blinding snowstorm, and located the broken-down motor home. He then borrowed a barn with a dirt floor, tore apart the transmission and rebuilt it. Another satisfied customer was soon back on the road.

Car and truck transmissions have changed greatly since Best Western Transmission opened its doors thirty-nine years ago, but a philosophy that puts customer satisfaction number one has kept the company growing. Russ calculates that eighty percent of the company's business comes from referrals and repeat business.

BELL, GOULD & SCOTT, P.C.

The fundamental principles of 'Strength + Integrity' have guided the law firm of Bell, Gould & Scott, P.C. for more than three decades. The firm provides a full range of civil legal services for individuals, businesses and local governments.

The firm was founded in its original form in 1982 by Greg Bell and Ed Stirman, friends at the University of Colorado School of Law. Greg began his career in Fort Collins with an old, established firm and then joined what appeared to be a promising collection of rising young attorneys. However, that firm broke up in late 1982 and Bell continued on his own in collaboration with Ken Wolf. At that time Ed Stirman was working for a firm in North Denver, but was eager to return to Fort Collins. His availability provided the opportunity for the two friends to team up, so they leased some space, hung out a shingle, and the firm was born.

Christine A. Carney, another friend from law school who had been practicing criminal defense law in the Pueblo area, joined the firm in 1987. Christine practiced with the firm until 1997 when she was appointed to the bench as a county court judge. Like Christine, Ed left the firm in 1993 to become a county court judge. After retiring from the bench in 2009, Ed and his daughter, Laurie, both worked at the firm before branching out to form the Stirman Law Office, LLC.

In 1995, Richard 'Rick' Boge joined the practice, bringing an excellent business sense, a quality California law school education, and a love of skiing and bicycling to the firm. Jed Scott joined the firm in 2001 after law school at the University of Wyoming's College of Law. In addition to his general litigation practice, Jed has a Master of Laws degree from the University of Denver in environmental and natural resource law.

Matt Gould joined the firm in 2007, after receiving his law degree from the University of Tulsa. A former software engineer, Gould has an extraordinary knack for attention to detail, and extensive knowledge and experience in construction and real property matters.

Peter Linder, who joined the practice in 2010, received his law degree from the University of Colorado Law School after earning undergraduate and master's degrees in music. His focus is on transactional matters, negotiation, alternative dispute resolution, and litigation.

In more recent years, Greg's practice has emphasized transactional planning to avoid the litigation he used to do, estate planning, and business law—an area that he taught to advanced students at the Colorado State University Business School for over ten years. Greg also works with several Northern Colorado municipal governments which are represented by the firm.

Bell, Gould & Scott is located in the historic Andrews House at 322 East Oak Street and on the Internet at www.bell-law.com.

American Legacy Firearms, Inc. is the leader in high quality limited edition, one-of-a-kind firearms that simply cannot be found anywhere else. These fine American Legacy Firearms, some engraved or gold-plated, are meant to be passed down from generation to generation; father to son, mother to daughter.

The company was founded in 2004 by Steve Faler, who began with three employees and a small, one-room office. American Legacy Firearms quickly became very popular and the company posted a first-year profit of $100,000. Employment has now grown to more than twenty employees, with annual sales of more than $6 million. Sales have increased from 10 to 20 a month to 500 per month and production has increased 500 percent since the start in 2004.

In early 2011, American Legacy began offering officially licensed products approved by the National Rifle Association, including the NRA rifle, NRA pistol and NRA shotgun. Later that same year, the company started working closely with Alan Gottlieb, founder of the Second Amendment Foundation. The company now sells products approved by that organization, including the SAF pistol and the newest edition of the SAF rifle, which commemorates the fortieth anniversary of the Second Amendment Foundation.

American Legacy's selection of engraved limited edition firearms come in several forms including gold plated, blued and nickel plated. The stocks and forearms may be engraved with most anything the customer can imagine. Receivers, frames, cylinders and barrels can be engraved as gifts that will be treasured for generations.

The limited edition, plated and engraved firearms manufactured by American Legacy are also fully functional and customers are encouraged to shoot the firearms, whether it is at a shooting range or hunting game animals.

American Legacy Firearms is headquartered in Fort Collins, with a sister company and production facility— SWS Engraving—located in Hope, Arkansas. The company employs twenty-one at the administrative office and thirty people at the production facility.

American Legacy is proud to be the top donor to the Second Amendment Foundation and one of the top ten corporate donors to the NRA. The company often donates or sells at cost for certain raffles and other fundraisers.

For more information about American Legacy Firearms, check their website at www.americanlegacyfirearms.com.

AMERICAN LEGACY FIREARMS, INC.

Above: Left to right, CEO Chantel Pritchett and owner Steve Faler.

Below: Our beautiful Second Amendment Foundation Pistol. We produce only 100 per state, and we engrave the number of the edition on the left grip.

MOUNTAIN WHITEWATER DESCENTS

Above: The Mountain Whitewater Descents rafting office was built in 1854. Trees with the bark still on are the beams that support the floor of this beautiful building.

Below: The Cache La Poudre River is Colorado's only Wild and Scenic River, which is like a national park for rivers. In Fort Collins backyard, rafting enthusiasts make their way down the picturesque canyon.

Adventure must be an enormous part of Brad Modesitt's DNA.

Growing up, his family taught Brad to appreciate and enjoy the outdoors. After graduating from Colorado State University with a degree in wildlife biology, he and his brother canoed 2,400 miles from Fort Collins to New Orleans, then he continued the adventure by biking 10,000 miles and sailing 3,000 miles to Southern Chile.

When he returned to Colorado in 1994, a good friend recommended that he become a raft guide. Brad followed that advice and began his career as a rafting fanatic. In 2000, he opened Mountain Whitewater Descents. "Our business has always been about adventure and bringing small adventures to the general public," Brad explains.

Brad feels his family background inspired his desire to experience the world. A grandfather, John Ambler, was the first to discover the West Buttress route up Mount McKinley with Bradford Washburn in 1951. He later climbed all the Fourteeners in Colorado twice and skied down thirty-six of them. Brad's grandmother, Betty Ambler, first

kayaked down the Middle Fork of the Salmon River in 1953.

Brad's father, Larry Modesitt has climbed all of Colorado's Fourteeners, runs marathons, and one year—as a birdwatcher—he saw the fifth most birds of any American.

In 2011, Brad and his wife, Lindsey, and their two children set off to sail around the world. "We sailed for fifteen months before the High Park fire closed our business for much of the season and we had to sell our boat to save the business," he says. "But we visited twenty-two countries and sailed 6,000 miles teaching our kids how beautiful the world can be."

Mountain Whitewater Descents offers whitewater rafting, kayaking, paddleboarding, guided trips and rentals on the Cache La Poudre River. "The fact that my degree from CSU is in wildlife biology helps me educate our guests on the great outdoors while we share Colorado's only Wild and Scenic River," Brad comments.

Mountain Whitewater Descents is headquartered at 1329 North Highway 287 in a building constructed in 1854, which makes it the second oldest building in Larimer County.

The company operates Fire & Water, a multifunction event center with five main departments: bar, restaurant, concert venue, facility rental and wedding site. The 3,000 square foot bar and restaurant will seat 100 patrons. The concert venue features a large stage, separate bar and multilevel seating for 1,200.

Reflecting Brad's love of nature and the outdoors, Mountain Whitewater Descents is a leader in environmental efforts and was an organizer of the Cache La Poudre River Clean Up. The firm was honored as an environmental leader in 2008 by the Fort Collins Chamber of Commerce and received the Chamber's Environmental Business Award in 2011.

To learn more about Mountain Whitewater Descents, please visit www.raftmwd.com.

HOUSKA AUTOMOTIVE SERVICES, INC.

Houska Automotive Services, a sixty-two year old, third-generation family business, offers the finest in auto repair from oil changes to complete rebuilds.

In 1952, Charlie and Martha Houska started the business in a two-bay garage at 899 Riverside Avenue, a location on the outskirts of town. The business is still in the same location today but is now in the heart of a bustling community.

Houska Automotive has grown from the original 2 repair stalls to 24 repair stalls and 8 tire and lube stalls.

Charlie and Martha's son, Dennis, took over the operation after graduating from Colorado State University in 1974. Recently, Dennis' son, L. J., has taken on more of the day-to-day responsibilities of the shop, although Dennis says he has no plans for retirement.

Both Dennis and L. J. worked in the shop as boys and take pride in continuing the family legacy at Houska Automotive.

"We both started working here by the time we were twelve year-olds," says L. J. "We were always helping by sweeping floors and washing windows."

Dennis adds that much of the family environment at Houska Automotive stems from its many long-time employees. Many have worked with the company more than twenty years, and some more than thirty. The company now employs forty people.

Many Fort Collins residents know Houska Automotive for its annual 5K run, the Houska Houska, which benefits the Northern Colorado bone marrow donor registry and the new Poudre Valley Hospital Cancer Center.

The race actually got its start as a fluke, according to Dennis. One year, the family had wanted to run the Bolder Boulder over Memorial Day weekend but missed the registration deadline.

"We'd been running the Bolder Boulder, but hadn't planned for that year and were going to have to pay a late fee to enter," Dennis explains. "At the last minute, we decided to do a 10K out of our house."

Four people, including Dennis, his wife, Noreen, L. J., and a family friend ran the 10K together. The family friend, Bill Liskey, dubbed the race the Houska Houska. The Twenty-second Annual Houska Houska will be run this year, with 100 percent of the proceeds going to the local Bone Marrow Registry and the new PVH Cancer Center.

In addition, Houska Automotive provides a free Women's Car Care Clinic two times each year and supports such community efforts as the annual blood drive, a Christmas card contest to benefit Irish Elementary School, Respite Care, Project Self-Sufficiency car give-away, Red Cross, and many others. The company has been a Climate Wise Partner since 2005.

For additional information, please visit www.houskaautomotive.com.

Top: Our employees celebrating at the Speakeasy Grand Opening of Houska Tire & Oil addition to Houska Automotive in April 2013.

Above: Left to right, the three generations of our business, L. J. Houska, Charlie Houska (in photograph in the background), and Dennis Houska.

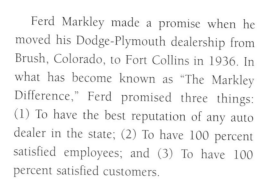

MARKLEY
MOTORS, INC.

Ferd Markley made a promise when he moved his Dodge-Plymouth dealership from Brush, Colorado, to Fort Collins in 1936. In what has become known as "The Markley Difference," Ferd promised three things: (1) To have the best reputation of any auto dealer in the state; (2) To have 100 percent satisfied employees; and (3) To have 100 percent satisfied customers.

For more than seventy-eight years, Markley Motors—now operated by the fourth generation of the Markley family—has worked each day to keep the founder's promises.

After operating successfully for several years, Ferd passed the dealership on to his two sons, Gene and Bob Markley, and went on to serve in the Colorado State Legislature.

In 1959 the Markley's purchased the Chrysler-Plymouth dealership and for two-and-a-half years operated two dealerships.

The Dodge facility was located at 246 North College and the Chrysler-Plymouth store at 300 South College. Ferd passed away in 1960 and, in 1961, Gene and Bob consolidated the two operations in greatly expanded facilities that took up most of the 200 block of North College.

In 1968, Bob decided to purchase a Volkswagen dealership in Greeley and sold his share of the partnership to Gene. After graduating from the University of Kansas, Gene's son, Doug Markley, joined the business.

The new Honda Civic was introduced in 1974 and soon became very popular because of its great gas mileage during the OPEC oil embargo. Honda awarded the much sought after Honda franchise to the Markleys in January 1975 and Honda went on to become one of the top selling autos in northern Colorado and the U.S.

Gene and Doug terminated the Chrysler-Plymouth-Dodge lines in 1979 and purchased the Buick-Pontiac-GMC Truck franchise for Fort Collins. Markley Motors also operated the Saturn franchise from 1990 until 2009, when General Motors discontinued Saturn and Pontiac production.

In late 2009, the Buick-GMC dealership was moved to the former Saturn facility at 3325 South College Avenue. The Honda operation was then moved to 3401 South College. Both facilities have undergone major remodeling and updates in recent years.

Markley Motors continually strives to invest in improving the quality of life in northern Colorado. The Markley family believes in giving back to the community that has given them so much and supports a long list of civic and charitable activities.

The fourth generation of the Markley family is now involved in the firm with Carrie Markley-Baumgart acting as COO, Cindy Markley-DeGroot as marketing director, and Justin Markley as assistant Internet manager. A fifth generation is still in school but already working part-time at the dealerships and learning the business.

Top: A

Highli

Above

Benz

RANCH-WAY FEED MILLS, INC.

Ranch-Way Feed Mills has been a major supplier of high-quality feed products in the Rocky Mountain Region for nearly 150 years. Founded in 1868, Ranch-Way is the oldest continuously operating business in Fort Collins.

The venerable firm began when Elizabeth 'Auntie' Stone and Henry Clay Peterson established the first grist mill on the banks of the Poudre River in what is now downtown Fort Collins. Water from the river was used to power the mill.

These early settlers in the Fort recognized a prime business opportunity when miners started moving to Colorado to 'strike it rich' and began plans to build a flour mill. Milling equipment was brought in from Buffalo, New York, and by 1869 Stone and Peterson began grinding wheat at the mill.

Electricity replaced water and steam power in the early 1920s and the mill stopped flour production and began manufacturing livestock feed in 1948.

The mill has had several owners over the decades. Colorado Milling and Elevator Company, founded by J. K. Mullen, took ownership of the business in 1885 and operated it as Lindell Mills. A group of Wyoming investors purchased the mill in 1968 and members of the same family still own and operate it today.

Ranch-Way Feeds produces a full-line of feedstuffs for animals ranging from alpacas to zebras and everything in between. This includes steam-flaked grains, pellets, wafers, and blocks. The mill has also produced 'Easy Feed' organic feeds since 2010. All the feed is produced from the finest quality ingredients and strict quality control measures are in place to insure that all incoming ingredients meet high standards.

Feed is sold throughout the Rocky Mountain region to stores, ranches, dairies, horse barns, zoos, the Division of Wildlife and others.

The staff at Ranch-Way is a dedicated, knowledgeable, service oriented group of individuals who are committed to giving customers the best possible service and products in the industry. Ranch-Way provides employment for more than sixty people at the mill and in a retail store at 546 Willow Street in Old Town Fort Collins. The company also employs six people in a company-owned retail store—The Feed Bin—in Santa Fe, New Mexico.

With an annual payroll in excess of $3 million, Ranch-Way has a major economic impact on the local economy. During the past ten years, Ranch-Way has invested more than $12 million in property and equipment, using local and regional contractors and suppliers. Ranch-Way owns nearly seven acres in Old Town and pays more than $100,000 each year in property tax.

Ranch-Way also invests heavily in the community. In 2014 the company committed to support the Animal Sciences Building Renovation at Colorado State University. The company also supports such activities as the Larimer County Fair, Larimer County Humane Society, 4-H, FFA, and many others.

A member of the Landmark Preservation Commission said, "When you look at Ranch-Way you are looking at the evolution of a mill."

THE SUPPLY CACHE, INC.

When wildland firefighters put their lives on the line to protect our natural resources and personal property, there is a high likelihood they are wearing protective equipment from The Supply Cache.

The Supply Cache (TSC) sells PPE (personal protective equipment) such as clothing, gloves, helmets and eye protection, as well as line packs, radio harnesses, weather instruments and all the other firefighting tools needed by those who fight wildland fires.

The business was organized by Diane Bauer and Jim Felix after a friend who was involved in search and rescue (SAR) brought Diane a radio chest harness and asked if she could make one for him. The harness worked well and the friend soon returned to ask Diane if she could make a dozen more to sell at a SAR conference in California. Before the conference ended, people were calling Diane to see if she would make them harnesses.

"It didn't take much thought to figure out there was a ready market for radio harnesses," Diane says. In addition, Diane and Jim recognized that without connections to agencies such as the U.S. Forest Service, wildland firefighters had difficulty in purchasing other needed gear. "We recognized there was a niche that wasn't being served very well and felt we had the expertise to fill that niche," Diane adds.

Diane's experience was in retail store management and Jim's passion was for fighting wildland fires. When a friend in Denver offered to help them get started by housing the fledgling business in his warehouse, The Supply Cache was born.

An old Singer industrial sewing machine was donated by a friend and Diane and Jim selected ten products they thought would be good sellers. Diane took product photos for a one-page flyer, which was mailed to a carefully selected mailing list and the response was overwhelming. The company was incorporated as The Supply Cache, Inc., and the founders moved the business from the Denver warehouse to an unfinished basement space in Fort Collins.

TSC had a presence on the web from the early days of the Internet (www.supplycache.com), upgrading software regularly. The web business has grown exponentially and now more than half the firm's orders come via the web. TSC's largest customer is the U.S. Forest Service. After outgrowing several sites, the company now has a permanent home at 1980 Caribou Drive.

The company currently has eight full-time employees, a part-time embroidery specialist and a part-time warehouse person, plus Diane, who continues to manage the operation. Jim resigned in 2013 to pursue other interests.

It has long been TSC policy to give back to the community that has made the success of the business possible. The company was honored with a Humanitarian Award from the Wildland Firefighter Foundation in 2007 for ongoing support provided to families whose firefighters are lost or injured in wildland fire incidents. TSC staff has volunteered many hours at Harmony House and continues to give back to Fort Collins in a variety of ways, most recently donating a large quantity of discontinued clothing to Homeless Gear of Fort Collins.

When you are visiting or doing business in Fort Collins, make your stay more pleasant by checking in at the Quality Inn & Suites located at 4001 South Mason Street. The management and staff at Quality Inn & Suites pride themselves on creating a comfortable home away from home where guests can work and relax.

Quality Inn & Suites is located along the historic Mason Corridor, a five-mile north-south byway within the City of Fort Collins. The Mason Corridor includes bicycle and pedestrian trails and links major destination and activity centers along the corridor, including the downtown commercial, cultural and business centers, Colorado State University, Foothills Mall, and South College Street retail areas. The corridor is centered along the Burlington Northern Santa Fe Railway property, located a few hundred feet west of US 287.

The Quality Inn & Suites offers 66 large, luxury rooms including 13 suites with 2 separate rooms. Hotel amenities include an indoor pool, exercise room, free wireless high-speed Internet access, free hot breakfast, free daily newspaper, free coffee and free local calls. All guest rooms feature separate bedroom and living areas, a refrigerator, microwave, coffeemaker, iron, ironing board and hairdryer. Guest laundry and copy and fax services are also available.

The Quality Inn & Suites was built in 1997 and operated for two years as a Ramada Inn. The property was purchased in 1999 by Creative Hotel Associates and the name was changed. The hotel was then operated by several different companies until it was purchased by Timberline Hospitalities of Casper, Wyoming, in February 2012. The facility was given a major remodeling and facelift when it was purchased by Timberline and is now positioned to take advantage of the current rebound in tourism.

More than 30,000 guests enjoy their stay at Quality Inn & Suites each year. The hotel is affiliated with Choice Hotels of Rockville, Maryland, which operates nearly 1,600 hotels

The Quality Inn & Suites is managed by General Manager Jayson Brown. Kindra Bielefeld is sales director. The hotel staff ranges from eighteen to twenty-five people, and hotel employees are involved in a number of community activities. The hotel is also a RamFam sponsor and an enthusiastic supporter of CSU athletic programs.

POUDRE SPORTS CAR

After growing up in Long Island, New York, and working on the classic sports cars of the era, Stephen Schroeder made a trip west and fell in love with Northern Colorado. Stephen had always wanted to have his own business working on sports cars and decided to open a shop in the area.

Poudre Sports Car, specializing in BMW, Porsche, Mercedes Benz, Audi and all British makes, was opened on Olive Court in the North End of Fort Collins in 1972. The shop started small, with only one bay, no lifts and only a few tools. However, local sports car owners recognized the level of skill Stephen offered and the shop was moved to a larger facility across the street after only a year to handle the growing volume.

By 1975 the shop had expanded to six employees and was in need of an even larger facility. The shop then moved to the old 7-Up bottling plant at 445 North College.

The company's growth slowed in 1980 with a downturn in the economy and Stephen was forced to move the shop again, this time to 201 Commerce Drive. Most of the employees had to be laid off and Stephen's wife, Cydni, worked the front office while his father, Gibbs Schroeder, helped in the shop. The Schroeder's first child, Zachary, was born during this period and with both parents working at the shop, the engine building room was converted to a nursery.

The shop began to grow again as the economy recovered and in 1983, the shop moved to a larger facility on Webster Drive and additional employees were hired. The Schroeder's second son, Stefan, was born in 1984, and the engine room once again became a nursery.

Poudre Sports Car began to grow rapidly after receiving its dealership license in 1984. Cydni and Gibbs were able to retire and a full-time manager was hired. The growth also prompted a move to the company's current location at 5806 South College in 1990. The shop has been expanded twice since that move, more than doubling its shop space.

Zach and Stefan started working in the family business after school and during summer breaks, and both eventually became full-time employees. Both sons continue to work at Poudre Sports Car, continuing a strong family tradition.

Adam Jaspers joined Poudre Sports Car in 2011 to help grow the business and within a few years the business had doubled, both in size and volume.

Poudre Sports Car has grown tremendously since its modest beginnings, but the company still believes in the foundation of honesty, expertise, loyalty and value that has made it the premier high-end sports car repair and sales facility in Northern Colorado.

F&C DOOR CHECK & LOCK SERVICE, INC.

Fred Hepp, owner of F&C Door Check & Lock Service, says he has never had a desire to be the biggest, just the best. His hundreds of satisfied customers will testify that he has achieved that ambition.

F&C sells hollow metal window and door frames, wood jambs or frames, and hollow metal and commercial wood doors from such well-known producers as Schlage, Von Duprin, LCN Closers and many others. The company also supplies pivots for aluminum doors, concealed closers, and even barn doors. In addition, F&C is a licensed, bonded and insured full-service locksmith.

Fred followed the lead of his father, Fred Hepp, Sr., who started in the industry in 1957 by repairing doors and installing closers. Fred began working in Chicago in 1969 repairing door closers part-time for $1.25 an hour. He was only thirteen years old at the time and made sure he always gave his mother $5 a week from his wages.

His father eventually bought F. W. Kline & Sons in Chicago and when Fred got out of the military, he went to work for the family firm and began learning the fine points of door closer, floor closer and concealed closer repair from the people who started with Louis C. Norton in 1916. Along the way, Fred learned locksmithing from Hugh Hefner's private locksmith in Chicago and various other professionals.

Fred moved to Colorado in 1985 with the dream of opening his own door closer and locksmith company and riding his motorcycle in the mountains.

F&C was founded in 1985 with only $1,200 and a desire to build a successful company. When Fred considered selling half interest in the new business for $5,000 to help raise capital, his father advised against the move and sent his son $6,000. "That helped a ton and helped me get over the top," Fred says.

After a couple of years in business, Fred realized that doors and locks were not enough to grow the company, so he went into the hollow metal frames, hollow metal and wood doors business and focused on commercial, industrial, retrofit and new construction business.

The company endured growing pains in the early days but a big contract with Larimer County, along with $600 received when Fred hit the Lotto, helped the company survive.

In 1990, Fred purchased a building with a garage on South Link Lane for $63,000. The building had no heat and needed upgrading but, once again, Fred's father came to the rescue with a $15,000 loan to finish the building.

Fred says he owes the success of F&C to his father and such loyal employees as Sean Fagan, who started with the company in 1987 and is still there. Others who have made important contributions include Tony and Louis Christensen, Justin Aschenbrenner, Daniel Clutter, Mike Tucker, Frank Leon, Joyce Osello, Candis Bowen, Daniel Congelosi, Andrew Perry, David Armstrong, Blake Paulus and Michael Henessee.

Everyone at F&C works by the company motto, "Our Desire is to Serve, the Ability to Repair."

FORT COLLINS DODGE, CHRYSLER, JEEP & RAM

Fort Collins Dodge, Chrysler, Jeep & Ram sells and services new Chrysler Corporation vehicles as well as all makes and models of pre-owned cars and trucks. The dealership also offers a complete line of parts, accessories and after-market products.

The dealership is owned by Doug Moreland, who moved from Reno, Nevada, to Denver in 1980 and became a partner in Cherry Creek Dodge. After completing a buyout of his partner, he began looking for other investment opportunities in the auto industry. This led him to Fort Collins where he purchased Foothills Auto Plaza in 1986. Foothills Auto Plaza became the second of what eventually would become eighteen dealerships in three states.

When Doug was considering the purchase of Foothills Auto Plaza, he contacted the district sales manager for Chrysler Corporation, Mike Downey, to ask his opinion of the purchase. Mike, a resident of Fort Collins, told Doug that he could not go wrong owning a business in such a great town. Mike is now Doug's partner in the dealership.

Foothills Auto Plaza was sold in 1999 to Lithia Automotive, which operated the dealership until 2009 when Doug and Mike repurchased the business and changed the name to Fort Collins Dodge, Chrysler, Jeep and Hyundai.

In the beginning, Doug's partner in Fort Collins was Jerry Cash, who stayed with the company until its sale to Lithia. Steve Hardy, a current partner and general manager, came to the dealership in 1990 and remained until 2003. He returned as general manager when Doug and Mike bought the company back from Lithia.

As with other automobile dealerships, Fort Collins Dodge, Chrysler, Jeep & Ram has had its ups-and-downs during the uncertain economy of recent years. "We have been fortunate to experience exceptional growth over the years and have reached the point where we are at the limits of our capacity," Doug explains.

The dealership is located on South College Avenue between Creger and Colboard Streets. The Hyundai dealership was moved to allow for the rapid growth of the Chrysler business and Crossroads Hyundai is now located at the Motorplex in Centerra.

"One accomplishment in which we take particular pride is the number of jobs we have created since we have been here," Doug comments. When he purchased the dealership in 2009, it had approximately forty employees. The company now employs 115 at the main Chrysler store in Fort Collins and twenty-five at the Hyundai dealership.

Total vehicle sales have increased from an average of eighty per month in 2008 to a monthly average of 240 in 2013. The service and parts operations have expanded and grown each year since 2009. To handle the growth, Fort Collins Dodge, Chrysler, Jeep & Ram is now reviewing plans to remodel or relocate to a larger, more modern and user-friendly facility.

It was May 1957, Lee Stark was headed to Estes Park looking to buy a restaurant. Lee missed his turn and ended up in Fort Collins where he happened to notice a small building for sale and the Charco Broiler was born. Lee asked his cousin and his wife, Gib and Lynn McGarvey, to move their family from New Mexico to help run the restaurant when it opened in the fall of 1957; they were business partners for nearly fifty years.

The Charco Broiler started out as a simple coffee shop and small galley kitchen. The blackboard hanging from the wall was the only menu, showing a steak sandwich for $1.75 and a handful of burgers. Coffee and sweet rolls were 'served' in the morning on the honor system, with customers leaving money in a cigar box on their way out the door. Four years after its opening, the Charco Broiler became the third establishment in the area to obtain a liquor license.

Today, the Charco Broiler has grown to a current seating capacity of more than 250 guests and a staff of seventy-one employees. The restaurant owes much of its success to the hard work of its many long time employees, including a dozen employees who have worked for over twenty years.

The restaurant is currently being run by Stan and Carol McGarvey, with the help of their two sons, Chad and Austin. The Charco Broiler is proud to be family owned-and-operated, now for three generations.

As an organization, the Charco Broiler feels it is essential to do its part by being more environmentally friendly and by supporting the local community and businesses. The restaurant is always looking to partner with other family-owned companies in Fort Collins and the surrounding area to provide the best products available.

The Charco Broiler's commitment to serve quality food with exceptional service at reasonable prices has remained unchanged. "We cook every breakfast to order, we make all of our soups and stews from scratch, we hand cut every steak, and we make our famous cream pies fresh every day," says Stan. "We make every effort to remain true to our unique character, but are always striving to improve."

The Charco Broiler is pleased to have served the Fort Collins community for nearly sixty years and will happily continue to do so for generations to come.

GILSDORF GARAGE, INC.

Left to right:

Gilsdorf Garage in the early 1970s.

Classic cars from the 1950s parked in front of Gilsdorf Garage in 2007.

A 2014 photograph of Gilsdorf Garage. The garage has serviced the automotive needs of Fort Collins for sixty-four years.

Mark Johnson says he can hardly believe it himself. On November 1, 1950, Ed Gilsdorf opened his one bay shop at the southwest corner of Shields and Mulberry, behind Watty and Son's Sinclair station. As business increased, the old building was added onto until 1964 when the new building was built. This building received a 2,000 square foot addition in the early 1990s.

Ed's great-great grandfather came to America from Germany in 1849 and settled in Platte County, Nebraska. Ed was born in Platte County, found his way to California as a young man and worked for Lockheed in Southern California during WWII, building B-52s. He later moved to Colorado in 1946 with his wife, Mary, who he met while in California. According to John Gilsdorf, Lockheed would not let Ed be drafted, as he was a valued employee doing a great job, which speaks for his quality craftsmanship, which still exists at Gilsdorf Garage today.

In 1974, Ed retired, built a motor home and moved to Sequim, Washington, selling the family business to his son John, who started working in the shop in 1970, and Colby Van Cleave, in March of 1974. Colby retired in 1982, and John then bought out his half interest. Under John's careful management, the business grew and prospered, adhering to the quality principles of its founder Ed. After earning all of his ASE certifications along with his AAM certificate as an automotive shop manager, and running the shop successfully for twenty-nine years, John retired in the fall of 2003, moving to Alamogordo, New Mexico, in 2004. John still tinkers with his vintage cars, owns and manages residential properties, and hits the road on his motorcycle in the good weather.

The current owners are Mark and Doreen Johnson, who have carried on in the Gilsdorf Garage tradition of providing quality service at affordable prices. Mark is originally from Southern California, and worked in transportation management at a major railroad for twenty-five years, spending half that time in Detroit working on transportation solutions for the Big Three automakers. In 1991, Mark came to Denver to become the national manager of automotive customer service for the railroad. Mark's hobby interest has always been automotive, owning his first car—a Model A Ford—at thirteen, and many more vehicles since.

When not working on the railroad, he could be found in his garage spending many hours on automotive projects. A graduate of USC in Southern California, majoring in accounting and marketing, Mark brings valuable business acumen to Gilsdorf Garage, always looking to improve the quality and service provided to his valued customers. When performing final quality control checks on customer's cars, Mark says, "I always look at the quality of our service through a customer's viewpoint. I know if I'm happy with the job, our customers will be too."

Gilsdorf Garage is one the few shops in Fort Collins that are AAA approved, a Napa Auto Care Center providing a twelve month 12,000 mile warranty on repairs, and carries a BBB rating of A+. Mark feels Ed would be proud of how well he and John have carried on the quality craftsmanship tradition at Gilsdorf Garage.

We hope that you have enjoyed reading this story behind a local Fort Collins tradition and, if you are looking for a shop to handle all of your automotive needs, please stop by and get acquainted. You will be treated in a friendly and courteous manner, and your vehicle will be serviced by some of the best techs in town.

LA-Z-BOY FURNITURE GALLERIES

There is much more than meets the eye in regard to the history of La-Z-Boy Furniture Galleries in Fort Collins. Today, the store stands proudly at the corner of Harmony and Timberline Roads, and boasts the fifth largest sales volume among all La-Z-Boy stores across America. But the humble beginnings of the store dates back to 1959 when Rick's Furniture and Appliance opened at 1007 North College Avenue.

Rick's was the name given to the store by F. D. Rickard, the founder of the company. The store, famous as the major appliance store in Fort Collins, also sold new and used furniture, often taking in trades for partial payment of new goods.

The articles of incorporation of the company were amended in 1966 when Harold Brett Allen invested in the company, along with J. L. Pflipsen. The partnership was a tremendous success and Harold's wife, Mildred, became a driving force in the company's expansion and growth.

In 1973, Mildred's son, Brett Allen, joined the company and, in 1974, Brett's eventual partner, Ken Knipp, became a director of the business as its acting controller. The company also adopted the dba, of Fossil Creek Galleries and relocated from Old Town to 5816 South College Avenue. The company expanded its offerings into high-end case-goods and upholstery and enjoyed tremendous growth while earning a reputation as the premier retailer of high-end upholstery and case-goods.

In 1978 the company officially dropped the name Rick's Furniture and Appliance and adopted Fossil Creek Galleries as the legal name of the company.

In 1992 the company again took big steps and embarked on a major transformation. Partners Allen and Knipp transformed the store through a license agreement with an up-and-coming nationally branded furniture retailer and officially became La-Z-Boy Furniture Galleries.

The company thrived for eleven years under the La-Z-Boy name brand and the direction of Allen and Knipp. A decision was made in 2003 to sell the business and it was purchased by Jason Johnston, who brought with him a host of new business practices. He launched a comprehensive in-home design service, innovative merchandising tailored to Northern Colorado, and an aggressive discount pricing model along with many other innovations. Jason also relocated the company to Harmony Road in 2005.

Under Jason, store sales have nearly tripled. Today, the La-Z-Boy Furniture Galleries in Fort Collins is the number five volume store among more than 300 stores nationwide.

Jason and his wife, Bonnie, have three children; Sydney, Colton, and Jacob and enjoy living and working in Northern Colorado. Jason is excited about La-Z-Boy's future outlook for continued innovation and growth in Fort Collins.

President Jason Johnston.

Ed Carroll Motor Company, Inc.

Ed Carroll Motor Company, Inc., in Fort Collins, a family owned-and-operated Audi, Porsche, and Volkswagen dealership, is proud to have served the Fort Collins area since 1967.

The dealership was founded by Ed Carroll, who began selling VWs to pay his tuition while studying civil engineering at Colorado State University in the 1950s. In 1965, Ed became a partner in Boulder Valley Volkswagen in Boulder, becoming the youngest VW dealer in America at the age of twenty-seven. Two years later, Ed and his partner were awarded the VW franchise for Fort Collins. With the flip of a coin, Ed sold his interest in Boulder Valley Volkswagen, moved to Fort Collins, and opened Ed Carroll VW. The new dealership, located south of Drake Road, was so far out of town that the building was surrounded by nothing but darkness each night.

The Audi brand was added in 1975 and Porsche in 1979 and Ed Carroll Motor Company now operates from modern, fully-equipped facilities on six acres at 3003 South College.

John Carroll, after receiving his MBA from the University of Colorado in 1988, began buying into the business. He completed the 100 percent buyout in 2005.

"It is our customers who have made our business flourish over the past four decades by repeat business and referrals," comments John. "Our goal is to always exceed our customer's expectations, whether they are purchasing a new or used car, having their car serviced, or buying parts or accessories."

Ed Carroll Motor offers a huge selection of new and used Audi, Porsche and Volkswagen models, along with an outstanding service department. Customers may browse the inventory through the convenience of the website and get a quote on a vehicle, research financing options, or contact the dealership with any questions.

The service technicians at Ed Carroll Motor are second to none. All are factory trained and use original manufacturer parts. The parts and accessories department is one of the most extensive in Colorado, Wyoming, and Nebraska.

The dealership employs a total of sixty-five people, including a number of long-time employees. Parts Manager Jack Robinson recently retired after forty-seven years with the company. Craig Roosa, Paul Bollacker, Jack Flanagan, Dan Cline and Scott Jones have all been with the company for more than thirty years. Janet Boucher, Doug Drake and Rich Conner have more than twenty years. Trevor Valdez, Adolf Zoch, Jon Vermouth, Pete Steiner, Dave Hess, Ryan Barnum, Leslie Dolifka and Mike DeMallie all have more than fifteen years.

Since it was opened in 1967, Ed Carroll Motor has posted more than $1 billion in sales, including approximately 42,000 new and used cars sold. As the oldest VW dealer in Colorado, Ed Carroll Motor Company has sold more than 20,000 VWs.

"Our motto is 'A Comfortable Place to Buy Your Next Car' and we have experience, knowledge and great customer service that can't be matched in Northern Colorado," says John.

To learn more about Ed Carroll Motor, visit www.edcarrollmotorco.com.

Heritage Health Products was established in 1993 by Karl Schakel, and other Colorado partners, as a multilevel vitamin and herbal nutritional product company. Karl Schakel, seventy-two years old at the time, had already enjoyed a long and successful career as an entrepreneur.

The Schakel family moved to Fort Collins from Wyoming in 1971 to be closer to Stapleton International Airport for Karl's extensive domestic and international travel. Karl became a wealthy rancher in the 1960s, and then proceeded to start and establish a number of new businesses that grew and prospered over the years. One of the most successful, Western Agri-Management Company, developed and managed large agri-business projects in several western states, as well as Chile, Paraguay, Venezuela, Egypt, Saudi Arabia and other countries.

Heritage Health Products was a natural extension of the decades of expertise gained by Karl in developing agricultural products in more than sixty countries and feeding the world's poorest countries. With operations in more than a dozen countries, Western Agri-Management led a scientific rediscovery of the proven benefits of natural herbs, from nutritionals to medicinal. As the company looked for ways to share this experience and expand its business, Heritage Health Products made great sense as a meaningful contribution to improving the human condition—a core mission of the Schakel family.

As successful entrepreneurs, the Schakels looked for ways to combine their nutritional background with their worldwide business knowledge, and this led them to using network marketing for Heritage Health. Together with co-founder Wayne Harding, the Schakels sought to promote the spirit of achievement from a sound work ethic leading to personal wealth and success.

This approach, combined with a driving commitment to quality, led to phenomenal growth that reached tens of millions of dollars in just a few short years. Thousands of distributors enrolled in more than twenty countries sold millions of bottles of thirty different natural health products and witnessed the results of well-engineered nutritional designs.

Meanwhile, Karl's eldest son, Pete, established a regional mortgage brokerage business called First Western Funding. The firm prospered for more than twenty-four years and helped finance hundreds of homes for new owners in Northern Colorado.

In 1995, the second son, Karl G., took the reins of Heritage Health and led its growth to a multimillion dollar sales enterprise developing and exporting natural nutritional products with fifty employees in Fort Collins and had over 20,000 independent distributors marketing the product line.

The Schakel family has started more than thirty independent businesses as entrepreneurs over the past forty years. In addition, the Schakels were extensively involved in real estate development in the Fort Collins area, including the Eagle Lake development and the Mountain Air Industrial Center.

HERITAGE HEALTH PRODUCTS

Top, left and left: Karl Schakel.

Above: Karl G. Schakel.

ANLANCE PROTECTION, LTD.

financially. This was followed by two high-profile 'close protection' assignments—one for the staff of Pope John Paul II during World Youth Day, and the second for former Vice President Dan Quail.

The firm's early days were filled with what Wilson calls 'learning experiences' that reinforced his personal motto, "There has to be a way."

Right: Barry Wilson.

The year was 1983 and Barry Wilson had hit bottom. He was broke, homeless and living in his car. With the support of family and friends he started painting houses to earn a few bucks and slowly began rebuilding his life. Today, Wilson heads Anlance Protection, Inc., a security agency employing nearly thirty people and grossing more than a $1 million a year.

Things began to turn around for Wilson in 1985 when he was practicing martial arts in his front yard. A neighbor who ran a small security firm took notice of his moves and asked if he would be interested in helping with some security assignments. Wilson jumped at the chance and began working plainclothes security, anti-theft operations, personal protections and surveillance.

"I discovered I had a knack for keeping people and circumstances calm during intense moments," Wilson explains. "I also realized I needed more skills and training."

Wilson enrolled in a private personal protection training academy, although it took several years to pull together the funds to complete the courses. When he graduated in 1991, he organized Anlance Protection, Ltd., along with Operations Director Paul Triffet.

Cash was tight and hours were long in the early days and gross earnings the first year totaled only $16,000. Wilson continued to spend half his time painting houses to earn enough to survive.

The struggling security agency got its big break with a contract to provide anti-theft services for two grocery chains: Steeles and Leever's. Those jobs saved the company

One of these 'learning experiences' came when the firm was protecting a show horse and decided to use a guard dog team and handler to assist surveillance and back-up. When movement from intruders was detected in the paddock, the handler called a warning, and the fierce guard dog was turned loose. Unfortunately, Wilson was also hidden in the paddock and a vicious guard dog was bearing down on him. "I barely got out of the way, although the dog bit into my boot before his handler called him off," Wilson recalls. The 'learning experience' Wilson took from this adventure was, "Always communicate your whereabouts."

Currently, the Anlance staff totals twenty-six, with plans to expand to thirty. The customer base includes local government facilities, businesses, corporate headquarters, manufacturing, schools, medical facilities, associations and individuals throughout Northern Colorado.

KEN'S AUTOMOTIVE

The motto of Ken's Automotive is 'Real Life Answers to All your Automotive Needs' and the expert technicians at Ken's work hard to keep you and your car safe and on the road.

Locally owned and operated since its inception, Ken and Sue Reynolds opened the shop at 200 North College in 1973. They quickly outgrew the two-bay shop and moved to 1219 North College, then a good sized four bay shop. As the years went on and business kept growing, bays were added on to the size it is today of nine bays. The shop was designed to be a premier exhaust shop, specializing in custom exhaust fabrication. Within a few years, Ken's Automotive had earned the reputation as 'the place to go' for complete automotive care, as well as custom exhaust work.

When Ken decided to retire in 2007, he sold the company to two long-time employees, Scott Melbye and Bob Jensen, aka: Toad (a character from the movie *American Graffiti*) who was one of Ken's first employees. Scott, sometimes known as "Peaches" (he was always just peachy) began with the shop in 1987 and brought with him an expertise in front end suspensions and alignments.

At Ken's Automotive, ASE certified technicians with years of experience provide everything from an oil change to complete Engine Diagnostics. Services include, but are not limited to, auto maintenance, brakes, emission failure repair, alignment and suspension, undercar services, and heating and cooling services. Ken's also provides diagnostic services and service for electrical systems and transmissions. Towing and shuttle services are available along with a unique loaner bike program. The technicians use only the highest quality replacement parts, filters, oils and components.

Ken's Automotive is one of the few independent shops in the region qualified to offer service for hybrid vehicles. In 2013, Scott and lead technician Allen Burch attended the Automotive Careers Development Center for eight days of intense training on hybrid vehicles. They were in class with experts from around the world, as well as a team from the Honda R&D department. Scott and Allen learned the fine points of hybrids and electric vehicles. The shop has a charging station on the front of the building that is available for free public use, first come first serve.

When asked "Why hybrids?' Scotts response was, "We are making this transition because we recognize the need in our community to be able to provide an alternative for repairs and maintenance to our growing hybrid/EV population. As our own knowledge has grown, so has our desire to contribute to the Green Energy Initiatives our city is becoming known for. This is an easy cause to get behind because it is part of our company culture to leave a better environment for future generations."

Ken's Automotive currently has ten employees. The company is very supportive of such community activities as NFCBA Coats & Boots Program, Smile Foundation, Larimer County 4-H Foundation and local clubs, Santa Cops, Northern Colorado Youth Hockey Association and the CSU Athletic Department.

Scott and Bob's objective has always been to provide a service to their customers that emphasizes the correct fix at a reasonable price and they take pride in standing behind their work. If a customer's expectations are not met, every effort is made to correct the problem.

For information on Ken's Automotive, visit www.kensmuffler.net.

FORT COLLINS CLUB

Membership in the Fort Collins Club is not just about working out and changing how you look, it is about changing your life and how you feel. The Club wants its members to have the latest in research equipment and motivational tools to take life over the top.

The FCC was the first club in Northern Colorado to incorporate a social aspect to the fitness club concept. That still rings true today, with the latest in fitness and training facilities as well as a restaurant and lounge for members to enjoy a meal or beverage before or after their workouts.

The FCC was opened in 1984 by Super Clubs, Inc., and was sold to Sports and Fitness, Inc., of St. Louis in 1990. The club was acquired by George Girardi and Todd Heenan in 2000 and reorganized as THK Fitness Enterprises, Inc. Heenan first came to the club as manager in 1990 but left in 1995 to run a group of clubs in Kansas City. He returned to FCC in 1999 and he and Girardi bought the club in 2001.

When THK Fitness acquired the club it was generating annual revenues of $1.6

million. An expansion in 2008 expanded the facilities from 40,000 square feet to more than 55,000 square foot and helped raise revenue to its current rate of $3 million. Membership has grown to more than 6,000 with a staff that now totals 140.

With a full-service fitness center and gym, the FCC is uniquely qualified to help its members meet their personal fitness needs and goals. The club offers a wide variety of facilities and programs where members may work out, relax with friends over good food and drinks, or shed some stress in the day spa.

The club's fitness offerings include aquatics, basketball leagues, a climbing wall, court sports, yoga/pilates and many others. In addition, the FCC provides health seminars, physical therapy, personal training and a wellness program. The club is very family oriented, with a wide variety of activities for the kids. The Conference Room at the club is a perfect place for meetings, seminars, special events or birthday parties.

The FCC started the Dig-Or-Die volleyball tournament, which is now one of the largest volleyball tournaments in Colorado. The club also originated the Fort Collins Sprint Triathlons. The club is involved with many local charities, including Ramstrength, an organization dedicated to helping local families stricken by cancer, and a large sponsor of the Fort Collins Thanksgiving Day Run, the largest run in Northern Colorado.

The FCC offers month-to-month agreements that may be canceled with a thirty day written notice. Very affordable monthly dues give members full use of the entire facility, including scheduled classes. A personal Life Traits Fitness style evaluation provides custom fitness plan, recommendations and free classes.

For more information about the Fort Collins Club, visit www.fortcollinsclub.net.

What does it take to open a small business in Fort Collins and keep it open for thirty plus years? According to Mike and Jeanann Deans, it takes a little luck, a little talent, and a lot of hard work! Mike left the family's custom home business in Scottsbluff, Nebraska, in 1983 and leased 1,500 square feet of retail space adjacent to Kmart at the corner of Drake and College. He and Jeanann opened their doors in the spring of 1983. The original business plan was to specialize in high-end jetted bath tubs and custom bathroom fixtures with a minor emphasis on the then fledgling home hot tub business.

So much for the original plan. The business quickly switched from being a bath store to a spa store. Mike soon realized that the new self-contained hot tubs—with all the plumbing, pumps, and heaters all contained under the skirt—would be the future of hot tubs. This new manufactured format allowed a customer to 'buy today, and use tonight'. The timing was right, Fort Collins was perfect for this new concept and business really took off.

After an incredible start, Mike partnered with his brother, Bill, to help with the service and logistics. Mike, Jeanann, Mary and Bill worked tirelessly—promoting, selling, servicing and performing every aspect of running a small business themselves. Employees were added and the business continued to grow.

In 1985, Mike approached Bill about selling out. Mike's vision was to not only sell the product but to manufacture it as well. He went on to establish Dynasty Spas in Athens, Tennessee. Dynasty is now one of the top three spa manufacturers in the world.

Meanwhile, Bill and Mary continued to develop Mountain Mist Spas. "From the very beginning, our philosophy has always been to treat our customers the way we would want to be treated," says Bill. "Our customers were not only clients; many of them were our friends as well." Bill and Mary expanded the showroom four different times to accommodate the growing business and addition of more employees. A second location was opened in Longmont in 1990 and a third added in Greeley in 1995.

"The true measure of any business is not how it operates when things are going great. It's how you overcome obstacles and setbacks without giving up," Bill feels. "For example, in the course of two weeks in 2001, we endured 9/11, our general manager, Albert Heine, suffered a heart attack, and a faulty sign transformer totally burned down our Greeley store. It was not a good month, but we picked up the pieces and kept going."

The company's biggest challenge came in 2008 when the housing market tanked. "Downsizing a business proved more difficult than growing a business." Bill explains. "But as a team, we rose to the challenge and refocused on our core values of honest customer service, hard work and not giving up. We came out of the recession a leaner, meaner and more efficient operation."

In 2011, Bill made the difficult decision to step away from day-to-day-operations and retire. The business remains in the family with Mike's daughter, Kara, and her husband, Corey, taking over in 2012.

Today, Mountain Mist Spas remains committed to providing its customers with the best buying experience—period. "There really is no secret to the success of our business," says Bill. "It's simply believing in your product, treating people honestly, hard work, and never giving up. Only in this country can you start with practically nothing and by your own hard work and perseverance turn it into a fulfilling career that not only provides a great living, but so many great friends and customers along the way. God Bless America!"

THE MARKETPLACE

191

Fort Collins streetcars three-way meet at College and Mountain, c. 1940s.

BUILDING A GREATER FORT COLLINS

Fort Collin's real estate developers,

construction companies, heavy industries,

and manufacturers provide

the economic foundation of the city

SPECIAL THANKS TO

Anderson Consulting

Engineers, Inc.

Water Pik, Inc.

Top, left: Founder John Mattingly.

Top, right: Founder Dr. Gerald Moyer.

Below: One of the original oral irrigators.

Water Pik, Inc., has been an important part of Fort Collins for more than fifty years.

The Water Pik success story actually began back in 1955 when a local dentist, Dr. Gerald Moyer, started fiddling around with oral irrigation as a means of cleaning and preserving his patient's teeth and gums. After noticing the problems his older patients suffered with their gums, Dr. Moyer searched for a solution and came up with the idea of developing a device that could spray a forceful, steady stream of water into a patient's mouth, which would rid the gums of food particles and bacteria while also massaging the gums.

In 1958 he contacted his friend and patient, CSU hydraulic engineer John "Matt" Mattingly, and they spent the next several years developing and prototyping the idea. The first product patent based on the water pulsating technology was granted in 1966. Over the years, the company has acquired more than 500 patents, and Water Pik products have been recognized for award-winning design and technology.

Today's Waterpik® Water Flosser is based upon the same principle and design as the original model—a powerful miniature pump sends a pulsating jet of water through a plastic syringe-like tip to clean the teeth and gums.

By the fall of 1961, thirty of the prototype units of the original design had been produced and Dr. Moyer began loaning them to his patients. One of those patients, Gene Rouse, was so enthused with the product and its potential, he began lining up local investors to further develop and market the product. A group of seventeen local investors,

about half of whom were local dentists and physicians, met on February 26, 1962, and committed to investing $50,000 in the start-up. They also elected the first board of directors for the company, which was incorporated as Aqua Tec Corporation. Rouse was elected the first president.

Eighty thousand shares of stock were issued, 50,000 to the investors at $1 per share and 30,000 to the co-inventors, Mattingly and Dr. Moyer. The new company leased a 1,000 square foot house on Highway 14, and the work of producing and marketing the product began. Production was done in the basement, while shipping, warehousing and billing took place on the upper floor.

The first non-shareholder employee was hired in April 1962; and, by the end of 1962, the growing corporation had six employees. Rouse and Dr. Moyer identified the dental community as the target market for the device. Along with board members, they began attending dental conventions on their own time and at their own expense to promote the product, which dentists would sell to their patients. A convention in Dallas in 1962 provided the first stream of revenue and really got things rolling with orders for 300 units. Initial test marketing of the product for retail sale began in Denver in 1963, and units began moving off drugstore shelves in Fort Collins, Denver, and other

Colorado communities. Aqua Tec made its first media purchase, an ad in *Life* magazine in the fall of 1963. Additionally, popular radio personality Paul Harvey became the spokesperson for Water Pik in the early years and this helped drive consumer awareness of the new oral hygiene product.

The significant growth that resulted from taking the product directly to the consumer allowed the company to move from the rented house to its present location at Prospect and Riverside in Fort Collins. The original 10,000 square foot facility at 1730 East Prospect Road has been expanded many times over the years to its present size of 245,000 square feet.

By adding new classes of distribution (such as department, appliance and hardware stores) to supplement drug store and dental professional distribution, significant sales growth occurred in 1965 and 1966. International distribution, which began in Italy in 1963, was added throughout Europe, Canada, the Far East and many other areas of the world. To finance this growth, additional shares were offered at $5 per share, and the number of stockholders, mostly local, grew to around fifty.

With sales and production capabilities continuing to rise, stockholders began investigating markets for their stock. In April 1967, stockholders approved the sale of Aqua Tec to Teledyne, Inc., a Los Angeles based conglomerate. Lore has it that Teledyne's purchase of Aqua Tec was based, in addition to its desire for innovative technology, on Teledyne's desire to get its name better known to the consumer. At the time, Teledyne was known for its

four main business segments of defense and aviation, specialty metals, industrials and insurance. Teledyne was founded in 1960 and remained a Fortune 500 company for thirty-five years until its merger into Allegheny Teledyne in 1996. The local company remained Teledyne Aqua Tec until 1975, when it became Teledyne Water Pik. Locally, it was usually referred to as Teledyne, in reference to its corporate parent.

It was during this time that Water Pik's second major product category came into being with the development and introduction of the massaging showerhead. Put into test markets in the fall of 1973, after three years of research and development work on the concept, the Shower Massage by Teledyne Water Pik was introduced nationally as the Original Shower Massage in the fall of 1974. It came in two models, a wall-mount and hand-held.

Above: "The Little Green House,"
original rental house of Aqua Tec, 1962.

Bottom, left: In 1973 the Original Shower Massage was introduced.

Bottom, right: President Mel Cruger, 1987–1996.

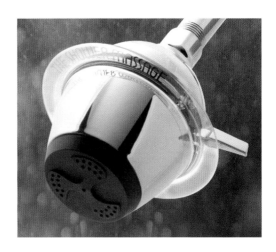

Water Pik celebrated its fiftieth anniversary in 2012. It has become a household name in water flossers, replacement shower heads and other consumer and professional dental products, and has posted superior financial results for the past eight years.

with outsourced production. Its products may be found online at www.waterpik.com and in various retail stores.

The city of Fort Collins and Colorado State University have played key roles in the growth and development of Water Pik and the company places great importance on being an economic and social asset to the community.

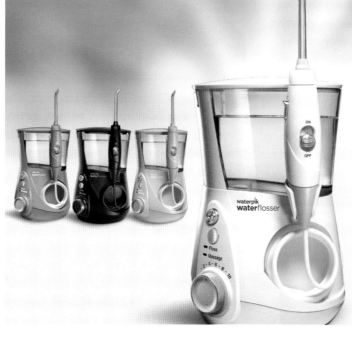

Water Pik participates in such community-based environmental programs as Climate Wise and employee birthdays are recognized by tree plantings in El Salvador through the Fort Collins-based nonprofit organization, Trees, Water & People. Water Pik recognizes its relationship with CSU by honoring excellence in the classroom with the Water Pik Excellence in Education Award.

Water Pik employees contribute to a number of Fort Collins civic and charitable organizations, including United Way, Fort Collins Chamber of Commerce, Poudre School District, Colorado State University, the Giving Guide, Habitat for Humanity and Larimer Humane Society.

Above: The new Aquarius Designer Series.

Below: Current showerheads and water flossers.

Throughout its various ownership changes, Water Pik has remained headquartered and committed to Fort Collins, the community in which it was founded more than fifty years ago and where it employs 175 people

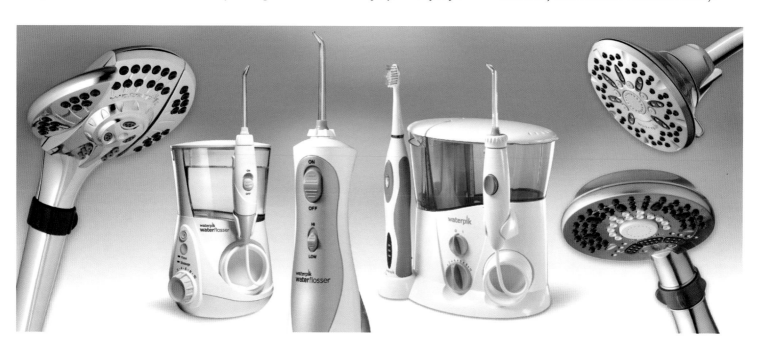

Water Pik is truly a homegrown success story that incorporates local resources to help create new product categories that are sold worldwide.

Above: President and CEO Richard Bisson, June 2012.

Left: In 2012, WaterPik celebrated fifty years.

HORIZON MECHANICAL SOLUTIONS

In April 1988, Sylvia and Asher Haun and their two sons, Darren and Kyler, were visiting Fort Collins, trying to decide whether to sell everything they owned, move to Fort Collins, and start a new life by starting their own business. Asher had experienced a major heart attack just a few months earlier, and that made the whole family realize they needed a change in their lives. Asher was part owner in a business in Pueblo with other family since 1980, and it was just time to make a change. It was a given that the new business would be a heating and air conditioning company, since Asher had been involved in that industry since 1967, and Sylvia had also been part of that previous business since 1980. That industry had been an important part of their lives since getting married in 1968.

Driving one weekend on a visit to their prospective new hometown, the sun was going down over the mountains, and the sunset on the horizon was beautiful. At that moment, Horizon Sheet Metal was born. The name was agreed upon by the whole family and the mountain with the sun setting became the logo for the company.

The company was incorporated on March 31, 1988, and, in May, the company's first location was rented at 216 Commerce Drive, Unit 4. Sylvia and Asher lived in a sport trailer in the back of that unit during the week, going home to Pueblo on weekends to be with their boys, who were living with grandparents and waiting for school to finish. In July a home was rented in LaPorte, and the boys joined their parents in the new undertaking.

It was a tough start, not knowing any contacts in a new town. New employees were hired and with perseverance, dedication and long hours, the company started growing and expanding into additional units as they became available. Asher had always been involved in the construction of water and waste water treatment plants, so that was the direction Horizon continued to follow.

The company purchased its own building at 126 Hemlock Street in 1995. Several remodels have taken place since that purchase to finally achieve an updated office atmosphere. The fabrication operations are located in the rear areas of the building.

Both of the Haun's sons originally came to work for the company. Darren started working at the company upon graduating from Poudre High School in 1993, then left for a period of time to pursue working as a temperature control engineer. He returned to the company in 2000, and started a temperature control division, representing Distech Controls. He also is the technical coordinator for everything from keeping the network operating to closing out projects. He will continue the company once Asher and Sylvia step down after retiring.

Kyler came into the company after graduation from Poudre High School in 1995, but in 2008 decided to pursue a different direction, and left his position at the company.

The company's majority of projects still involve water and waste water treatment plants. Sylvia is the controller, handling all contract reviews, general operating functions, and financial decisions. Asher is the principal estimator, and project manager of the water and waste water treatment plant projects.

The company has added two major key personnel, Dennis Whitman and Bruce Roth, who have helped the company grow into the company it is today. It is anticipated that they will be key people, along with Darren, in continuing the business once Sylvia and Asher start reducing their involvement in the business to pursue more leisure time.

Dennis is the project manager for Colorado State University projects, does some estimating, and project manages multiple other projects. Bruce is the operations manager, along with estimating and project managing.

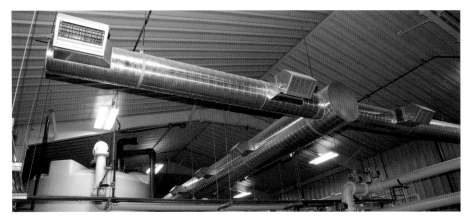

When the company was started in 1988, sheet metal was incorporated into the name because in Pueblo all the heating and air conditioning companies were called sheet metal companies. But as the industry evolved, sheet metal became associated with metal roofing and siding contractors, rather than the HVAC industry. Consequently, on the twenty-fifth anniversary of the company, in 2013, it was decided to update the company's image by adopting a trade name that better identified with the type of work that was performed, so Horizon Mechanical Solutions was adopted.

In addition to Colorado, Horizon has performed projects in Kansas, Nebraska, Wyoming, Texas, Arizona, Utah, Oklahoma, and both Dakotas.

Horizon Mechanical Solutions prides itself on the reputation it has developed over the years, and still considers itself a family operation. Sylvia and Asher have worked well together since 1980. Both have their part of the business they excel in and areas in which they are weak, they have employees that fill the voids. Learning to surround themselves with talented people has been their key to success. At Horizon, we work as a team to integrate each person's strengths to form a strong nucleus with which the company can continue to grow into the future as an example of what a change in life can become.

Opposite, top: Front row, left to right, Sylvia and Asher Haun. Back row: left to right, Bruce Roth, Darren Haun and Dennis Whitman.

Forney
Industries, Inc.

Forney Industries, headquartered in Fort Collins, is a nationwide leader in the distribution of metalworking and welding products, tools and equipment. The current Forney Industries catalog includes nearly 4,000 items, including three brands: Forney™, Industrial Pro™, and ForneyHide™ work gloves.

For more than eighty years, Forney Industries has found success because it is passionate about its customers and their success.

Right: J. D. Forney invented the instant heat soldering iron and launched Forney Industries, 1932.

Below: Farmers nationwide welcomed Forney Industries' new 110-volt/125 amp and 150 amp welders, 1936.

"As we have grown to cover North America, we have held true to the belief that, 'All Business is Local.' It is not a tagline, it is our mantra to bring a local, personal approach to our global environment," explains President/CEO Steve Anderson. "Local is the ultimate in attention and attentiveness. We at Forney Industries see individual faces, families, personal needs and opportunities as the key to successfully satisfying our customers and our employees.

"Executing the 'All Business is Local' philosophy is not easy. It begins with listening," Anderson continues. "Once we understand our customers' and suppliers' positions and concerns, only then can we treat them as they expect and deserve to be treated. No matter what the size of the client, we negotiate honestly, strive for mutual benefit, and deliver on our promises. It takes dedication from our entire organization to provide the exemplary service to our largest customers and suppliers, as well as the personalized touch our smaller partners and individual users desire."

Forney Industries was founded by James Donovan 'J. D.' Forney, who was an innovative inventor all of his life. He created not only the instant heat soldering iron and first 110-volt welders, but also vacuums, airplanes, and a two-man water ski sled dubbed the Aqua Sled.

J. D. launched his business in 1932 during the dark days of the Great Depression, selling the Forney Instant Heat Soldering Iron door-to-door across the heartland. In 1936, he invented and produced the first successful 110-volt/125-amp and 110-volt/150-amp welders intended for use outside the industrial setting.

By 1937, despite the nation's bleak economic times, the Forney nationwide sales staff had begun to expand and the company's product literature reflected that, "There's a Forney product in every town across the U.S.A."

The company's growth received a major boost in 1945 when the Rural Electric Associations (REA) began delivery of 230-volt service to farms and ranches. The sales staff procured permission from the REA to climb utility poles to connect welders for demonstrations and Forney welders added metal repair and tool hardening to farmers' capabilities.

In 1949, Forney moved its offices to its present location on Laporte Avenue in Fort

Collins, where the sales staff continued to grow. With 500 in-house employees Forney produced as many as 500 welders each week.

Forney's product line expanded in the 1950s to include products such as auto generators, battery chargers, more electric welders and welding supplies. A Forney central residential vacuum system and portable vacuum cleaner were introduced during this era, as was the 'Fornaire' an easy-to-fly, two-seat airplane designed for the consumer market.

The products became so popular that customers would trade cars, trucks and other items for Forney welders. The Forney Transportation Museum was incorporated as a nonprofit charitable organization in 1961 to house the astounding collection of transportation devices assembled over the years by J. D. Forney.

In 1963, Forney Industries switched its focus from welders to metalworking supplies, resulting in the product line increasing to 1,400 products. A dealer network was launched in 1968.

Sadly, J. D. passed away in 1986, after leading the company he created for fifty-four years. However, under the leadership of Ted Anderson, Jack Forney and now Steve Anderson, the company continued to grow through the 1990s as a leading manufacturer and distributor of metalworking and welding products. To help handle the increased business, an additional warehouse was opened in Horseheads, New York.

In 2011, Forney Industries purchased a new warehouse and distribution facility in Fort Collins, adding an additional 60,000 square feet of space, for a total of 185,000 square feet. That same year, the company launched a company e-store (www.forneyind.com), using Internet capability to sell both to dealers and end users.

The year 2012 saw the introduction of an innovative new line of work gloves (SKU 166) known as ForneyHide. The line covers seven categories and includes nearly 140 part numbers.

Forney Industries has enjoyed solid growth since 2010 and employs nearly 300 people across the United States, with almost a third being field-based

Forney-employed sales representatives. Forney Industries' brands—Forney, Industrial Pro and ForneyHide—may be found at more than 15,000 hardware, automotive, farm and ranch stores across the nation.

Forney employees are involved in a number of community activities, including Junior Achievement®, United Way®, and various organizations at Colorado State University and Front Range Community College.

"As we grow and enter new markets, we remain humble, nimble, and focused on delivering individual solutions to insure our customers' success," comments Anderson. "Because we are passionate about our customers and their success, we believe that only through change can we continue to provide our customers with the products and service they need to be successful."

Above: Manufacturing Forney welders in Fort Collins, 1963.

Below: Forney Industries today, with thirteen product categories and over 4,000 SKUs.

HYDRO CONSTRUCTION COMPANY, INC.

Hydro Construction Company, Inc., specializes in the construction of water and wastewater treatment facilities and related projects. Headquartered in Fort Collins, the company has constructed many of the major treatment facilities throughout Colorado and the surrounding states.

Above: Larry and Karla Rice.

The company was founded in 1974 by Larry Rice and his wife, Karla. Prior to opening Hydro, Larry had worked in the construction industry and had developed a number of strong business relationships. Larry and Karla had two children, loved the Fort Collins area, and believed it was a great place to raise their young family. After ten years in Fort Collins, they wanted to establish a business that would keep them in the area.

Like most fledgling businesses, capital was thin, but with a dream, hard work and determination, and $700 in the bank, the company was formed.

Accounts were established and Hydro landed its first contract within six weeks. Larry remembers that he was in southern Colorado working on the firm's first project when Karla called in a panic. Hydro had received a $5,000 bill for materials. He says his humor was not appreciated when he asked Karla if she could pay it from the household budget. "The confidence that the people had in us, plus a few miracles and persistence, led to our early success," Larry says.

The company continued to grow and eventually Larry and Karla felt confident enough to move the business from their basement into a rented space on Drake Road. In 2002, Hydro moved again to the location it still occupies on Lincoln Avenue. The five acre site accommodates the office, shop and equipment lot.

Over the years, Hydro has performed a number of important projects for the City of Fort Collins. These projects impact water use from raw water delivery to wastewater treatment. Among the many projects performed by Hydro are the Michigan Ditch Improvements at the top of Cameron Pass, Fort Collins Water Plant, Mulberry Water Reclamation Facility, and the Drake Water Reclamation Facility.

In the mid-1990s, a number of alternative means of construction delivery were introduced to the construction industry, including Partnering, Design Build, Construction Management, and Construction Manager at Risk. Hydro was at the forefront in the implementation of these new approaches.

At the turn of the century, Hydro was growing at the rate of fifteen percent per year by implementing new technologies and maintaining a culture that made sure the new technologies were useful and produced quality results.

By the early 2000s, Hydro was building or retrofitting water and wastewater plants for the City of Fort Collins, Greeley, Johnstown, Milliken, Wellington, Windsor, and others throughout Colorado and Wyoming. In recent years, Hydro has completed work in Arizona, Nebraska, New Mexico and North Dakota.

The increased water quality standards in the United States have enabled Hydro Construction to assist customers in building high-tech water treatment processes that continue to exceed regulation standards.

The company has also diversified into work for the Forest Service, building camp grounds throughout Colorado and Wyoming.

As the projects grew in scope and complexity, Hydro recognized the need for more skilled and educated employees. In the early 1990s, the company partnered with Colorado State University's Construction Management program and began hiring summer interns for jobs that could eventually lead to full-time positions. Many of the interns hired at that time are still with the company today and Hydro continues to benefit from this outstanding program.

Safety was a concern during the firm's early days, prompting the company to organize a campaign to make sure that employees of Hydro Construction focused on safety first. In 2011, Hydro was awarded the Workers' Compensation Safety and Cost Containment Award by the State of Colorado Department of Labor and Employment.

for the environment and constant pursuit of excellence."

Also in 2007, the company founded The Hydro Construction Community Fund. Hydro believes that giving back to the community is an honor. And Hydro does not just give back to the northern Colorado community but to the many other communities in which they work. Many organizations, including schools, nonprofits and health organizations have seen the benefit, and hundreds of thousands of dollars have been donated. In 2008, Hydro Construction was the first large donor for the PVH Cancer Center and The Healing Gardens will be in honor of that contribution.

Larry and Karla's son Rodney, a CSU graduate, started working full-time for the company in the early 1990s. In 2007, Larry and Karla sold their remaining stock to Rodney and retired.

"As part of the larger community, it's important that we think of the environment as we approach a project," comments Rodney. "Our responsibility lies in demonstrating to future generations the importance of respect

During the floods of 2013, Hydro worked with affected communities to assist with cleanup, broken pipelines and earth moving so that the lives of so many who were devastated could begin to return to normal.

The quality of the employees at Hydro is what distinguishes the company from others in the industry. The company has grown to approximately forty full-time employees, many of whom have been with the company ten to fifteen years. Hydro Construction is a 100 percent employee-owned company, which has a direct influence on the longevity of its personnel.

"Hydro Construction's success is attributed to our many excellent employees, business associates, friends and family we have had through the years," comments Larry. "All of you have our sincere thanks."

The increased water quality standards in the United States have enabled Hydro Construction to assist customers in building high-tech water treatment processes that continue to exceed regulation standards.

WOLF ROBOTICS, LLC

Below: The first company-owned building was at 1941 Heath Parkway.

Bottom: Wolf Robotics current facility at 4600 Innovation Drive.

With a vision to become the best in the world at automated fabricating, Wolf Robotics is contributing to the trend by American manufacturers to bring back jobs and operations to the United States.

Wolf Robotics, headquartered in Fort Collins, is a leading manufacturer and integrator of robotic welding and cutting equipment for off-road, construction, mining, agriculture, oil and gas, transportation, aerospace and fabrication industries. Wolf products include simple modular cells as well as complex custom engineering systems, large positioning equipment, robot carrier track systems and tower assemblies for upright or inverted robots and other peripheral products.

Although the current operation was not organized until 2003, the company roots date back seventy years to 1944. The business was started by Robert Heath, who repaired farm equipment and produced specialized farm machinery. John Mattingly became the company owner in 1948 and developed the first Ultra-Graph shape cutter in 1950. Mattingly expanded the business and then sold it to Bob Morris in 1956. Morris continued the expansion and developed a farm products division as well as manufacturing gas cutting equipment. Morris sold the farm products division to Gary Johnson and Eugene Mitchell in 1962, and later sold the gas cutting division. Johnson and Mitchell sold the company to ESAB in 1976.

Robotic welding was introduced by ESAB in 1978 and a new division was formed. The shape-cutting business was moved to South Carolina, and the robotics business was sold to ABB in 1993. Wolf Robotics was formed in 2003 after ABB sold the Fort Collins Division to Rimrock Corporation of Columbus, Ohio.

The company's original location was a rented building on Lincoln Avenue. The firm later moved to a larger facility once used by Citizens Printing and now the location of Sundance Saloon. The first company-owned building was at 1941 Heath Parkway where several large bay sections were added over the years. Wolf Robotics built its current 110,000 square foot facility at 4600 Innovation Drive in 1990.

The company's very first product was the Ultra-Graph shape cutter, a simple pantograph type single torch shape cutter that duplicated shapes from a metal template. The company owner at the time took the machine

to a company in Salt Lake City for a demonstration, but neglected to test the machine beforehand. When he placed the machine over a barrel for the cutting demonstration, it nearly blew everyone out of the building because of the build-up of acetylene and oxygen flowing into the barrel. Despite the surprise explosion, the demonstration went well and the sale was completed.

Wolf Robotics and its predecessor companies have been responsible for a long list of achievements that have helped place the company among the leaders in its industry. One of the first major developments came in 1966 when the company added pipe cutters and multiple torch equipment to its product line. Sales first reached the million dollar level in 1971 when the company entered into a joint venture with Liquid Carbonic. In 1978 the gas cutting division won a $2.3 million contract to produce large shape cutting gantries for XM-1 military tanks produced by Chrysler Corporation.

In more recent years, the company has introduced the Wolf Cell Control for complete control of welding systems from one central location and was the first robotics company to integrate submerged arc welders to robots. In 2009, Wolf engineered and installed an air bearing ride gantry that carries four robots for the cutting, grinding and finishing of wind turbine blades. In 2012 the company developed a load compensation mechanism to automatically offset the center of gravity on large welding positioned equipment.

Wolf Robotics had a core group of twenty-two employees when it was formed in 2003. Employment has now grown to more than 120 people as the company has maintained a yearly growth rate of fifteen to nineteen percent. Company revenue has grown from $1 million in sales in 1971 to more than $40 million annually in recent years.

Wolf Robotics and its employees are deeply involved in the Fort Collins community. Most recently, Wolf has supported the numerous robotic teams formed in local schools for competition in the FIRST program. Currently, the company provides financial aid and mentoring assistance to more than ten robotic teams. In addition, several Wolf employees serve on local college advisory boards to ensure that students learn what is required to succeed in the business world.

The company strongly supports and contributes to the United Way and supports organizations and charities employees are involved with. The company has been a member of the local Chamber of Commerce for more than twenty years.

Wolf Robotics has a progressive business plan for the future. By continuing to embody a mission of 'being the best' as a company, Wolf will be positioned to adapt to changes in the industries it serves. Focusing internally to create a positive work environment and attracting outstanding employees helps strengthen Wolf against its competitors. Continually innovating new technologies focused on customer's needs or problems represents Wolf's dedication to customer care and demonstrates the company's willingness to go the extra step for future customers.

Above: Ultra-Graph cutting machine developed by Heath Engineering, c. 1950.

Below: Robotic welding system producing chopping blades for agricultural equipment manufacturer.

OTTER PRODUCTS, LLC

The technological revolution has inspired thousands of entrepreneurial ventures, none more successful than Fort Collins-based Otter Products, which produces protective cases for smartphones, tablets and eReaders.

The company was founded by Curt Richardson, whose innate entrepreneurial spirit began as a child with yard sales and a lawn maintenance service, and was honed while he attended the Earl C. Martin Academy of Industrial Science. He found his passion for learning was best exercised through practice and, after a three year apprenticeship at a local molding company, he bought Genie Plastic Tooling. This was followed by several other successful start-up ventures.

Eventually, Richardson took his industry experience, set up shop in his garage, and created his first waterproof case prototype in the early 1990s. OtterBox was officially founded in 1998 with Richardson's wife, Nancy, as co-owner. The company's current CEO, Brian Thomas, started as an OtterBox salesman in 2003. Also instrumental in the growth of the company are President and COO Pete Lindgren, who was integral in developing the systems OtterBox needed to handle its rapid growth; and CFO Bruce Valentine, who helped guide the company through its first acquisitions.

Following the initial success of the OtterBox dry box line, the company created a line of custom cases for PDAs that incorporated an interactive screen membrane so users could access device controls. This innovative and customer-focused spirit has helped OtterBox evolve from the original waterproof box line into several lines of device-specific cases for smartphones and other handheld technology.

OtterBox grew so rapidly in its early days that it had a hard time finding a suitable location for its headquarters because employment growth kept outpacing capacity. Today, OtterBox has a 'campus' in the downtown area, with four large buildings housing customer service, Otter Relations (HR), sales, marketing, finance,

supply chain, engineering, product development and other activities. Distribution centers are located in Fort Collins and Frederick, Colorado, and other offices are located in San Diego and Boston.

OtterBox expanded globally in 2010, opening a sales and marketing office in Cork, Ireland, to handle the European, Middle East and Africa markets, followed shortly thereafter by an office in Hong Kong to manage the Asia Pacific region.

The company now employs more than 1,000 persons globally, including 700 employees in Colorado. The company posted an incredible 1,081 percent growth rate from 2009 through 2012.

The phenomenal success of OtterBox has resulted in major recognition for the firm. *Forbes* magazine named the company to its list of 'America's Most Promising Companies', *INC* magazine has included OtterBox on its *INC 500* list six times, and the Association for Corporate Growth awarded the company its prestigious Corporate Growth Award.

As OtterBox developed and evolved, Richardson looked for mentors to help him plan and strategize for a successful business. In 1999, he began studying the Entrepreneurial Myth ("E-Myth") program, which is based on the theory that most businesses fail because the founders are 'technicians' rather than managers or entrepreneurs; they are inspired to start a business, but lack the knowledge of how to run a successful business.

Leveraging the E-Myth and the theories of well-known business experts, Richardson and the OtterBox executive team developed a culture of continual, strategic improvement that allowed the company to grow at a rapid pace while maintaining its commitment to quality and customer satisfaction.

The OtterCares Foundation—committed to the principle that 'to whom much is given, much is expected'—was established in 2010 as the charitable arm of OtterBox. The foundation is an instrument of charitable giving, as well as an outlet for employees to become involved with the company mission through philanthropy and volunteering. OtterBox employees are given twenty-four hours of paid time off annually for volunteering.

Above: Curt Richardson working on early OtterBox prototypes in his Fort Collins garage.

Below: OtterBox headquarters in Fort Collins.

Blue Ocean Enterprises was founded by Curt and Nancy Richardson in 2011 to support emerging businesses, create jobs and make a positive impact throughout the communities they cherish.

Blue Ocean pursues the Richardson's entrepreneurial passions and humanitarian vision by investing in high-potential businesses, leading local revitalization through strategic investments in commercial real estate, and strengthening communities through its philanthropic organization, The Richardson Foundation.

CEO Jim Parke joined Blue Ocean in 2012 after having served as the company's general counsel. In his position, he manages all legal operations for the company and oversees the formation and acquisition of new business ventures, ranging from start-up companies to multi-national companies.

Blue Ocean Enterprises provides high quality, centralized professional services to its affiliated companies, including business mentoring, accounting, information technology, real estate, marketing and human relations services.

Its investment division, Blue Ocean Holdings, invests in growing, high-potential companies and has collaborated with emerging business leaders to create more than 1,000 jobs.

Blue Ocean Holdings is led by CEO Kurt Hoeven, who has worked alongside Curt Richardson since 1998. With a focus on community transformation, Blue Ocean Holdings is significantly impacting the redevelopment, restoration, and renewal of Fort Collins and Northern Colorado. A significant real estate investor with a growing footprint, Blue Ocean Holdings owns nearly 500,000 square feet of commercial space.

Blue Ocean Enterprises and Blue Ocean Holdings are headquartered at 401 West Mountain Avenue in Fort Collins and also maintain offices in San Diego, San Francisco and Kirkland, Washington. The organization employs more than 100 people.

BLUE OCEAN ENTERPRISES, INC.

BLUE OCEAN HOLDINGS, LLC

Left: Nancy Richardson helps a Poudre School District student select school supplies during the OtterCares-sponsored Pack2School event.

Below: Habitat for Humanity is a team effort.

FRONT RANGE INTERNET, INC.

In the last 150 years, Fort Collins has seen many changes. One of those changes, a big one, was the birth of the Internet and the World Wide Web. Front Range Internet, Inc., (FRII) was a part of bringing them to the people of Fort Collins.

It was 1995. Brad Ward and Andy Neely were roommates at CSU. Brad had graduated in 1994. About to lose their school Internet accounts, and unable to find a good, reliable Internet Service Provider (ISP) in town, they decided to start their own.

This was not as far-fetched as it might seem. Brad and Andy had studied computer science and had started a software company together. Bill Ward, Brad's father, had a professional background that was both technological and entrepreneurial. Working together, the three came up with a plan to bring Internet to the people of Fort Collins. On Halloween day, FRII opened its doors.

In the beginning, FRII's primary focus was to deliver exceptional Internet service to local residents. It did not take long, however, before they were growing beyond that. Their reputation for exceeding customers' expectations meant that more and more customers were seeking them out. In the first year, their growth outpaced their business plan.

This growth had been entirely organic. However, as FRII continued to grow, they also expanded by acquiring other local and regional businesses. The first, in 2000, was Verinet, another Fort Collins ISP. Verinet's owner wanted out of the ISP business, but wanted to find a company that would take care of his customers and had staying power. He chose FRII. This acquisition was the first of many for FRII, as the years would show that most regional ISPs could not survive.

By 2004, FRII had outgrown its Old Town location. Rather than moving out of town, though by now they were serving communities up and down the Front Range, they made the decision to stay in Fort Collins. Fort Collins was home, and FRII liked being part of the community. They moved to their current location on Eastbrook Drive and expanded their data center.

With the expansion of FRII's data center, they turned even more toward enterprise and business customers, but they were still, at their core, an ISP. The data center expansion allowed them to serve even more customers who needed websites hosted, or virtual private servers, or to colocate equipment in a controlled environment. And with the expansion, FRII continued to grow.

Although FRII already had a presence in markets throughout northern Colorado, over the next few years FRII focused on growing this presence even more. But this did not mean they were neglecting their hometown. In 2007, when Fort Collins chose to provide wireless to patrons in Old Town, it was FRII they asked to implement it. FRII was active in the community, supporting nonprofits and providing service to community businesses. They were a local business that could compete with the national players when it came to service and reliability. FRII provided the Old Town wireless with pride.

FRII was also developing its very-high-capacity fiber based services at this time. They began working with The Reflections Group and Garry Myall, serving new technology campuses, industrial parks, and multifamily developments. In 2012, Garry joined the FRII family as principal technology consultant.

It did not take long for FRII to realize that Garry brought more to the company than his consulting services. With his vast industry experience (which included director of communications and general manager of Computer Operations at Microsoft Corporation, and principal consultant at Microsoft Telecommunications), he would make a great executive. Bill was the chief executive officer. Brad was the chief operations officer. Now Garry was appointed chief information officer. (Andy had left to pursue different opportunities a few years earlier.)

In 2014, FRII decided to hire a chief technical officer, as well. Chris Bissell had started with FRII in 1995, doing tech support. Using various mentors at the company, he expanded his technical skills and knowledge, working his way into positions of greater and greater responsibility. While doing this, he also went to business school. He was a natural fit when FRII decided they needed a CTO.

Chris and Garry were integral to the most recent of FRII's expansions, the tripling of their data center. As before, FRII chose to keep the expansion local.

Today, FRII is far more than the small ISP dreamed up by two friends in 1995. Today the ISP is an important, but secondary, part of their business. Their focus now is on data center services, such as disaster recovery. As Northern Colorado's largest commercially available data center, they are uniquely suited to it.

Though they now have international and Fortune 500 customers, they still feel like a hometown company. Because they are. Whether supporting community organizations such as KRFC, Partners Mentoring Youth, and the Autism Society of Larimer County, or providing Internet to businesses throughout the town, FRII is a part of Fort Collins. They take pride in that fact.

Opposite, bottom: FRII's technical support bay is state-of-the-art.

Above: Brad Ward, Bill Ward, Garry Myall, and Chris Bissell cut the ribbon to celebrate the expansion of FRII's data center.

Below: Inside a cabinet in FRII's data center.

UDY CORPORATION

Chances are you have never heard of a hay core sampler called the Colorado Hay Probe, or the Cyclone Sample Mill used in laboratories to grind samples to a consistency necessary for accurate test results. However, if you are a farmer, rancher, food processor or even a brewer, these products developed by the Udy Corporation impact your business every day.

From its 10,000 square foot laboratory and production facility at 201 Rome Court in Fort Collins, Udy Corporation develops and produces competitively priced analytical test and sampling equipment for food and feed industries throughout the world.

The firm was founded by Dr. Doyle Udy, an analytical chemist who was looking for better ways of testing proteins in foods, particularly for the wheat industry.

In an interview with an industry publication several years ago, Dr. Udy explained how he became an inventor within the area of food and feed analysis: "Many opportunities to become better acquainted with the problems of plant breeders, flour millers, bread bakers and even the producers of cereal grains pointed to the need for improved cooperation among many groups," he said.

"The landowner especially needed more incentives to grow the most advanced seeds developed for specific end-use products. The producers of higher quality grains needed a remunerative reward other than the usual payment for bushels alone. Feasible analytical means to ascertain the better quality products would be required."

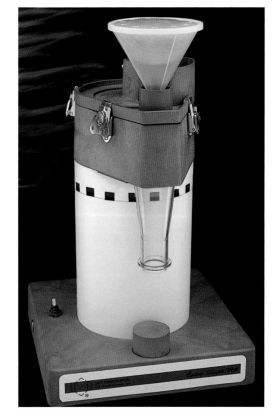

To develop these analytical techniques and products, Dr. Udy, a graduate of the University of Wisconsin, founded the Udy Analyzer Co., later changed to Udy Corporation in 1960. The firm was located originally in Pullman, Washington. One of the first products developed by the new company was the Udy Protein Test method, which created a faster, simpler and safer method of testing for total protein in food and feed.

Among the key individuals in the company's early years were Dr. Udy, his wife, Madeline, his son, Douglas Udy, Bill Lear, Caryl Griscavage and Barry Kroemer.

Udy Corporation moved its operations to Boulder in the early 1970s and then to Fort Collins in 1982.

When Dr. Udy decided to retire in 1995, the firm was purchased by long-time customer William F. 'Bill' Lear, a food scientist who graduated from Colorado State University. The company continued to enjoy steady growth of its core products under Lear's direction. Recognizing an opportunity for further growth, Lear purchased Alpha Plastic & Design from Don and Billie Johnson in the summer of 1999. "I wanted to expand our manufacturing capabilities as well as to obtain more outlets for service work on a local basis," Lear explains.

Alpha Plastic & Design is a manufacturing/service division of Udy Corporation, which allows the company to not only develop new products and techniques but to manufacture the testing equipment as well.

Among the products produced by Udy Corporation are Udy Protein Systems, which provides quick, easy and affordable protein analysis with non-hazardous chemicals; the popular Colorado Hay Probe, a low cost, easy to use hay and forage core sampler; and the Cyclone Sample Mill, which produces a uniform particle size in a variety of materials.

The company currently employs ten people who work in an environmentally friendly

'green' facility partially powered by solar panels. The company and its employees are involved in such civic projects as Special Olympics and CSU activities. The company also helps promote science education in the high schools by contributing material for robotic programs.

All Udy products are sold worldwide to laboratories, schools and such organizations as the U.S. Department of Agriculture through a network of sales representatives.

"We are very good at what we do," asserts Lear. 'We are in a niche business but try to be innovative and are always looking at new ways of doing things. We promote service and quality and our growth has been slow but steady, thanks to a very loyal customer base."

RLE
TECHNOLOGIES

Respecting the past. Appreciating the present. Driving the future. This is how RLE Technologies, which celebrated thirty years in business during 2014, views its place in the world. RLE has learned from past successes and failures and is now able to enjoy the present while assuring a bright future through responsible corporate practices and great people.

Above: The RLE Technologies founders,
left to right, Don M. Raymond, his father
Don A. Raymond, and Roy A. Lae, Jr., 2001.

Below: RLE's F200 Environmental
Monitoring User Interface.

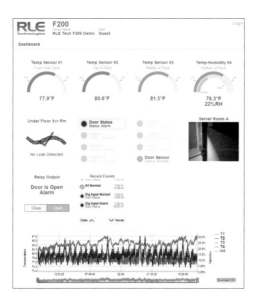

RLE Technologies (RLE) is committed to producing the highest quality, most innovative critical facility environmental monitoring equipment and systems in the world. Statistics show that one in five environmentally sensitive spaces such as data centers, retail space, libraries, and museums will experience damage and downtime due to changing interior environmental conditions every two years. RLE has taken on the challenge to see this threat mitigated for its customers.

Raymond & Lae Engineering, Inc. (RLE) was founded in 1984 by Don M. Raymond, his father Don A. Raymond, and brother-in-law Roy A. Lae, Jr. Don M. and his father, while working at Ball Aerospace and Emergency Power Engineering respectively, had three epiphanies that would shape their future: the importance of environmental awareness in critical facilities, the value of reliable design, and the

critical need for reliable environmental sensors across many market segments.

So like so many entrepreneurs, Don M. and Don A. saw a need and decided to fill it. They quickly teamed up with Roy to form Raymond & Lae Engineering, Inc. a company built on four foundational principles:
1. People first;
2. Fiscal responsibility;
3. Product quality; and
4. Innovation.

Fast forward to today: After relocating from Southern California for the enhanced lifestyle and business environment that Fort Collins offers, you will find RLE a thriving company with customers all over the world and a bright future ahead. RLE is a zero-debt organization that values not only the business, but what the business can bring to its employees, its customers, and its community.

RLE enjoys a position as one of the premier leaders in environmental monitoring equipment worldwide with nearly nine million feet of conductive fluid sensing cable installed globally. The company is also aggressively expanding its reseller and distribution channels to further penetrate global markets, Europe and Australia in particular.

While RLE's eye is fixed on expanding sales internationally, it still thinks locally when it comes to manufacturing and supply chain. RLE proudly wears the "Made in America" label and actively seeks to utilize local and domestic supply chain resources whenever and wherever possible. It is just one more way RLE seeks to pay back the community and country that has helped them be so successful.

RLE honors its tradition of innovation by actively expanding product offerings into both new areas such as hydrocarbon sensing cable, and by continually improving established products. For example, RLE recently released an entirely new WireFree sensor technology that is redefining how companies deploy and manage environmental sensor networks.

Perhaps most importantly, RLE fully realizes the value of our greatest asset—our employees. RLE benefits from a rare longevity by today's standards with nearly forty percent of the

current employees having been with the company ten years or longer. This continuity is a testament to the company's commitment to people and also affords RLE the power of retained knowledge and expertise that most companies only dream of.

RLE also actively promotes family values and work/life balance for all employees by encouraging them to participate in family functions and community activities whenever possible. Many employees are deeply involved in the Fort Collins Community, supporting a number of organizations such as the Child Advocacy Center, Rist Canyon Firefighters, Midtown Arts Center, Night Lights and many others. RLE believes that Fort Collins has been good to the company and, as such, the company owes it to the community to help make it an even better place to live for everyone.

As for the future of RLE, the sky truly is the limit. And even though serendipity has been kind to RLE, the firm feels it is its foundation and preparation for the future that will carry

it above the clouds. Given its great people, outstanding products, innovative philosophy, and strong business position, the future of RLE truly is bright!

RLE's Mission: "We exist to prevent disasters, preserve our client's reputation, and provide peace of mind."

Above: Thirtieth anniversary team.

Below: RLE's Flagship Leak Detection Cable.

BUILDING A GREATER FORT COLLINS

MAXEY COMPANIES, INC.

Maxey Companies, Inc. began in 1969 when Loren Maxey, an agricultural engineer, and his wife, Kathy, purchased a small manufacturing business in Fort Collins. Along the way, Maxey needed to design and build trailers for the center-pivot irrigation business he already

owned, and word soon spread about the high quality of his products. As an engineer, Maxey insisted that every trailer he built was of the highest quality and precisely engineered.

The manufacturing facility evolved into Maxey, Inc., which built innovative trailers and truck bodies for construction, farming, ranching and municipal use throughout Northern Colorado, Southern Wyoming and Southwestern Nebraska.

Maxey designed and developed his first patented product, the MAXEY® Snow Mover in the winter of 1971-1972. The product, designed and developed for the Winter Park Ski Area, greatly improved the ski-ability in the mountains where wind or lack of snow were problems.

Maxey's next patented snow grooming product was the first commercially manufactured snowmobile trail-groom. The equipment was given the name Wisconsin Special in recognition of the Bo-Boen Snowmobile Club, which purchased the first implement in 1975.

Under the direction of his son, Carl Maxey, the company expanded into selling other trailer lines in 1993 under the business name Max-Air Trailers. Maxey Truck Equipment was added to the Maxey family of operations to provide the same customers with the truck bodies and accessories they needed to do their jobs.

Maxey also designed and built the first Half-Pipe snow groomer for the snowboarding community in 1999 after three years of product development. The first half-pipe machine was created by a machine built on Vail Mountain that winter.

As the business developed, Maxey's wife, Kathy, was active in the business. Frederick E. Urben joined the company in 1973 as vice president and sales manager and was instrumental in the growth of trailer and truck body manufacturing and truck equipment distribution for the company.

Eventually, the family of businesses was rolled into one—Maxey Companies—which is still owned by Carl and Loren Maxey and Fred Urben. Loren Maxey is now retired, Urben is semi-retired, and the company is now operated by Carl R. Maxey.

Customers for Maxey products include public and cooperative utilities, municipalities, construction, energy, mining and manufacturing. The company's trailer sales operation serves all types of customers whether they need a trailer for their profession or their passion.

Maxey has developed long term manufacturing relationships with original equipment manufacturers accounts and specialty trailers for over-snow vehicle transport. The demands of this customer base have allowed the company to grow into markets where design specifications meet critical customer expectations on capacity and life-cycle cost.

After several years of development, the company introduced a line of trailers used to transport wood fired pizza ovens used in catering and special events. This venture has grown to more than 350 customers worldwide in partnership with The Fire Within in Boulder, Colorado. The company is committed to the development of features in the product line that meet the needs of a very special customer in a unique market outside of Maxey's traditional customer base.

The company, which now employs thirty-five people, has grown from one 6,400 square

foot building to five buildings in three locations—providing 39,000 square feet of space on fifteen acres. Company headquarters and the manufacturing facility are located at 2101 Airway Avenue in Fort Collins. The trailer sales location is at I-25 and Prospect Road and truck fitting, parts and service at 2220 East Lincoln Avenue.

The Maxey Companies and its employees have been long-time supporters of a number of community activities, including Colorado State University and its athletic programs, American Red Cross, United Way, Foothills Gateway, Larimer County Fair and Rodeo, Larimer County Junior Livestock Auction and the Fort Collins Area Chamber of Commerce.

Whether customers need custom manufacturing of trailers, truck bodies, snow groomers or other related equipment; trailers from well-known manufacturers; truck accessories for commercial vehicles; or maintenance, service, and parts for anything we make or sell—one name is all they need to know: Maxey.

WOODWARD, INC.

Woodward's leadership in energy control and optimization solutions is built on a foundation of strategic vision, quality performance, and core values. Woodward focuses on controlling energy by integrating components into systems. The result is high-quality emissions performance, reliability, and fuel efficiency to help ensure a better environment.

With a focus on community, Woodward promotes the values of honesty, loyalty and hard work. This legacy in work ethic—known in the company as the Woodward Way—continued with the opening of the Fort Collins plant in 1958.

Woodward, Inc. was founded in 1870 in Rockford, Illinois, as Woodward Governor Company after Amos Woodward invented his first water wheel governor. Amos handed over the business to his son Elmer, who handed it down to his son-in-law Irl Martin. It remained within the Woodward family for over 100 years.

For over 140 years, Woodward has innovated products for control of water, wind, and gas turbines as well as steam, gas, and diesel engines. Since its formation, Woodward has grown to more than 7,000 members and more than twenty-five facilities in fourteen countries—one of these locations being Fort Collins, Colorado.

The decision to move to Fort Collins was a result of Woodward's success in the twentieth century and perhaps a dose of chance. As CEO, Martin considered expanding operations to Nebraska, Kansas or Colorado. He thought metropolitan areas were too large and impersonal to cultivate the Woodward Way.

The board of directors was convinced that a small college town was desirable and many were intrigued with Colorado Springs. Walt Thorell, a loyal Woodward member, was on his way to scout Colorado Springs when he stopped in Fort Collins to visit an old friend. During his stay, he became certain that Fort Collins, the home of Colorado A&M College (now Colorado State University), was the perfect place for Woodward to expand.

By 1958, more than 250 people were employed at the Fort Collins location and Woodward's relationship with CSU grew to be mutually beneficial. Woodward engaged CSU students, starting with fifty-six CSU students who worked on construction. Many of these students were mechanical engineers and decided to stay with the company upon graduation, which further intertwined Woodward and the Fort Collins community.

Fort Collins later became headquarters for the Engine & Turbine Controls Division. In 1966 growing demand for these products led to a requirement for a larger space for manufacturing. Operations were moved from the company's downtown location to a new forty acre lot at the corner of Drake and Lemay. In 1973 additional administration and manufacturing buildings were added. This allowed all Woodward members to locate to the newer facility. The innovation in this plant led to three new business units: Turbomachinery Controls, Engine Controls, and Manufacturing.

Success at the Fort Collins location led to an expansion in production across the Northern Colorado area. Another production plant was built in Loveland in the early 1990s due to increased demand.

Above: Fort Collins, 1958.

Below: Architect's rendering (right) shows office building built by Woodward Governor Company at its engine and turbine controls division facility located in Fort Collins. Cantilevered roof and exposed steel framing members of butterfly-shaped structure area are featured in the bottom photograph (left).

In 2007, Tom Gendron, Woodward's current CEO, recognizing the potential in Northern Colorado announced, "In the past several months, we have relocated a few key leaders and functions to Colorado, which we believe has improved communication and realized efficiencies." This press release officially announced the headquarters relocation from Rockford to Fort Collins. Continuing to expand in Colorado, other additions included a testing facility in Windsor, which further ensured the quality of Woodward products and systems.

Fast forward to Fort Collins 150th year anniversary and Woodward employs more than 1,300 people in Colorado, sustaining over 2,500 additional community jobs indirectly. However, Woodward's community philosophy, as stated in its Constitution, is to provide more than just jobs in the areas in which it operates. Woodward is deeply committed to supporting programs and organizations, both financially and through volunteerism, which ensures that the communities in which it operates are desirable places to live and work.

Woodward continues to grow around the world and at home in Fort Collins. The company purchased over 100 acres along the Poudre River (with over thirty acres donated back to the city for development) with plans to begin construction in 2014. The new facility will bring hundreds of new jobs and capital that will continue the prosperous relationship between the company and the community. Woodward will stay true to the values that are rooted in its Rockford history, while focusing on what it will accomplish well into the future. In doing so, Woodward continues to add new chapters to its legacy of innovation.

Above: Group from Rockford that set up initial Woodward operations in Fort Collins. Taken in late 1954 or early 1955, Irl Martin can be seen standing furthest on the left.

Below: Woodward, Fort Collins.

KUCK MECHANICAL CONTRACTORS, INC.

Kuck Mechanical Contractors, Inc., is a local, family owned construction company that specializes in the design, custom fabrication and installation of a wide range of heating, ventilating and air conditioning (HVAC) projects—both renovations and new construction.

Russ Kuck.

Kuck Mechanical was founded in 1999 by Ted and Bob Kuck. However, the family legacy dates back from the 1930s when Theodore Alfred Kuck began his sheet metal career in the shipyards. This led to the establishment of his own sheet metal business in Sheboygan, Wisconsin, in 1942. The trade was passed down in the family to his son, Russell Kuck, who is still an estimator in his son's business. This craft and dedication were then also passed to Theodore's grandsons—Ted, Bob and Dave. Dave just recently joined his brothers in the operation, and the three men represent the family's third generation of sheet metal craftsmen. A fourth generation is up-and-coming.

Ted and Bob started their business in Ted's garage in rural Fort Collins, with the office located in the basement. They soon filled the garage to capacity with sheet metal equipment, much of which is still being used in their new fabrication facility today.

As with any new venture, the brothers made many sacrifices to get the business going. Times were tough and even transporting equipment and supplies were a challenge. The steep, rocky road to the early shop was often impassable during the winter, and the brothers had to transport all of their supplies and machinery themselves. In more than one instance, the company's delivery truck could not make it up the hill, weighed down at times with over 15,000 pounds of raw steel. Often, additional trucks had to be called in to help the delivery vehicle make it to the top.

The brothers also faced an unusual problem because of a non-compete clause Ted had with a previous shop of which he had been part owner. The new company was forced to conduct all its business outside a sixty mile radius of Fort Collins, which led to additional and different challenges. However, this proved to be a big advantage in the long run because new relationships were established with companies outside the area that the brothers had not worked with in the past. Many of these long-term customers are still an important part of Kuck Mechanical today.

All the hard work and innovation paid off and Kuck Mechanical grew a million dollars in volume every year for its first twelve years. The garage was enlarged but, after a couple of years, the brothers decided to purchase land in the Northern Colorado area and build a new manufacturing facility and office space. In the following years, they also added an additional lot for storage and a separate facility for a mechanic shop and training facility.

Kuck Mechanical, which has become a major competitor in the local market, provides design build, commercial construction, and heat, ventilation and air conditioning services. In addition, the company provides in-house and custom fabrication in its 20,000 square foot manufacturing facility, which is fully equipped with state-of-the-art sheet metal manufacturing equipment that can fabricate all standard and custom metal products. Projects range in price from $5,000 to $5 million or more.

Customers for the firm's commercial construction are involved in healthcare, education, office, retail, municipal, recreation, laboratory facilities, industrial construction and wastewater and water treatment plants. Almost all have been retained as repeat customers over the years.

Kuck Mechanical prides itself on providing premium craftsmanship and solutions that fit within the customer's schedule and budget. Depending on the customer's needs, Kuck Mechanical can prepare accurate conceptual drawings as well as solid estimates on hard-bid products. The Kuck brothers take quality seriously and are dedicated to exceeding their customer's expectations every time.

Over the years, Kuck Mechanical has built an impressive resume of commercial HVAC projects along the Front Range, Mountains, Western Slope, Wyoming, and into Nebraska and Texas.

The company has grown from three employees to more than ninety, and revenues have grown from $250,000 to an average of $12 million per year in sales. Kuck's talented craftsmen provide the highest quality work through their capabilities, experience and dedication. The company strives for continuous improvements in the training and education of its workforce and has established a Certified Apprenticeship Program.

Kuck Mechanical was honored to participate in ceremonies that commemorated the 137th anniversary of the military order that established Fort Collins near the banks of the Poudre River in what is now Old Town. Kuck designed and installed the stainless steel frame that holds the plaque commemorating this significant event in the community's history. The plaque is located at the CSU engines lab in north Fort Collins and includes a picture of Lieutenant Colonel William Collins and a copy of his order establishing the fort.

Also included is a copy of the document, signed by President Abraham Lincoln, establishing the 6,000 acre military reservation and a drawing of the fort as it appeared in 1866.

Kuck Mechanical is also a contributor to many other organizations and charities, including local schools' fundraising and athletic programs.

Kuck Mechanical is a family owned company that takes its business relationships seriously and personally. The company's reputation is based upon its ability to meet its client's schedules, budgets and quality demands.

In the future, the company will continue to strive for an employee-friendly environment. Kuck is dedicated to providing continuing education and training to assist and encourage their employees to continue to maintain the quality craftsmanship that has always been a vital part of Kuck Mechanical.

Kuck Mechanical Contractors takes care of business by taking care of its valued employees and customers.

For additional information, please visit Kuck Mechanical Contractors on the Internet at www.kuckmechanical.com.

Left to right: Ted and Bob Kuck.

TST, INC. CONSULTING ENGINEERS

TST, Inc. is a professional team of inspired dream-makers, a collective of talented individuals who love what they do. Staffed by engineers, planners, landscape architects, surveyors and municipal strategists, TST specializes in community and municipal development.

TST was founded in 1977 by Donald N. Taranto, Larry E. Stanton and Darold E. Tagge. The firm has grown into an award-winning organization that is well prepared to address the challenges and opportunities of the twenty-first century.

Taranto, Stanton and Tagge began with a total staff of three, primarily providing services for municipal clients. In 1985 the original partnership was divided to form two entities: Taranto, Stanton & Tagge Colorado and Taranto, Stanton & Tagge Nebraska; then, in 1989, the company was incorporated to form TST, Inc. with offices in Fort Collins and Denver. The Fort Collins and Denver operations were split in 1994 and the Denver office incorporated as TST, Inc. Consulting Engineers of Denver. TST Infrastructure joined the family in 2001.

The firm has been instrumental in helping to craft the varied communities in Northern Colorado that have been recognized as some of the finest places to live in the United States. For thirty-seven years, TST has designed and helped to construct the infrastructure, projects and communities that have been honored by such publications as the *New York Times*, which described Fort Collins as "the happiest place on earth."

Whether engaged in creating the experience-based communities of tomorrow, providing the civil engineering design for a municipal infrastructure project, or providing the surveying and construction services to realize a project dream, TST is a cornerstone in the engineering, planning and construction services industry in Northern Colorado.

A talented and dedicated staff at TST brings decades of experience and a focus on world-class services to each project, large or small. Matching the best team and experience for each project creates successful outcomes that go beyond typical expectations and traditional levels of thinking. This is the culture and philosophy that enables TST to call itself 'dream-makers'.

TST's work in the private sector has encompassed all aspects of land planning and engineering development from projects as small as two acres to as large as 5,000 acres. TST has completed a broad mix of commercial, industrial, residential and mixed-use applications. The firm specializes in complex projects where inventive thinking and innovative solutions are key to a project's success.

Municipal engineering is a second specialty of the Civil Engineering Group. From serving as municipal engineers and planners for growing municipalities to providing design services for municipal infrastructure; creating Metropolitan Districts to new technology applications in water distribution; wastewater innovations to green industry, the Civil Engineering Group is dedicated to providing value-added solutions.

TST's construction Services Group provides a blend of services in the construction phases of projects. Services include construction observation and surveying support. As infrastructure construction nears it completion, TST provides final landscaping and public site furnishing plans.

As award-winning planners and designer, TST brings a renewed spirit, integrated vision and style to community and land development projects that create true market differentiation, increased project velocities and success. TST also works to create municipal and public environments that enhance the experience of the public realm and seek to create twenty-first century environments for our communities that continue the legacy of excellence in Northern Colorado.

TST Company values guide the firm and all its employees in goal setting and decision making. The core values consist of service to clients and productivity. The client is the most important part of TST's business and the firm seeks to earn its clients confidence and trust through professionalism and performance that exceeds their expectations. TST accomplishes extraordinary results

through commitment, sound organization and planning. The firm promotes a family atmosphere and works as a team to create innovative ideas and solutions. The most effective tools and technology available are utilized to provide exceptional service.

Today, TST is a leading provider of engineering, planning and construction services that envision a positive, productive and healthy future in our region and beyond.

TST has an outstanding record of engineering innovation, expansion of expertise and providing the highest quality service to its clients. The firm's growth and reputation are the direct result of individual efforts and close cooperation by all the personnel. TST's future success depends on the continuation of these efforts and adherence to the highest professional standards and ideals.

HENRY HERSH TRUCKING, INC.

Top: Henry 'Hank' Hersh, Sr., 1945.

Above: Left to right, Hank Sr., Hank, Jr., and Scot Hersh, 1962.

Right: Loading material with an end dump, 2013.

Below: Big Thompson Flood, 2013.

It was probably inevitable that Henry A. 'Hank' Hersh would make a career of the trucking business. As a youngster, he helped his father haul poles and produce by horse and wagon from the Masonville area, where he was born and raised. Hank started his own business after getting out of the Army in 1945 following World War II.

Hank began small with only one truck, which he used to haul hay. He then began some over-the-road hauling, delivering back-packs for the Army from a manufacturing plant in Loveland to California during the Korean War.

In 1955, Hank began hauling raw oil to the asphalt plants operated by Sterling Paving Co. in Fort Collins. This led to moving Sterling's equipment and hauling gravel and asphalt products to all sorts of job sites in Colorado and Wyoming. As the business grew, Hank bought additional trucks and hired more drivers, including his brothers.

"We have done paving jobs and helped build roads all over Colorado, Wyoming, New Mexico, Kansas and Nebraska," explains Hank's son, Henry G. Hersh.

Today, Henry Hersh Trucking is headquartered in Fort Collins and specializes in hauling heavy equipment and construction materials. The company provides a variety of lowboys and flatbeds to accommodate any type of hauling, in addition to double-drop and single-drop trailers. "Essentially, we can move almost any type of heavy equipment that needs to be moved," Hersh says.

Henry Hersh Trucking has always been a family owned and operated business, with Hank, Sr., running the operations and sons Hank, Jr., and Scot driving trucks. Hank, Jr., and Scot took over operation of the business in 1992 so Hank, Sr., and their mother, Jean, could have some time to enjoy life. Hank, Jr.'s wife, Annette, runs the office for the company, with Scot driving and helping run the company.

The company that began with 1 truck and 1 owner-driver hauling hay has now grown to 14 trucks and 18 trailers hauling construction-related materials. The company currently has twelve employees.

"We feel we have the most reliable and professional drivers in the industry and it shows, as they not only drive the trucks, but maintain them," Hersh says. The drivers are responsible for keeping up the maintenance on the trucks and for keeping them clean the way Hank, Sr., took so much pride in.

The Hersh family would like to thank all their employees for their dedicated service because, "Without employees, we have no company," as Hank, Jr., says. Hank and Scot both feel that by hiring drivers who honestly care about their equipment it ultimately presents our fleet as 'one of a kind'.

"We try to keep a small company atmosphere because we believe we can offer better service to our customers and control how we get things done in a timely fashion while giving proper attention to our customer's needs," says Hersh."Our business plan is to keep this a family-owned and operated company as long as we can."

Chadwick Electric, Inc., has provided electrical services to businesses and residential communities in Northern Colorado and Southern Wyoming for more than four decades. Chadwick family members have been electrical contractors for four generations and have worked in the Fort Collins area since 1958.

Judy McEntee started working for her dad's electric company in Fort Collins in 1963, earning $1 per hour while attending Fort Collins High School. Judy married Gale Chadwick in 1965 and a year later, Gale asked Jim Chance and Judy's dad, Leland McEntee, who operated C&M Electric, for an apprenticeship. He was hired for $1.75 an hour. Leland died unexpectedly six months later, but Gale continued working for Jim for three more years. At that time, he began working for Jack Giuliano at Jack's Electric until he received his Master Electrical License in 1971 and he and Judy decided to go into business for themselves.

"Jack Giuliano was very busy at the time and gave us a contract to wire an eight-plex. That helped us get the business started," Judy recalls.

"At first all of the bookkeeping was done by the old method—double entry," Judy explains. "It was a major change when we started using a peg-board system of accounting that used NCR-type paper and would copy information automatically onto individual ledger cards."

A huge improvement came in 1977 when the company invested $22,000 for its first computer system and had an accounting program written for the business. CB radios were used for communication in the field in the early days, followed by bag phones and pagers and today's cell phones.

The company operated out of the Chadwick home until 1995 when they purchased a commercial warehouse at 1305 Duff Drive. The company has expanded at this location over the years and employment now averages around thirty persons.

The four Chadwick children—Blye, Tye, Tad and Pauli—all worked in the business as they were growing up, and all are still working in the electrical trades in various capacities. Gale and Judy retired in 2005 and the company is now operated by Blye, and the service division is managed by Tad.

Over the years, Chadwick Electric has wired more than 6,000 apartment units, over 1,500 single-family homes, more than 800 finished basements, and several hundred commercial projects. The company has responded to countless service calls, including many after-hours emergency calls.

Chadwick Electric, which has worked with many of its customers and contractors for more than twenty years, believes that being competitive in the future means servicing its customer with the highest quality and courtesy possible and by operating at the highest measurable standards of the industry.

Additional information is available at www.chadwickelectric.com.

Gale and Judy Chadwick, 2004.

ARAGON IRON & METAL CORP

Written by Leslie Barela, third generation of the Aragon family.

Aragon Iron & Metal Corp is a family business that was started in 1951 by Martin and Louise Aragon. Martin and Louise worked hard to start recycling here in Fort Collins, originally starting their business in their home on Loomis Street. Before they began their own business, no job was too rough or tough for the Aragons. Martin hauled peaches and coal, and helped with the monumental task of the relocation of a cemetery.

In the late 1940s, the Aragons began purchasing recyclable metals from their house on Loomis Street. Once they had accumulated enough for a truckload to Denver, Martin and his sons would load their truck and off to Denver they went to sell their metal. Meanwhile, Louise would clean houses and their daughter would help take care of the family home and meals.

They eventually bought the property they currently reside at. In addition to the purchase of metals, they began purchasing cars and trucks for recycle. The purchase of vehicles lead to the beginning of the parts department and furthered their recycling efforts with the processing of red metals.

In 1974, Martin and Louise incorporated their business, making their children part owners as well. In 1978, they bought additional property adjacent to their existing location and were able to expand. During the years that followed, Aragon's began to exceed their capacity and saw a time where the building was too small to house the office and warehouse that was needed. In 1989 the Aragon children decided to build the office/warehouse building they currently reside in.

Since 1989, Aragon's has seen many changes within both the metal industry and the mainstream economy. From local steel recycling to worldwide shipping, the metal industry has exceeded the ideas Martin and Louise had for their company.

As times changed, so did operating necessities. Aragon's began purchasing additional trucks and equipment to serve the company's needs. Aragon's provides industrial pick-up service with semi-trailers, roll-off and lugger boxes. They also welcome walk-in recycling from aluminum cans to vehicle disposal; they are able to recycle all your metal materials.

Since 1951, Aragon's has recycled for many businesses, farms, and local community members. They have been at their current location for more than fifty years and have been a steady place for recyclables to be taken. Five family members, spanning the second and third generations of the Aragon family are currently active in everyday business. They serve Northern Colorado and Southern Wyoming and continue to realize the importance of recycling for our future and meet the dreams Martin and Louise had for their family business. The Aragon family began their business to support their family but it has become more, it is now a way of life locally and globally.

A business founded on a simple handshake has grown to become one of the largest mobile warehousing and storage firms in northern Colorado. Today, American Storage Trailer Leasing of Fort Collins, Inc., offers more than 300 semi-trailers for mobile warehousing and storage of household or commercial items.

"In the beginning, we had several over-the-road semi-trucks and delivered a wide variety of freight throughout forty-eight states," explains co-founder Anna Dee Hallam. "Along the way, we started renting a trailer here and there and realized the need for this type of service."

The company was organized in 1990 by Hallam and Sid Whittemore. Whittemore, who was Hallam's accountant, was already in the storage business and Hallam asked if he would be interested in having a division in Northern Colorado. "He thought about it a few days, then called me back and asked when I wanted to start," Hallam recalls. "With just a handshake, he said he would back anything I could build. We formed a business relationship that is still going strong today."

Hallam admits that when she first started delivering semi-trailers for storage, she could not "back a trailer for anything. My customers were very patient and I finally learned."

American Storage Trailer Leasing has grown from one truck and one trailer at the beginning to a total of 280 units. Anna Dee married Ron Hallam in 2005 and the two now operate the business.

American Storage Trailer Leasing has grown by offering reasonable rates and dependable, on-time delivery for mobile warehousing and storage. The company's professional drivers can deliver trailers to the customer's location for loading and then move the trailer to any desired location for a small monthly fee. The trailers may also be stored in American Storage Trailer Leasing's secured facility.

American Storage Trailer Leasing also offers twelve acres of outside storage for trailers, RVs and boats. The facility has a six-foot solid fence with three strands of security wire, an on-site manager and coded keypad entrance gate. Short-term and long-term leases are available and access is available during daylight hours, seven days a week.

AMERICAN STORAGE TRAILER LEASING OF FORT COLLINS, INC.

In addition, the company has used trailers and containers for sale.

American Storage Trailer Leasing is always available to help when the community is struck by floods, fires or other catastrophes. At such times, the company donates trailers to charitable organizations to help the community get back on its feet.

Looking to the future, Hallam hopes to upgrade the company's fleet and add newer units and additional storage containers.

American Storage Trailer Leasing is located at 311 North U.S. Hwy 287 in Fort Collins. For additional information, check the website at www.americanstoragetrailerleasing.com.

EXPONENTIAL ENGINEERING COMPANY

Above: The owners of the company in 2009. From left to right: Benj Hoffner, Greta Gibbens, Eric Jungen, Patrick Ghidossi, Mickey Pitt, Tom Ghidossi, Tim Wallick, Dave Rightley and Mike Reed.

Below: The Hydroelectric Plant on Boulder Creek outside Boulder, Colorado. This plant was built in 1909 and EEC was a part of the design team that upgraded the hydrogenerator and electrical facilities in 2011-2012 to provide more efficient power production.

In 1992 two engineers met at the old Bennigan's Restaurant on College Avenue and decided to start a company that would focus on relationships. The founders—Thomas Ghidossi and Richard Holstad—chose Fort Collins as headquarters for the new company because it was a nice, affordable community located close to the clients the partners hoped to attract.

Exponential Engineering Company (EEC) came into existence on January 8, 1993, as a full-service power engineering consulting firm. The company provides professional electrical engineering consulting to Rural Electric Associations, municipalities, investor-owned utilities, industrial and commercial facilities, architectural/engineering firms and government entities, as well as private individuals.

EEC started in a one-room office in midtown with only a phone number and two computers—one an early laptop, the second a desktop with a monitor that was moved from place to place as needed.

Cell phones had not come into existence at the time, so the engineers would set up a few appointments in Colorado, Wyoming, or Nebraska, then stop at pay phones along the route to see if a potential client might be available in the next town.

The founders had hoped to hire one or two additional people after the first few years, but as it turned out, the company had a staff of five by the end of its first year. EEC's original clients included Wheatland Rural Electric Association in Wyoming; Fred Wilson & Associates; Reedy Creek Energy Services; Walt Disney World in Florida; and EDAW in Fort Collins.

A number of key employees have helped EEC grow and prosper while helping maintain the firm's commitment to a family-friendly and open atmosphere. These include Eric Jungen, Mickey Pitt, Benj Hoffner, Greta Gibbens and Dave Rightley.

In order to better serve more of Colorado and hire some very talented employees, the firm opened an office in Wheat Ridge in 2003, Cortez in 2006, and Steamboat Springs in 2010.

Revenues for the firm have grown from $2 million in 2006 to $5.9 million in 2013. EEC is currently working on 160 active projects with a total of 310 active clients.

In keeping with the company's operating philosophy, EEC employees participate in many activities beyond the scope of their job descriptions, from raising money for the Larimer County Food Bank to delivering presentations about engineering at local schools and mentoring students. EEC donates approximately $20,000 annually to local and national charities.

Over the past two decades, Exponential Engineering Company has grown from a small staff and client base to more than thirty employees operating out of four offices across the state. "We're dedicated to providing the high quality, cost-effective service that brings success to our clients, and we stand behind our work," says Ghidossi.

SCHRADER OIL CO.

In Fort Collins, Colorado, the name Schrader has been synonymous with the sale of petroleum products since 1937.

In that year, Wayne H. Schrader came to Fort Collins to operate the office and distribution warehouse for the Texas Company (Texaco). Wayne H. sold gasoline, diesel fuel, motor oil, fuel oil and other petroleum products to service stations, automobile dealerships and contractors in Larimer County. Wayne H. also acquired two service stations, which he leased to operators during this time. Wayne H. was well known in Fort Collins as having the reputation of being an honest businessman, who provided good service.

Wayne K., son of the senior Wayne, was born in 1929, was quite young when his father first started in this business. However, as he became older, Wayne K. helped his Dad by performing maintenance work, such as painting gasoline pumps and tanks and cutting weeds around the locations.

When he turned sixteen, he also drove delivery trucks to customers ordering gasoline or lubricants. After graduating from Colorado, A & M College in 1952, and a brief career as a County Extension agent, young Wayne K. was hired in 1954 by Texaco. His job was selling and delivering Texaco products in Larimer County to farms and ranches. When Wayne H. retired in 1963, Wayne K., then thirty-four years old, was hired and given the responsibility for both positions.

Wayne K.'s desire was to own his own company as a distributor, rather than a commissioned employee of Texaco. However, Texaco denied that request. When the opportunity came in 1966 he purchased the Phillips 66 distributorship, including five operating service stations. The new independent marketer business was, and still is, called Schrader Oil Co.

During the next forty-eight years, the company has grown to own and operate over twenty convenience stores, called Schrader's Country Stores. The company also expanded in 1971 to include the distribution of Propane gas, used for home heating and other commercial uses.

Joining the parent company over the years have been three children: Perry in 1975, Steve in 1977, and daughter Jennifer in 1992. Today the company also includes four grandsons: Casey, Clayton, Eric and Kyle. Strong supporters of the Fort Collins community, the Schrader family have supported a variety of entities, including various projects at Colorado State University and many philanthropic needs in the city. Phyllis and Wayne K. were honored with the Multiple Sclerosis Society's Hope Award in 2000 for their outstanding contributions to the community. Through the years, Wayne K. and Steve have served on the boards of the Colorado Petroleum Marketers Association and the National Oil Jobbers Council.

With a new generation of Schraders continuing the family oil business that has grown to more than 180 employees, the company plans to continue its success by offering what it has since 1937—convenience for its customers. Through unrelenting dedication to providing the best service possible, Schrader Oil Co. will persistently work to be the consumer's choice in Northern Colorado.

Above: Wayne Schrader delivering fuel in North Park to the Soil Conservation District.

Below: The Schraders from left to right, Susie, Phyllis, Steve, Wayne, Julie, Perry and Jennifer.

L&L ACOUSTICAL, INC.

Above: Fred Lockman.

Below: Jerry Lockman.

Brothers Fred and Jerry Lockman established L&L Acoustical, Inc., forty-two years ago with a vision of providing Northern Colorado with an impeccable turn-key product and service for both contractors and homeowners. The company provides full, in-house service consisting of drywall stocking, hanging, finishing, priming, and texturing including several types of hand textures and clean-up. The company specializes in residential and multifamily construction.

Fred Lockman, Jr. and Jerry E. Lockman founded the company in January 1972. L&L Acoustical started with only six employees but soon became one of the leading drywall contractors in Northern Colorado and presently employs over fifty people. During the early years, Fred and Jerry made regular trips to the gypsum plant in Florence, Colorado, which, at that time, was the closest gypsum board manufacturer. Along with their brothers Dale and Bill, the Lockmans established Lockman Drywall Supply, Inc., the first gypsum board supply company in Fort Collins.

The company's superintendents have been with L&L Acoustical, Inc. for more than thirty-five years, providing customers with the daily, on-site attention they deserve. Bill Lockman, the lead texture professional, has been with the company thirty-seven years and has developed some of the firm's specialty textures.

Unfortunately, Jerry passed away in 1977, leaving his portion of the company to Fred. When Fred passed away in 2004 his wife Karen, acquired sole ownership of the company. L&L Acoustical is currently operated by Karen, her son, Gery Lockman, and daughter, Aundrea Lockman-Pringle.

In response to a changing economy, L&L Acoustical introduced its Home Servicing division in 2011. This service is designed for homeowners who are looking to repair or update their homes. The division specializes in acoustical texture removal, retexturing or adding accent walls, repairs after water damage and remodeling. No job is too small or too large for the servicing division to handle.

In an effort to diversify and better serve their customers, Karen, Gery and Aundrea, established L&L Insulation, LLC in 2011. In 2012, Kevin Miller joined the team as operations manager. Kevin brings twenty years of experience and a passion for his work that is unmatched. L&L Insulation is BPI certified; blown-in blanket certified and specializes in all phases of thermal applications. L&L Insulation is a preferred contractor with Xcel Energy and Poudre Valley REA and is a BBB accredited company. Saving energy on existing homes is a strong passion of the division.

L&L hires the most experienced, productive teams to provide only the highest quality drywall and insulation solutions. Their mission is to service each customer with the professionalism and workmanship they deserve. Whether it is a complete custom home or existing, L&L strives to provide the highest quality product available.

The principles and passion that guided Fred and Jerry remain the guiding light for the company as it moves into the second generation. The founding vision of "Providing quality craftsmanship and service for Northern Colorado" will continue to remain the company's mission statement and vision.

Access to safe and reliable utilities services has been a hallmark of Fort Collins for more than a century.

Concerns about typhoid fever, coupled with two devastating fires over a two-year period, prompted creation of the city's first waterworks in 1882. By 1910 the water works system had grown to forty miles of distribution mains and was considered one of the finest facilities in the west.

A city sewer system was under construction in 1888 and sanitary sewer districts were established in 1891. Before the first sewage treatment plant came on line in 1948, all sewage drained into the Cache la Poudre River.

Fort Collins Light and Power Company was organized in 1887 to provide an electric lighting system for the growing city. The first streetlights were carbon arc lamps located at the center of selected intersections. By 1900 the power plant supplied electricity for forty-five commercial arc lights and 5,000 incandescent lamps.

Fort Collins Electric Utility, a municipal electric utility owned by the citizens, was organized following a public vote in 1935 and the Department of Utilities was formed a few years later.

The utilities infrastructure grew as Fort Collins continued to grow, fueled by a robust farming economy and the new Agricultural College (now Colorado State University). The city established a Public Works Department in the early 1900s, and obtained senior water rights and built the Poudre Canyon Water Treatment Plant. To increase raw water supplies, the city obtained and improved Joe Wright Reservoir and Michigan Ditch in the 1970s.

In more recent years, Fort Collins' second water treatment plant was constructed in the late 1960s. The city began its water conservation efforts and laid the foundation for a comprehensive water quality plan in the late 1970s.

Also during this era, utility staff began experimenting with an underground electric distribution system. Today, 99 percent of the electric system is underground and its reliability rate is 99.9982 percent, an award-winning statistic.

In 1980 the Stormwater Utility was established after the Poudre River Floodplain was mapped to better access flooding risk.

The water utilities (water, wastewater and stormwater) and electric utility merged into one utilities organization—Fort Collins Utilities—in 1998.

Fort Collins Utilities was the first in the state and among the first in the nation to offer its customers the option of purchasing clean, renewable wind power in 1998. Mass deployment of advanced meters, which eliminates manual readings, began in 2012.

Today, more than 400 employees of Fort Collins Utilities maintain and administer 539 miles of water mains and 437 miles of sanitary sewer systems. Light and Power provides electric service to more than 68,000 homes and businesses.

Looking to the future, Fort Collins Utilities has designed the "Utilities for the 21st Century" initiative with the vision of protecting and preserving the quality of life in Northern Colorado while delivering the high level of service customers expect.

FORT COLLINS UTILITIES

Above: The City of Fort Collins gets half of its drinking water from Horsetooth Reservoir, part of the CB-T system that brings water from the western slope of the Rocky Mountains to the eastern foothills and plains. The other half comes from the Cache la Poudre River.

Bottom, left: Part of Fort Collins' high-mountain water supply, a system of ditches and wooden stave pipe was constructed by early settlers along steep mountainsides at elevations of more than 10,000 feet.

Bottom, center: Electric crews, as well as water field crews, provide 24/7 service to customers.

Bottom, right: Safety is the top priority for all utility crews who receive extensive field training, including confined space and respirator training.

COLORADO IRON & METAL, INC.

Top: The current owners of Colorado Iron & Metal, Inc., from left to right, Marty, Kent and Dan Garvin.

Above: Conserving natural resources through metal recycling.

Colorado Iron & Metal, Inc., is dedicated to conserving natural resources through metal recycling. The company is a full-service scrap metal recycling enterprise that focuses primarily on metal recycling.

The company was organized in 1995 by Kent D. Garvin, who admits he knew little about the metals business when he purchased an existing small metal business operated by a man he had known earlier in Minnesota.

Garvin had been operating a successful towing and automotive repair business in southern Minnesota but vacations in Colorado had ignited a desire to live in the shadows of the Rocky Mountains.

He sold his business in Minnesota and spent two-and-a-half years looking for a new business to purchase. He finally came to terms with the owner of Nelson Metals in 1995 and moved to Colorado to pursue new opportunities.

"One of my nephews, Marty Garvin, relocated with me," Garvin recalls. "We loaded a twelve foot U-Haul with the bare essentials to set up a small apartment and, with a hope and a prayer; we headed west to seek a new future. The reality of what we were doing set in quickly when I realized I really didn't know anything about the metals business, didn't have any employees, and the former general manager had quit before the ink was dry on the purchase agreement."

Fortunately, scrap commodity prices were at an all-time high when Garvin purchased the business and renamed it Colorado Iron & Metal. The company was doing about $250,000 in annual sales when Garvin took over and sales doubled the very first year. By 2008 the company was grossing $10 million annually.

"Within the first year I had to make decisions about the primary focus of the business and decided to emphasize our scrap and metal sales operations, which eventually evolved into a metal fabrication business as well," Garvin explains.

Colorado Iron & Metal recycles both ferrous metals (iron and steel) and non-ferrous such as aluminum, copper, brass and many others. The company has a large buy-back center where people may drop off their metals for cash, as well as an extensive container/roll-off service to pick up metals at industrial and commercial businesses. The scrap metal is processed by sorting and segregating the different materials and alloys by chopping, stripping, bailing and packaging the product into containers suitable for shipping throughout the world.

The company uses sophisticated electronic metal analyzing equipment to determine the specific type and grade of metal being recycled. Currently, the company handles several thousand tons of metal each month.

The company now employs sixteen people, including the owners; Dan, Marty and Kent Garvin. Dan and Marty took control of the business in January 2014 and plan to expand with additional scrap yards.

Colorado Iron and Metal is owned by committed Christian men who strive to manage their business with Biblical values and principles. The company supports many local and national charities, especially faith-based organizations such as Lutheran Family Service, Salvation Army and many others.

WALKER MANUFACTURING COMPANY

It all started with a golf car in Fowler, Kansas. Max Walker, who had always had a flair for innovation and design, developed the Walker Executive Golf Car—the first gasoline-powered golf cart—in 1957. Electric carts of the day would often run out of power and leave golfers stranded on the course, and the gasoline-powered golf car soon became very popular.

The Walker golf car business lasted until 1963 when Max sold his design and tooling to another company in Kansas. After selling, he started looking for another outlet for his talents and this resulted in the Walker Power Truck, a runabout vehicle for industry, and an agricultural tractor cab cooler called the Byco Evaporative Cooler. In 1974, Walker Manufacturing moved its operation from Casper, Wyoming, to Fort Collins.

Seventy thousand coolers were built over an eleven year period, but Max and his sons, Bob and Dean were also working on a new product that would eventually become the company's sole product—a very maneuverable and compact riding lawn mower aimed at the commercial landscaping industry.

Max's sons had joined the company in the mid-1970s and together they designed and built a lawnmower that was fast, easy to operate and delivered a beautiful cut. The early prototypes were built for private homeowner use but as improvements were added, the mowers began to attract attention from commercial cutters. Walker Manufacturing participated in its first national power equipment show in 1981 and national marketing started a year later.

Walker Manufacturing was soon enjoying a steady growth rate of ten to fifteen percent per year. The company currently has forty-six distributors throughout the world and more than 1,200 dealers offer the Walker mowers. Thirty percent of Walker's business is in the export market. Since 1980, Walker has manufactured more than 130,000 machines.

Bob Walker, who now serves as president of Walker Manufacturing, feels one of the company's major strengths is its personal relationships with customers. "These days, big corporations have virtually no personality so one of the things we try to do is have a personality," he says. "We try to treat customers like real people and offer a more personalized relationship."

In 1990, Walker Manufacturing moved to a new facility in Fort Collins. That facility has grown to 216,000 square feet on sixty acres, which provides plenty of open space for testing the mowers. The company employs 160 people and remains very much a family business.

"Our father always said he'd rather have his own hamburger stand than be a part of McDonald's, and we've tried to continue that attitude," says Walker. "We still do our own product design and our manufacturing is still in-house."

Bob and his brother, Dean, who serves as vice president, are equal partners in the business. With Dean's sons now working for the company, Walker Manufacturing is poised to become a third-generation family business.

The Walkers are people who live with gratitude; thankful to the Lord for the opportunities they have enjoyed to be in business, and thankful for a great place to live and work in Fort Collins.

Above: Walker factory located southeast of Fort Collins on sixty acres.

Below: Third generation Walker family member, Ryan Walker, testing a Walker Mower.

Bottom: Walker Mower at work on landscaped property in Florida.

RAW URTH
DESIGNS, INC.

Above: Modern sensibilities meet rustic charm with the Leadville Range Hood harmoniously integrating rustic iron planking with the floating shelves and beam details creating an awe-inspiring stylish kitchen.

PHOTOGRAPH © 2012 KIMBERLY GAVIN.

Below: Elegantly poised in this urban farm kitchen, our Washed Steel Montrose, built from recycled steel, adds flair without being overstated with it's strapping, rivet and crown details.

EMILY FOLLOWILL PHOTOGRAPHY.

Raw Urth Designs is a unique metals company producing range hoods, countertops, fireplace surrounds, and other custom products. All pieces are handcrafted one at a time in Raw Urth's Fort Collins studio.

According to co-owner Amy Sasick, Raw Urth came about as the result of needing to fill a need they had for fantastic metal work.

The year was 2004 and Amy and Stefan Sasick were operating a landscaping business in Austin, Texas, and searching for a company that could supply unique steel work for their customers. Amy's designs were based on creating an outdoor environment through the use of hardscapes created from stone, wood and steel. However, the Sasicks were having difficulty finding the steel elements they needed. On Valentine's Day, they decided that the solution was to make the steel themselves. "We told each other 'Happy Valentines', borrowed my sister's camper, dropped the kids off at Nana's and headed to New Mexico for a week of blacksmithing camp."

On the way home, Amy and Stefan realized their paths had made a decisive turn. With an antique anvil found in a friend's garage, a hand-crank forge that needed work, and a bag of leather gloves, Raw Urth Designs began.

Working in the garage of their new home in Bellvue, on the outskirts Fort Collins, the Sasicks started hammering out the look and style of Raw Urth. As word got out and jobs began to come in, the garage soon became too small. Stefan and Amy then jumped with both feet and moved their operation just north of Old Town. "We made it a firm goal to really put our hearts and energy into the new business and leave our landscaping business behind," Amy explains.

Range hoods soon became Raw Urth's premier product. As an alternative to stainless steel and copper hoods, Raw Urth hoods are created with clean, modern lines and rustic, timeless finishes in both traditional and contemporary collections. All products are made in-house, with care and attention to detail. When they returned to Vegas and the International Builder's Show a few years later, their products were received with enthusiasm from builders looking for a fresh approach.

Additional products, including countertops, backsplashes, fireplace surrounds and mantels and wall panels were added as the company grew. The products are produced in steel, stainless, bronze, brass, zinc, pewter and aluminum with the most unique finishes and patinas the market has to offer. Raw Urth has clients across the United States, Canada and Caribbean, along with consulting services to clients across the seas.

Raw Urth has assembled a team of fifteen uniquely talented artists, metal smiths, draftsmen and administrators. The employees are actively involved in the Coats for Kids project, which distributes coats, gloves, boots and hats to kids in need in Northern Colorado. Raw Urth fully outfits about ten kids each year and helps facilitate more through the North Fort Collins Business Association.

For more information about Raw Urth Designs, visit www.rawurth.com.

Evergreen Landscape & Sprinkler Co. had its beginnings in 1980 when an industrious high school student, Bob Toomey, began a rototilling business called Bob's Rototilling. In 1983, Bob added grounds maintenance and snow removal to his list of services and incorporated the growing business as Evergreen Landscape & Sprinkler Co. Evergreen is now one of the larger firms of its kind in the area, offering total grounds maintenance for both commercial and residential customers.

Four year-round contracts helped the company get its start and Bob employed several friends from high school in the new venture. One of those friends, Jeff Sergi, worked for the company off-and-on during the early years. Bob's parents, Sheila and R. M. Toomey, also helped out, with Sheila heading up the pruning crew and handling the flower planting.

When Bob started the business, he worked out of an old barn at the corner of Taft and Drake Streets that they rented from Coach O'Donnell. When Bob and Jeff went to the barn one morning to get their equipment for the day's work, they encountered a family of skunks that had taken up residence in the barn. Since neither boy had much interest in a smelly encounter with a skunk, the humane society was called to evict the unwelcome visitors. But, since they could not retrieve their equipment, Bob and Jeff lost an entire day's production.

The company began to grow as Bob signed contracts with several management companies and additional services such as sprinkler installation and maintenance and snow removal were added to Evergreen's list of

services. Key individuals responsible for the growth, in addition to Bob, include irrigation tech Jeff Sergi, landscape supervisor Jory Wilcox, new construction supervisor Steve Feese and office manager Cathy Toomey, Bob's wife.

Fort Collins' Christmas Blizzard of 2006, which dumped twenty-one inches of snow into eight foot drifts, was a challenge for the company. The city declared a state of emergency and Evergreen crews worked around the clock from December 22 to December 29 helping customers dig out from the storm. Since employees could not get home, the office turned into one big slumber party.

The high school student's after-school rototilling service has grown into a thriving business with $2 million in annual revenue. Evergreen provides a total package of landscape renovation and construction services, including everything from turf mowing and snow removal to tree and shrub planting and pruning and outdoor lighting.

Bob serves on the board of Foothills Gateway Foundation and Cathy helps with the organization's annual charity event. Evergreen also supports the Larimer County Child Advocacy Center, CSU athletics and other CSU organizations.

EVERGREEN LANDSCAPE & SPRINKLER CO.

Above: Bob and Cathy Toomey.

Mountain-n-Plains, Inc.

Left to right: Justin Morrison and Charlie Koons.

Mountain-n-Plains, Inc., ("MnP") was founded in 1979 by Charlie Koons, and was originally called Mountain 'n' Plains Property Management, Inc. Charlie was introduced to property management when she sold an investment property and traded her role as a landlord to become a manager for the buyer, who would not close the deal unless Charlie agreed to manage the property. Soon thereafter, word of Charlie's hard work, dedication and ethics spread throughout Fort Collins and neighboring communities. These core values formed the foundation of MnP, and remain the premise on which the company stands today.

MnP began with 3 properties, growing immensely over the past thirty-five years to managing more than 500 single-family homes and more than 60 commercial projects today. The firm's residential portfolio consists of everything from cozy apartments to sprawling estates, while the commercial portfolio consists of medical, industrial, office, retail, mixed-use communities, undeveloped land and associations.

In the beginning, the company had a one-room office upstairs at 1405 South College, near the Colorado State University campus. When deciding on a business name, Charlie

combined her family roots on the plains of Western Kansas, with her own roots in the foothills of Colorado, inspiring the name "Mountain 'n' Plains."

While attending a family wedding in the summer of 1997, Charlie discussed her succession plan with her second cousin, Justin Morrison, who was working for a general contractor in San Diego, subsequent to serving as an infantry officer in the United States Marine Corps. After one visit to Northern Colorado in 2001, Justin and his wife, Deb, a school teacher, fell in love with the area and left California to raise a family in Fort Collins. Six years later, in September 2007, Justin and Deb bought the company and shortened the name to Mountain-n-Plains, Inc. while maintaining the same familiar logo Northern Colorado residents have learned to trust. Charlie is still involved in the day-to-day success of MnP as the employing broker and manager of the residential division.

Since 1994, MnP has remained one of few Accredited Management Organizations® (AMO) in Colorado. AMO designations are awarded by the Institute of Real Estate Management (IREM), the most recognized and respected real estate management organization in the world, and must be led by a Certified Property Manager® (CPM). Both Justin and Charlie have earned this title during their careers.

MnP remains active in the Fort Collins community, focusing its efforts of both time and money in a number of youth-based organizations including, but not limited to, Partners Mentoring Youth, Respite Care, Colorado Youth Outdoors and several local schools.

As MnP's business continues to grow with the community, their goals to efficiently and ethically serve clients will remain unsurpassed. Mountain-n-Plains, Inc., believes living and conducting business by these standards, maintaining a great team of employees and valuing strong relationships will further their success. Justin and the Mountain-n-Plains team look forward to being a part of, and giving back to, the great community of Fort Collins for many years to come, as it continues to be the best place in the world to live, run a business, play and raise a family!

RMB Recycling Center

Rocky Mountain Battery Service of Fort Collins (RMB) was established by Dean Hoag and Fred McClean in 1982 and is still locally owned and operated at 1475 North College Avenue. As the business expanded, the name evolved into Rocky Mountain Battery & Recycling or, eventually, RMB Recycling Center.

Dean and Fred both worked at Salt Creek Freightways in Denver and, as the firm was going under, some friends who also worked for the company started Rocky Mountain Battery in Wheatridge, Colorado. When a store was opened in Fort Collins, Dean and Fred were offered the opportunity to purchase it. Dean, a business management graduate from UNC (Greeley) had always wanted to own a business.

Dean was living in Coal Creek Canyon near Golden at the time and moved his family to Fort Collins in 1984. Fred resided in Broomfield, then Arvada.

The company sells reconditioned auto batteries and new batteries for autos and light and heavy trucks, as well as batteries used in agriculture, industries, lawn and garden equipment, golf carts, motorcycles, ATVs, watercrafts, snowmobiles and most any other machine that uses a battery.

In 1985, RMB expanded into recycling non-ferrous metals such as aluminum, copper, brass, lead, stainless steel, radiators and lead-acid batteries. The company also buys non-ferrous metals at prices established by current market conditions. RMB was also a U-Haul dealer at both locations for fifteen years.

In 1987, a second location was opened at 2929 North Garfield Avenue in Loveland. This location sells batteries and buys non-ferrous metals. Fred was manager of this store until his recent passing in June 2014.

The company expanded into the pallet business in the 1990s and now buys, reconditions and sells four-way (40 inches by 48 inches) wood pallets for shipping. Pallets are sold to commercial accounts as well as the general public. Prices depend on the grade of the pallet.

RMB is also a collection center for many recycled materials and provides a drop-off facility for steel items. RMB also recycles E-waste, which includes all electronics, computers and microwaves. The company accepts computers and all computer accessories, typewriters, small fax machines, printing cartridges, VCRs, phones and most other electronic items. Some fees apply.

Recycling containers and pick-up service for commercial accounts are available through the main location in Fort Collins.

The firm is active in both the Fort Collins and U.S. Chambers of Commerce and NFIB. Dean is the current president of North Fort Collins Business Association (NFCBA) and has been actively involved since 1985. NFCBA is noted for Project Smile and the Coats & Boots Program, both organized to help underprivileged elementary school children. Dean has also served on various boards for the City of Fort Collins and was active in naming the new Gateway Bridge for the Northside in 1995.

Dean has also served as president and a head coach for the Fort Collins Buckaroos Girls Fastpitch softball organization. His daughters both played in the league.

For additional information about RMB Recycling Center, visit www.rmbrecycling.com.

Dean Hoag.

MILE HIGH LAND & HOMES, INC.

Below: Left to right, Briana Aragon, Norman Wyatt and Ronni Aragon.

Mile High Land & Homes, Inc., was founded in 2001 by local natives Ronni Aragon and Norman Wyatt. The firm specializes in residential, rural and mountain, farm and ranch in Larimer County.

Their original area of expertise was the mountains of Northern Colorado, especially Bellvue, Red Feather and Livermore. They have since expanded into the Fort Collins/Loveland residential market. Over the years, Mile High Land & Homes, Inc. has sold thousands of acres of land and homes in these areas. Between 2010-2014, Mile High Land & Homes, Inc., was involved in forty-one percent of the sales in the Bellvue area. The company has persevered through changing market conditions, difficult wildfire seasons, and the floods of 2013, which dramatically changed the landscape and market. They were the first to sell acreage in Bellvue following the High Park Fire and many of their sales were used to help determine value of affected land.

Company listings vary from seasonal cabins to custom homes and vacant land for new construction or recreation. Their sale of the 931 acre Crystal Mountain Ranch in late 2012 was the largest land sale in Larimer County that year and positioned them as leaders in local land sales. After Larimer County instituted the Land Use Code in 1972, new construction was required to have a building permit.

However, the mountains were a unique setting for building structures the county may not otherwise see. Mile High Land & Homes, Inc. sold many cabins that were built without permits and are extremely knowledgeable with these unique types of sales.

Ronni Aragon, a third generation Larimer County native, graduated from Colorado State University with a business administration degree, majoring in finance and real estate. Continuing education is a constant pursuit, and she is also a Resort and Second Home Property Specialist. Over the years, she has worked for builders, developers, real estate agents and various government entities. Her years of experience made her the perfect fit for managing broker of the company.

Norman Wyatt received his undergraduate degree in parks and recreation management at Mesa State University and his master's degree in public health administration from the University of Northern Colorado. He managed the aquatics program for the City of Fort Collins, supervised lifeguards and taught CPR and first aid to city employees prior to becoming a licensed broker. Norman's love of the outdoors and hunting positioned him as the leading salesperson at Mile High Land & Homes, Inc. He recently received his GREEN designation from the National Association of Realtors and is also a Certified Negotiation Expert.

Briana Aragon, their daughter and fourth generation Larimer County native, joined the team in 2013 and has already graduated from the Fort Collins Board of Realtors Academy. She holds an undergraduate degree from Colorado College and a master's degree from Penn State, where she focused on literature and languages. Briana lived and worked in Italy, Mexico, and Thailand before settling in Colorado, and her travels have equipped her with both perspective and adaptability. She is quickly becoming an instrumental part of the firm, focusing on residential sales in the Fort Collins/Loveland area, and is eager to help her generation achieve home ownership.

Mile High Land & Homes, Inc., continues to be active in the community through the Larimer County Food Bank, Poudre School District, and most recently through donations for the High Park Fire recovery and floods.

OBERMEYER HYDRO

Obermeyer Hydro is the world's foremost designer and manufacturer of pneumatically operated water control gates. In addition to water control gates, the company designs and supplies hydro turbines, inflatable dams, inflatable seals for tunnel boring machines, as well as engineering and manufacturing services to the energy and aerospace industries.

Obermeyer Hydro was founded in Connecticut by Henry Obermeyer in 1988 and relocated to Northern Colorado in 1990. The company's markets are driven by growing worldwide demand for municipal water, irrigation water, flood protection, increased dam spillway capacity, increased dam storage capacity, wastewater treatment, stormwater management, groundwater recharge, wildlife habitat enhancement, inland navigation, and hydropower, and water recreation (including swimming, ice skating, boating, fishing, and kayaking.) In each of these markets, the company continues to answer, in an environmentally responsible manner, the historic societal needs of millions of people with novel and disruptive technologies.

Obermeyer Hydro's patented pneumatically operated gates allow large rivers to be precisely controlled with minimal construction and, unlike fixed weirs, without increasing flood risk to nearby and upstream inhabitants. Unlimited spans without unsightly overhead structures assure unrestricted channel capacity to safely pass flood flows. Lowering of the gates during seasonal high flows clears retained sediment, thereby perpetually renewing full storage capacity while supplying clean water to treatment facilities, agricultural users, and hydropower plants.

Above: A water quality gate, Guiyang City, Guizhou Province, China.

Bottom, left and right: Boise Whitewater Park.

RAND-SCOT, INC.

From tragedy can often come great achievement. Such is the story of Joel Lerich and creation of the EasyPivot Patient Lift.

An auto accident in 1974 broke Joel's neck and left the young mechanical engineer a quadriplegic. After several months of rehabilitation, Joel was sent home where he quickly mastered most daily tasks. One task, however, proved to be a menacing obstacle—transferring from place to place. He never felt completely safe when a traditional sling-type lift or sliding board was used to transfer him from bed to chair or chair to car. Joel was also concerned about the long-term effects of lifting on his wife's health.

Realizing he would face the issue for the remainder of his life, Joel drew on his years of mechanical engineering experience and began to study the mechanics of the 'standing pivot transfer,' a transfer technique often used in hospitals and rehab centers. Studying the advantages and disadvantages of the standing pivot transfer technique led to the invention of the EasyPivot Patient Lift.

Joel and his wife, Barbara Hoehn-Lerich, a mechanical draftsman and designer, experimented with several early prototypes, some of them constructed from defunct gas pipes removed when retrofitting their home for accessibility. They studied ways to reproduce the simplest of transfers learned in the rehab center, the standing pivot. Through determination and research, the EasyPivot Patient Lift was developed and patented. With the EasyPivot Lift, neither the size, strength nor the ability of the caregiver or patient are factors in a smooth, easy transfer.

Joel and Barbara started Rand-Scot, Inc., in 1980 to manufacture and market their streamlined 'transfer machine.' A building was purchased at 401 Linden Center Drive for the new company and still serves as company headquarters.

In 1995, Rand-Scot acquired the Saratoga Cycle Company. Their stationary bikes enable disabled patients to exercise more easily, compared with regular gym equipment

The BBD Cushion Company, which produces pressure relief wheelchair cushions, was acquired in 2000. The BBD Wheelchair Cushion, along with the Saratoga Cycle series and EasyPivot Patient Lifts, allow Rand-Scot to solve three parts of an individual's healthcare puzzle. Rand-Scot continually adapts its equipment to individuals, and prides itself on responsive engineering to meet these special needs.

Steve Jacobson and Fred Ekstam were instrumental in Rand-Scot's early success in the 1980s. Steve went on to work for Advanced Energy and Fred, already a retired engineer once, retired again in 2007 when he was nearly eighty years old. Kate Stephens, who began working as Joel's caregiver in 1998 while a student at Colorado State University, joined Rand-Scot after graduation and is now the marketing director. Erin Thames, also once a caregiver, became the office manager and was instrumental in keeping the company running smoothly for the next decade, especially during Joel's greatest health challenges as a quadriplegic. John Schulein has been with the company for twenty-five years and as production/shop foreman keeps Rand-Scot relative and sustainable. He and Kate work together, combining their expertise in adapting equipment to patient's myriad and multiple needs. Zip McCrea and engineering student Daniel L. complete Rand-Scot's essential personnel.

"We have been in business for thirty-four years," says Barbara, president of Rand-Scot since 2010. "We remain true to the American tradition of industry providing sustainable jobs and manufacturing quality products that help solve difficult problems. For our future, we will continue to produce quality products that help disabled individuals enjoy a better quality of life."

Foothills "A" for Aggies
(Colorado A & M college).
COURTESY OF JANE BASS.

The original 1887 Larimer County Courthouse.

COURTESY OF JANE BASS.

SPONSORS

ABOUT THE AUTHOR

WAYNE C. SUNDBERG

Wayne Sundberg is a Fort Collins icon. A teacher of history, an activist for historic preservation and an avid writer of history, Sundberg is known as "Mr. Fort Collins History".

Sundberg taught history and geography at Lincoln Junior High School for twenty-seven years. He also taught Fort Collins history as an affiliated professor at Colorado State University.

Sundberg was the chairman of the Landmarks Preservation Commission, where he advocated for the preservation of historic Fort Collins homes and buildings, and the "Old Town Historic District".

He was also an original organizer of the Fort Collins Municipal Railway, helping to restore a portion of the city's trolley line.

He is the author of a previous general history of the city, *Historic Fort Collins* and also *Fort Collins First Water Works*. In addition to books, Sundberg has written numerous articles on Colorado historical topics.

Among his awards and recognitions are the Pioneer Association's 2010 Pioneer of the Year. He was honored by the Colorado Historical Society for his book on The Water Works, and the Colorado Education Association and the Poudre School District have recognized him for his efforts to introduce junior high school students to Fort Collins' rich history.